Energy, Economic Growth, and Geopolitical Futures

Energy, Economic Growth, and Geopolitical Futures

Eight Long-Range Scenarios

Evan Hillebrand and Stacy Closson

The MIT Press
Cambridge, Massachusetts
London, England

All statements of fact, opinion, or analysis expressed are those of the authors and do not reflect the official position or views of the CIA or any other U.S. government agency. Nothing in the contents should be construed as asserting or implying U.S. Government authentication of information or Agency endorsement of the author's views. This material has been reviewed by the CIA to prevent the disclosure of classified information.

MIT Press books may be purchased at special quantity discounts for business or sales promotional use. For information, please email special_sales@mitpress.mit.edu.

This book was set in 10/13 pt Palatino by Toppan Best-set Premedia Limited. Printed and bound in the United States of America.

Library of Congress Cataloging-in-Publication Data

Hillebrand, Evan E.
Energy, economic growth, and geopolitical futures: eight long-range forecasts / Evan Hillebrand and Stacy Closson.
    pages   cm
Includes bibliographical references and index.
ISBN 978–0-262–02889–9 (hardcover: alk. paper)
1. Economic development—Forecasting. 2. Energy development—Forecasting. 3. Geopolitics—Forecasting. I. Closson, Stacy, 1971–. II. Title.
HD82.H4796   2015
333.7901′12—dc23
2014034247

10   9   8   7   6   5   4   3   2   1

We dedicate this book to our former colleagues at the Central Intelligence Agency and the Department of Defense, from whom we learned to think globally.

Contents

Preface

This project began with an idea to impose some structure on the myriad efforts across several disciplines to describe the future based on the present scenario. A host of publications—professional, journalistic, and academic—have attempted to describe the trajectory that will lead us, in many cases, to a post-American world. We noted that in these efforts, the key drivers—whether they be energy, the global economy, or geopolitics—were often isolated from a broader interplay with other factors. The availability of energy resources, economic growth, and relations within and between nations are so codependent that it makes little sense to consider the long-term future for one key driver based on fixed assumptions about the others. This book therefore portrays the interconnectedness of these three major drivers over the next 40 years in eight different scenarios.

Our first step in this effort was to organize a conference in which 12 academics, former government officials, and think-tank analysts joined 75 graduate students and professors of the Patterson School of Diplomacy and International Commerce at the University of Kentucky to speculate about possible long-range global futures. On the first day of the conference, the invited guests presented their individual and diverse views on the future of energy availability, macroeconomic growth, and intra-state and inter-state relations.

Many of the speakers discussed the conundrum of how to ameliorate the cycle of volatile energy prices. Questions arose about whether alternative energies would have a chance to come to market and whether the United States, Europe, or Asia have the best financial and regulatory system for this. Technology futures were explored, from biofuel development to new methods of hydrocarbon development, fuel cells, and nuclear energy. Some warned about the impending strain on natural resources compounded by population growth and climate change and the political fallout from such events. Particularly, the question of whether there would be enough water to support agricultural development and clean energy production was raised, as well as the social tensions that could arise over tying food prices to energy prices if food (or other resources used to produce food) is increasingly used for energy production.

During the conference, debates on economic growth scenarios for the different regions of the world varied according to prescribed growth theories. There were those who argued that achieving a sustainable higher level of development required democratic governance and trust. Lack of these would impede significant positive growth in emerging economies. Others argued that the Chinese growth model was a new path toward modernization; economic reform could take place without liberal reforms in the near future.

Tension in the economic growth scenarios was highlighted as occurring between mere growth and the distribution of wealth. If wealth was believed to drive greater global harmony, more growth or less growth would affect national stability. A distinction was also made in terms of nations with and without hydrocarbon production. Future stability in the oil-producing regions would depend on the management of resources in Russia, Latin America, the Middle East, and Africa. In particular, the distribution of mineral wealth within these societies, and between government and business, would most likely determine future stability within these regions.

On the second day we convened a workshop in which we assigned six groups of 10 to 12 students each to mentors from the previous day's sessions. Some of the mentors had led this type of exercise at the National Intelligence Council. Each group developed a sketch for one of the scenarios discussed in this book. We assigned each group to work with a set of end points: high or low energy prices, strong or weak economic growth, and global harmony or disharmony.

The groups were encouraged to fill in as many details as they wanted, on a variation of several critical questions. Is the world energy supply plentiful or not, by the standard of the last 50 years? Will world economic growth be stronger or weaker, by historical standards? Do the Organisation for Economic Co-operation and Development (OECD) countries and the non-OECD countries grow strong simultaneously? Does hegemonic stability pass smoothly into some new form of great-power peace? If not, do discord and war result from the various potential combinations of resources, economics, and national interest?

At the end of the two-day exercise, we were left with a mass of raw material that formed the foundation for this work. Our task was to use the tools of social science theory and empiricism to develop, in ways that made sense, the groups' assumptions that motivated the scenarios. The results were trend-based scenarios, conditioned on quite different assumptions about the three major drivers.

Our larger task was to show how the drivers were not independent—how the assumptions about one affected the range of possible outcomes of the other two. We added two scenarios of low energy prices to the six scenarios developed at the conference in order to consider every possible combination of the three key drivers. What we learned about the first six scenarios influenced the logic of the additional scenarios.

An instrumental part of our scenario building was done with the quantitative assistance of the International Futures (IFs) model built and operated by Professor Barry Hughes of the University of Denver. With the material gleaned from the conference and the scenario-building workshop, we determined to use the IFs to impose some numerical consistency on the project. The IFs is a global model representing hundreds of relationships within and among 186 countries. This model has evolved since 1979 as a tool for thinking about the future.

The IFs is a global model with complex submodels focusing on 10 areas: agriculture, economy, education, energy, environment, governance, health, international politics, population, and technology. The behavioral relationships are based on theoretical and empirical specifications derived from the literature as well as from empirical work by Hughes and his colleagues. The model has a long history of use in assessing long-range global futures, including by the National Intelligence Council, the United Nations, and the Pardee Center for International Futures at the University of Denver. It is important to note that the model is used not to make forecasts but rather to impose consistency within and across the scenarios to draw out the rich details implied by the scenarios by sector and by country.

We wish for our book to involve you, the reader, in exploring alternative futures in two ways. The first is through reading the eight scenarios and determining which ones you believe are more likely than others to occur.

We reviewed the eight scenarios with our students at the Patterson School of Diplomacy and International Commerce in Lexington, Kentucky, who use the IFs model in their classes. They chose strong-growth over weak-growth economic scenarios while also being more pessimistic about the future energy market, choosing higher energy prices over lower. For geopolitics, they tended to favor scenarios with global harmony, but with lower levels of accord among the major powers and the continued existence of intranational conflict.

At the Pardee Center in Denver, Colorado, in contrast, while deeming strong-growth economic scenarios as more likely, the students opined that energy prices would remain lower long-term and that there would be more global disharmony.

Discerning what you and your peers believe to be the most likely combination, therefore, is an interesting exercise in debating how current trends influence our perceptions of the future of the energy market, the global economy, and geopolitics. Moreover, we believe that an appreciation for how the interplay of these three areas will determine the future is a useful exercise for government analysts, politicians, economists, businesspeople, and military strategists.

The second way that this book involves you, the reader, is by giving you the ability to actively participate in the exploration of alternative futures through the use of a highly interactive computer simulation model. The IFs model is freely available at http://pardee. du.edu/access-ifs. All the scenarios in this book are reproducible by any interested reader using the model software. Once you have downloaded and become familiar with the IFs model, you may reproduce or alter any of our scenarios by loading the "Sce" files found under "World Integrated Scenario Sets/HillebrandClosson Energy-Econ-Geopolitical." We provide data for each of our scenarios in the web appendix to this book available at http://mitpress.mit.edu/geopolitical-futures.

For this book, we used version 6.75, August 2013, but the model is regularly updated to reflect new or additional data. Our scenarios will work with new versions of the model, although the numerical results will change. The use of the model will facilitate your thinking from the present through 2100. You can explore what might happen as a result of your assumptions about potential policy choices or possible disruptive events.

This book provides a much-needed comprehensive look at the interplay of several key drivers over the course of four decades and offers different scenarios of the future. It allows each of the three drivers—energy prices, economic growth, and geopolitics—to be simultaneously endogenous, each affecting the others, and the effects changing over a multidecade period. This approach cannot give a unique prediction; it yields instead an infinite number of scenarios.

Our work offers the first attempt to bring together the three driving factors as endogenous variables, generating primary and secondary implications. We found that maintaining an assumption of the exogeneity of certain variables was unrealistic and likely to lead to less than helpful scenarios. Our book therefore demonstrates to practitioners in government and industry the value of not assuming that any one variable is the consistent driver; rather, it is critical to appreciate the interplay of all three drivers over time.

Likewise, there is much to be gained from combining a quantitative model with the more subjective and qualitative approaches usually taken in scenario analysis. Integrating the qualitative tool of the IFs model into scenario analysis is our methodological contribution both to practitioners and academics. More than proposing intuitive determinations or prescriptive offerings, we qualify our scenarios with the IFs and data. This book therefore provides a useful text for courses on scenario analysis, enhanced by the availability of the model and scenarios online for instructive manipulation.

Finally, we are the first to offer multiple scenarios not favoring one particular combination of factors but rather allowing for multiple scenarios to be generated. Thus, we offer no definitive long-term forecast for any of the three drivers. Rather, we show how different assumptions about any of the drivers can affect the outcomes of the other two, and we offer insights on how events are likely to unfold, given starting assumptions. We offer eight different scenarios that capture the main results of this exercise and suggest which ones are more probable than others and why.

We are grateful to the students, staff, and faculty at the Patterson School of Diplomacy and International Commerce. We could not have begun this project without their support and participation. In particular, we appreciate the support for the conference concept from our Patterson director, Ambassador (Retired) Carey Cavanaugh. The insights and mentoring from Patterson professors Karen Mingst and Robert Farley were extremely useful. In addition, the comprehensive presentations from the conference participants were highly beneficial to our scenarios, as was their mentoring of students in the workshop. They include Robert Aten, Robert Brecha, Yong Deng, Richard Engel,

Ralph Espach, George von Furstenberg, John Garen, Audra Grant, Paul Herman, Sean Kay, Steve LeVine, and Arch Puddington (see appendix A for affiliations).

Our concepts of Asian security were enhanced through participating in two workshops at the kind invitation of the Shanghai Institute of American Studies. We are grateful to all who reviewed drafts. The first draft was reviewed anonymously by four people, and their comments inspired us to continue the effort. The second draft was reviewed by Dr. Peter Hartley and anonymously by a second person, and their comments directed us toward completing the manuscript. Before submission, the second draft was reviewed by two major figures in international futures, our friends Paul Herman and Barry Hughes. Finally, we would like to specially thank Stephanie Hillebrand for superb editing and to Sabry Hanna for moral support and extraparental duties.

1   Modeling Future Scenarios

How can we think about the future? Will there be more wars or peace? What country or countries will dominate, and which ones will fade in geopolitical significance? Will the unprecedented 60-year surge in world economic growth continue or come to an end? Will shortages of energy or other resources constrain the global future?

There are many books and articles that describe global future scenarios for each of these questions. We offer a new approach that considers the interconnectedness of what we consider to be the key drivers of the outlook: energy prices, economic growth, and geopolitics. We set out to determine how a change in any one driver could affect the outcomes of the other two and how the various combinations of the three drivers could interact to create different futures.

We have constructed eight scenarios envisioning quite different views of the future. They cannot technically be described as forecasts; rather, they are projections conditioned on a large range of assumptions. The key assumptions, based on recent historical standards, are whether energy prices are high or low, whether economic growth is strong or weak, and whether nations live in reasonable harmony or disharmony.

Energy prices are determined by a number of factors affecting supply and demand and could take many different forms that affect countries and regions differently. The factors motivating strong or weak economic growth in each country are dependent on a host of other assumptions about the rate and nature of technological change, policy choices, and innovations in economic institutions. Finally, the state of harmony is affected by war and peace within and between nations as well as by whether countries choose to work together or apart in solving future challenges. Our purpose is to demonstrate how the codependence of the three key drivers ensures that it makes little sense to consider the outlook for one driver of the global system based on fixed assumptions about the other two.

This chapter introduces our approach to scenario building, both qualitative and quantitative. It places the model within the context of the recent history of long-range forecasting. Next, we discuss each of our three key variables within the context of the literature covering scenarios for energy prices, economic growth, and geopolitical futures. We then offer a summary of our eight scenarios. Although we cannot predict the most likely scenario, we do discuss the key challenges faced when certain variables are combined. We conclude with our assessment of how the interplay of the three variables is more or less likely to unfold in the coming decades.

Scenario Building

In each scenario, we consider how the three key drivers interact through three periods: 2010s, 2020–2040, and 2040s–2050. We have chosen three broad periods for several reasons. First, we do not wish to suggest that any scenario will produce a linear or consistent trend. For example, slow growth in 2010s could eventually turn into higher growth. Second, we want to show how assumptions about exogenous factors and policy choices in one period can lead (or not lead) to significant changes in subsequent periods. That is, short-term energy policies could result, by 2030, in a greater or lesser supply and, as a result, affect economic growth. Third, we want to keep the scope of the discussion manageable, so we have limited it to four decades.

We follow a general pattern of first addressing what happens to the American (and often European) economy in the 2010s, since we believe this will be the critical factor in future outlooks. We next address how China is evolving internally and is relating economically and politically to events in the West. After that are depictions of events in various regions, often by level of relevance to the particular scenario. Energy is blended into the economic and political discussions as appropriate. We conclude with an observation about the international system.

Although the economy is discussed first in each scenario, it is not always the key driver, nor is it consistently the main thread in different periods. In each scenario we identify the main threads, whether they change in different periods, and the challenges we faced in creating scenarios with a particular mix of three endogenous variables throughout four decades.

We distinguish each scenario by beginning in the 2010 decade with a set of assumptions for the key drivers of economic growth, energy prices, and geopolitics.

In the four high-growth scenarios, we assume that there is rapid technological change (as has been the case the last 60 years) and that many of the non-OECD countries successfully adapt new and old technologies in the process of catching up with the income standards of the OECD countries.[1] In these strong-growth scenarios, we make different assumptions about which countries will do better or worse at developing the political and economic institutions that facilitate growth. The thinking behind these assumptions generally follows the work of Acemoglu and Robinson (2012) and Helpman (2004), who stress the importance of establishing the rule of law, property rights, and competitive government institutions that are accountable to the people.

In the four scenarios that assume good energy availability and thus a low relative price of energy, we make different assumptions about what form energy abundance takes (oil, gas, coal, nuclear, or renewable) and where the energy is produced. Energy production by source and location, of course, affects economic growth at the national level.

In the four scenarios that assume global harmony, we make different assumptions about how the harmony is created: as the result of hegemony, a balance of power, or increased global governance. We also take into account that intra-state and inter-state conflict might move in opposite directions. That is, several countries may determine to act responsibly together to deter a conflict within one country.

In the four weak-growth scenarios, we assume factors such as limited technological advancement and adaptation in both OECD and emerging economies and the interaction between these two groups. We also make different assumptions about which countries will do better or worse at developing the political and economic institutions that facilitate growth. Also factored in are external constraints to growth, such as energy supply and pricing, natural disasters, and international events such as conflicts.

In the four scenarios that assume poor energy availability and thus a high relative price of energy, we suggest that this results from factors such as geological constraints, environmental regulations to curb hydrocarbon growth, costly renewable fuel sources, or rapid-demand growth from buoyant world economic growth.

In the four scenarios that assume global disharmony, the competition among the rising powers and the existing powers is considered important in creating the disharmony. We make different assumptions about how conflict destabilizes nations and the international system, including the ineffectiveness of global institutions. We also assume that where national institutions remain underdeveloped, the onset of energy production tends to destabilize the country.

The assumptions about each driver affect the outcomes of the other drivers. For example, if we assume that China will have very strong economic growth for the next 40 years and that the United States will stagnate, then the global power balance in 2050 will be drastically different from today's. At the same time, different assumptions about energy availability—or even differences in the assumptions about the kind of energy that will be produced and where it will be produced— will make a great deal of difference in the shape of the geopolitical order. A rich, energy self-sufficient China in 2050 would probably play a very different role in the world system than a rich China dependent on imported oil. Likewise, a prosperous, energy-rich United States with a diversified economy will respond differently to the rise of China than a less prosperous and less energy-secure United States.

Of course, some scenarios pose greater challenges in imagining the interplay of seemingly less likely combinations, such as weak economic growth and high energy prices alongside geopolitical harmony. We will discuss the assumptions made in each combination of the three key drivers, and we will address how this affects evaluating the scenarios in the conclusion.

Quantitative Assistance from the International Futures Model

This book offers a combination of theories and a computer model that inform the development of our scenarios. The careful use of the computer model has several advantages in combination with our mental models. First, the computer model is highly explicit, thus complementing our more abstract mental models. Second, the computer can attain a level of complexity and sophistication that often surpasses simple extrapolation or, at the very least, enhances it. Third, we can use the computer model to quickly investigate experimentally a variety of different assumptions.

As noted in the preface, our particular model is the International Futures (IFs) model developed by Barry Hughes at the University of

Denver. It has been discussed extensively by Hughes and Hillebrand (2006). The IFs model was inspired by the World Integrated model (Mesarovic and Pestel 1974) and draws on the Leontief World model (Leontief, Carter, and Petri 1977), the Baroliche Foundation World model (Baroliche Foundation 1976), and the Systems Analysis Research United model (SARU 1977). The IFs model has a long history of use in scenario exercises, including work done by the United Nations (2004), the National Intelligence Council (2004, 2008, and 2012a), the Pardee Center for International Futures (2009), and Hillebrand (2010).

The IFs model is multidimensional and capable of simulating 186 countries to 2100.[2] We focus on the effects of the interplay of the variables on the great powers and the rising powers, but the descriptive scenarios are tied to year-by-year quantitative estimates of hundreds of variables for 186 countries. The model projects gross domestic product (GDP) demand components and a six-way sectoral output for each country: agriculture, manufacturing, energy, services, materials, and information and communication technology (ICT). It also projects trade and capital flows, demographic change, and income distribution. Energy supply for six fuel types (oil, gas, coal, nuclear, hydroelectric and other renewables) is projected for each country, and the energy demand for each country is estimated based on economic activity, relative prices, and assumptions about efficiency changes.

The model is used to generate many numbers to provide a context and to illuminate the scenarios. Economic growth rates, energy supply and demand projections, measures of geopolitical power, and a variety of other factors are shown in the text for the existing powers and some regional groupings. Appendix D (available online at http://mitpress. mit.edu/geopolitical-futures) has country-by-country and scenario-by-scenario results for real GDP per capita, poverty head count, Gini coefficients of income inequality, comprehensive national power, world energy production, energy vulnerability, general population, and elderly population (65 and older).

All the numbers (there are millions of them) generated in these simulations can be accessed by interested readers, who can download the IFs model onto their own computers (see either the preface or note 2 of this chapter for the link), examine how we altered the model's assumptions for each scenario, replicate our results, and even alter our interventions and resimulate the model as they wish. Appendix B provides a more thorough description of the model and its use.

The numbers, however, should not be viewed as model-generated forecasts. Instead, we have assumed the key numbers and growth rates for important variables for the most pertinent countries based on our judgment and the story line we have developed for each scenario. Model simulations are used to expand the numerical story for all the other actors and to help us identify inconsistencies and insights, thereby allowing us to improve our initial story.

Long-Range Forecasting

Our work follows a relatively new phenomenon of long-range forecasting begun in the late 1960s by academicians and then applied by private industry. Perhaps the most important futurist for our purposes is Peter Schwartz, who began forecast modeling in the 1970s at Stanford University and then applied his knowledge to forecasting global trends for private companies. His first book, *The Art of the Long View: Planning for the Future in an Uncertain World* (1991), is considered to be the seminal publication on scenario planning, and his 2003 book, *Inevitable Surprises: Thinking Ahead in a Time of Turbulence*, examines how present forces will continue to affect the world on a long-term basis.

Also relevant is the work done by the World Future Society, whose founder, Edward Cornish (2004), offers methods for scenario planning in *Futuring: The Exploration of the Future*. The nonprofit organization examines the social, economic, and technological developments that are shaping the future.

Another contributor is the Millennium Project of the World Federation of United Nations Associations, which has published the *State of the Future Index* (SOFI) every year since 2001. SOFI aggregates the history and forecasts of a number of variables that depict the future outlook in many social and human dimensions.

The U.S. government offers its own long-range forecasting of global events in five successive unclassified reports produced by the National Intelligence Council. Each study examines a different set of key drivers. The 2008 study, *Global Trends 2025: A World Transformed*, features the climate and energy. The 2012 study, *Global Trends 2030: Alternative Worlds*, offers four scenarios that look at megatrends and their effects on global stability or instability.

Long-term forecasting is not just an American exercise. European government and nongovernment institutions are engaged in scenario planning reflective of strategic and economic interests. European forecasting has been done by the European Union Institute of Strategic Studies (2011) in *Futures Study to 2025: Citizens in an Interconnected and Polycentric World*. In this study, a network of policy officials from European institutions identifies four global trends: empowerment of the individual, sustainable development against a backdrop of greater resource scarcity, a shift of power away from nation-states, and growing governance gaps.

European energy companies such as BP engage in long-term scenarios that it publishes in its periodical, *Energy Outlook*. Royal Dutch Shell is a pioneer in future scenario planning, led by Pierre Wack in the 1970s and 1980s, which has enhanced the company's ability to foresee market turbulence. Shell (2013) considers the nexus of economic, political, and social forces, projecting implications for energy supply and the environment to 2050.

The aforementioned Millennium Project has partners globally that cooperate on its future studies in Europe, Asia, Latin America, and the Middle East. Our own work relies on a series of papers on global long-term economic growth by Fouré, Bénassy-Quéré, and Fontagné (2010, 2012) at the Center for Economic Perspectives and International Information.

Regardless of the discipline or the institution, previous long-range predictions have usually been restricted in scope. In general, energy experts consider the energy supply on the basis of known resources and technologies, and they estimate the demand based on the projections for economic growth made by others, but they neglect to think about the endogenous relationship between energy and growth, between energy and geopolitics, and among energy, growth, and geopolitics.

Good examples of this approach are the *Annual Energy Outlook* and the *International Energy Outlook*, both produced by the U.S. Department of Energy's Energy Information Agency. Unstated in the forecasts are assumptions about the global security arrangements and the national security policies of the key energy producers and consumers. Implicitly, global security and economic relationships remain unchanged: (1) most energy crosses international borders in response to voluntary and mutually beneficial market transactions, and (2) the Organization of Petroleum Exporting Countries (OPEC), if it continues to exist, does not try to exert significant pressure to increase prices for economic or political reasons.

Victor, Jaffe, and Hayes (2006) use a more sophisticated approach in *Natural Gas and Geopolitics: From 1970 to 2040*. But the chapters in that edited volume still follow a unidirectional line of causality: GDP growth causes energy demand, geological estimates and technological change assumptions drive energy supply, and energy supply and demand and prices affect geopolitics. Connections running from energy to GDP growth, from geopolitics to economics, or from energy to long-term geopolitical consequences are mostly not addressed.

Economic forecasters have tended to do the reverse: they couch their forecasts in terms of savings and investment, demographic change, and guesses about technological change, but they take the availability of energy to drive whatever economic growth is expected to be delivered in quantities and prices determined by the energy forecasters. They also tend to ignore the political transformation that most development economists think is necessary to achieve a modern economy or the geopolitical environment that would be conducive to long-term economic growth.

A good example of this is the Goldman Sachs BRIC study (Wilson and Purushotham 2003), which brought the rise of the eponymous four countries—Brazil, Russia, India, and China—to wide attention. In *The Next 200 Years: A Scenario for America and the World*, Kahn, Brown, and Markel (1976) assume that economic development will lead to democracy (or at least legitimate authoritarianism) and eventually world government. Their scenario includes nothing about how alternative political arrangements or strife between countries (except in the unlikely event of thermonuclear war) could affect economics.

When writing about the world economy over the past 50 years, Cooper (2002), in *What the Future Holds: Insights from Social Science*, comments that only a few in the economics literature have attempted to make long-term forecasts, and most of those leave the political dimension untouched.

Geopolitical analysts have tended to do the same thing. There is a burgeoning literature of intuitive predictions about where the world is headed based on an interpretation of history, an ideological perspective, or both. Ikenberry (2011) predicts that the next geopolitical order will be a kinder, more cooperative liberal international system than the previous years of hegemonic stability. This forecast is based on assumptions not just about the economic growth rates of the various players but also on a strong assumption about the relationship between economic interdependence and the geopolitical order.

There is also a long list of books describing an impending American decline, the rise of other powers, and a prescriptive agenda for preserving American power. Among them are *J Curve: A New Way to Understand Why Nations Rise and Fall* (Bremmer 2006), *The Post-American World* (Zakaria 2008, 2011), *Strategic Advantage: Challenges, Competitors, and Threats to America's Future* (Berkowitz 2008), *The Next 100 Years: A Forecast for the 21st Century* (Friedman 2009), *Why the West Rules—for Now: The Patterns of History, and What They Reveal about the Future* (Morris 2010), *The Next Convergence: The Future of Economic Growth in a Multispeed World* (Spence 2011), and *No One's World: The West, the Rising Rest, and the Coming Global Turn* (Kupchan 2012). The book that most closely addresses the nexus of energy, economics, and geopolitics is *Oil, Dollars, Debt, and Crises: The Global Curse of Black Gold* (El-Gamal and Jaffe 2011). However, it has a singular focus on the relationship between the United States and the Middle East.

In economics, we call the kind of work discussed above "partial equilibrium analysis." Each individual expert or group focuses on a single area of expertise, ignoring or downplaying the interdependence and the contingencies. This is all quite natural; the standard practice when making predictions is for something to be exogenous.

We present here the first work that offers multiple scenarios favoring not one particular combination of factors but rather eight different combinations of three key drivers. We uniquely treat all three key drivers—energy, economic growth, and geopolitics—as simultaneously endogenous and codependent. This allows the reader to appreciate how different assumptions about any one of the drivers can affect the outcomes of the other two. This, combined with the ability of the readers to model their own scenarios using the IFs model, should enhance the tools available to scenario planners and broaden the discussion to one of complexity in long-range forecasting.

Energy Shortfall or Abundance

One of our major concerns is the future availability of energy. Will there be a shortfall of supply and, consequently, rapidly rising energy prices, or will there be energy abundance? This book engages with both sides of the peak oil debate. Prominent media attention to oil has raised questions about resource depletion. Oil production peaked throughout the United States in 1972 and in the North Sea in 1999. When will the world's production peak? Reaching the peak does not mean we are running out; it merely refers to reaching the maximum production rate. Oil production will start to decline when it becomes too expensive relative to alternative fuels. Inaccurate or mendacious reserve estimates, limited technology, or financial constraints could hasten the arrival of the peak, but political forces could also force a move away from oil.

Generally, books about the future of oil provide a grim picture of impending resource depletion. Examples are *The Long Emergency: Surviving the End of Oil, Climate Change, and Other Converging Catastrophes of the Twenty-First Century* (Kunstler 2005), *The Coming Economic Collapse: How You Can Thrive When Oil Costs $200 a Barrel* (Leeb 2006), *Twilight in the Desert: The Coming Saudi Oil Shock and the World Economy* (Simmons 2005), *The End of Oil: On the Edge of a Perilous New World* (Roberts 2005), and *Peak Everything: Waking Up to the Century of Declines* (Heinberg 2010).

The Myth of the Oil Crisis: Overcoming the Challenges of Depletion, Geopolitics, and Global Warming (Mills 2008) provides a counterargument that the relative lack of new discoveries is more a result of underinvestment in technology and politics and that there is likely to be a recovery in the future. Likewise, *The Quest: Energy, Security, and the Remaking of the Modern World* (Yergin 2011) argues that technological advances will enhance the recovery of unconventional sources, thus lengthening the period of oil abundance.

The major energy bureaucracies—the U.S. Department of Energy, the International Energy Agency, BP, and Shell, among others—see a world with enough energy supplies to prevent a major increase in the relative price of energy in the coming decades. They admit that petroleum supplies from existing fields are declining, but they point out that new fields are being discovered in west Africa, Iran, Iraq, Brazil, China, the Arctic Ocean, Egypt, southeast Africa, and Australia. Furthermore, unconventional oil from tar sands and shale, as well as gas from shale, is set to expand dramatically because of market demand and technological advances in recovery. Likewise, advances in research and development are assumed to substantially increase the production of renewable forms of energy in the next 40 years.

Even if carbon-fuel resources are not as abundant as the optimists suggest, or renewable energies are not scalable in the near future, technological change is an endogenous process. Increasing scarcity and rising energy prices are expected to generate more research and more learning by doing as the capital stock of renewable energy sources expands, thus transitioning society to a different energy future (Hartley 2011).

The timing of this transformation is another source of debate. Hartley et al. (2013) believe that the transition to renewable forms of energy might not occur until around 2100, when, they estimate, about 80 percent of the world's recoverable fossil fuel reserves will be depleted. The European Union's energy policy sets a target of up to 75 percent renewable sources for final energy consumption by 2050 (European Commission 2012).

We could represent the contrasting ideas by a simple metric. Does the price of energy (relative to all other prices) rise sharply, leading to economic dislocation and political tension, or does it stay roughly the same? The difference between a peak oil scenario and a scenario of energy abundance (see figure 1.1) rests not on whether oil production falls, but at what rate and on whether there are adequate alternatives to replace oil in time to keep energy prices from rising exponentially.

In the peak oil scenario, oil production falls rapidly, and there is no ready alternative to replace this deficit. In the energy abundance scenario, the mix of energy sources is diverse, including conventional and unconventional hydrocarbons and several renewable energies. Which line of thinking is likely to be accurate? In our work, we explore the effects of different trends for energy supply and energy prices and examine how those differences might affect economic growth and geopolitics.

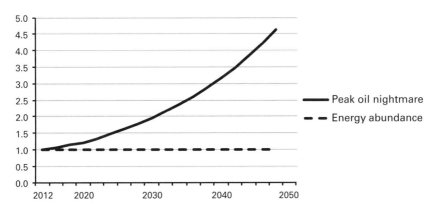

Figure 1.1
Relative Price of Energy Scenarios
Source: Authors

We start from the IFs model base case scenario and adjust parameter values and assumptions about exogenous variables to run simulations that match as closely as possible the logic of the story presented in each chapter. Energy production estimates in the IFs model base case scenario start with Energy Information Agency (EIA) data for 2010 and closely approximate the EIA (2013) projections through 2035.

The IFs model base case projection, like the EIA reference scenario, assumes no short-term peak in oil production, which continues to climb at least through 2035. For our scenarios, we run model simulations adjusting energy production by fuel type for each country, as required by the logic of the scenario. Such model changes can have quite dramatic effects on economic activity in the producer countries, on global energy prices, and on economic growth in the importing countries, as we will demonstrate in the scenarios.

Rising Prosperity or an End to Growth

The last 60 years of world economic growth have been extremely strong, by historical standards. From an average annual rate of per capita real GDP of roughly zero from the year 1 CE to 1820, and a 0.9 percent per year growth from 1821 to 1950, world growth surged to 2.1 percent per year from 1951 to 2010 (Maddison 2007; World Bank 2011). This occurred despite a huge increase in world population. The last 15 years in particular have seen not only a rapid expansion of world output but also some convergence, with the less developed countries (hereafter referred to as the non-OECD countries) growing much faster than the OECD countries.

Economic historians will forever argue over the causes of this phenomenal rise in output and living standards. Most would agree it was enabled by improvements in technology (see, in particular, Barro and Sala-i-Martín 1995; Helpman 2004; Romer 1986; Rosenberg and Birdzell 1987). Others have stressed that growth is importantly associated with the development of commerce-friendly institutions and attitudes (see, in particular, Acemoglu and Robinson 2012; Landes 1999; McCloskey 2010; North 1990), generally referred to as the Washington Consensus model (Williamson 2004).

Economic growth projections for 40 years can only be guesses, based on past trends, assumptions about future drivers, and insights about possible constraints. According to convergence theory, the lower a country's output per capita compared to the technology leader, the faster its growth rate could be, all other things being equal.

In 1980, for example, China's GDP per capita was only about 2 percent of the U.S. level. At the start of their growth surges, Botswana, South Korea, and Taiwan were 5.5, 7.1, and 9.5 percent, respectively (Maddison 2001). With the help of effective government institutions, good policies, and a benign international environment, those poor countries were able to advance very rapidly. Between 1990 and 2007, real per capita GDP in the non-OECD countries rose by 3 percent a year, three times faster than in the previous 40 years. There is no guarantee of future success, of course; many other countries remained poor during the same period—especially nonreforming communist countries, most countries ruled by noncommunist authoritarian regimes, and countries with civil disorder.

The literature contains a large number of long-range projections (see, for example, Duval and de la Maisonneuve 2010;, Fouré et al. 2010; Maddison 2007; Nordhaus 2008; Spence 2011; Van der Mensbrugghe et al. 2011). Fouré et al. present a detailed global forecast based on an estimated neoclassical economic growth model, which, given certain key assumptions, yields forecasts of continued strong world growth for the next 40 years, stronger than the last 60 years of world economic growth, and even stronger than the best years (1999–2007) of the globalization boom. This broadly optimistic forecast is similar to the ones that are reflected in the long-term analyses of the Energy Information Agency (2013), the International Energy Agency (2013), and the International Panel on Climate Change (2007).

Meadows, Randers, and Meadows (2004) have long represented an opposing viewpoint. Their work in the last three decades has consistently predicted that the world was near a tipping point: that world growth would soon slow and then go into reverse. Other authors predicting collapse from resource constraints are Campbell (2005), Slaughter (2010), and Leeb (2006).

Table 1.1 shows the range of global economic forecasts by these sources, compared to recent history. Why are there such great differences? The long-range forecast by Fouré et al. (2010), similar to many that appear in the literature, uses a trend-based economic model. The key determinants in such a model are the growth of the capital stock, the growth of the labor force, and the growth of technology. Although growth in technology is an intuitively useful concept, it is empirically

Table 1.1
World Economic Growth
(average annual percent change, real GDP per capita, PPP terms)

	1951–2010	2011–2030	2011–2050
World Bank	2.1%		
Fouré et al. (2010)		3.2%	3.1%
Meadows et al. (2004)		−1.8%	−2.5%

Source: 1951–2010, authors' calculations based on World Bank (2011) and Maddison (2001). Other numbers are from Fouré et al. (2010) and Meadows et al. (2004) plus an accompanying CD-ROM. Our calculations assume that Meadows et al.'s human welfare index is approximately the same measure as real GDP per capita. All per capita figures use purchasing power parity (PPP, base year 2005) exchange rates to convert national currency measures to a common standard.

awkward because it cannot be measured directly, and it is calculated in the recent past as part of observed growth that is not explained by the growth in capital and labor.

The basic reason for an ahistorically strong forecast in Fouré et al. and in many of the other works cited is the assumption that technological progress will continue at its recent strong pace in the OECD countries and that although Chinese and Indian growth will eventually slow down, growth will speed up in the rest of the non-OECD countries as many more join the convergence club by raising their level of technological efficiency to that of the OECD countries.

Even though the experience of the non-OECD countries has been staggeringly diverse in the past 60 years, most of these forecasts assume that all regions will join the convergence club. In Fouré et al. (2010), sub-Saharan African growth will speed up in the coming decades so that its real per capita growth rate in the 40-year period will be 4.5 percent a year. Implicitly, the forecast makes very strong assumptions about technological growth, institutional developments in the non-OECD world, good policy choices in both OECD and non-OECD countries, and a lack of major wars or resource constraints.

Spence (2011, 271) reasons that such an optimistic scenario is plausible because countries have "accepted the importance of decentralization, market incentives, and entrepreneurial capitalist dynamics." He adds that better problem solving and better governance, both domestic and global, will propel convergence.

The much more pessimistic scenario painted by Meadows et al. (2004) is based on concerns about resource constraints. In the World3 model of Meadows et al., the inability to provide enough food makes collapse inevitable. Campbell (2005), another pessimist, sees collapse from the depletion of carbon fuel resources, whereas Slaughter (2010) fears catastrophic climate change.

Most of the pessimistic authors are not very precise in their predictions, but in the projections from Meadows et al. (2004), problems with the global food supply do not just end the recent period of rapid world growth but actually shrink world output and incomes. Instead of extrapolating the positive trends of the late 20th century, they take the view that the high growth of the earlier period will lead to a drastic fall in income and population in the near future. In their base case scenario, the world "human welfare index," composed of world per capita food output, services, industrial output, and life expectancy peaks sometime between 2010 and 2015 and falls by more than half by 2050. No plausible range of assumptions, in their view, can do better than hold world average GDP per capita constant at the 2015 level.

Granted, some modeling efforts that take resource constraints seriously are far less pessimistic—for example, Van der Mensbrugghe et al. (2011) use the World Bank's Environmental Impact and Sustainability Applied General Equilibrium (ENVISAGE) model. Nor is Randers (2012) quite as pessimistic as Meadows et al. (2004).

Between the two extremes of growth and no growth as a result of resource constraints are the views of many authors who have written about various weaknesses that can undermine the projections of strong growth without pushing the world into a tailspin. Bremmer and Roubini (2011) worry that without a strong hegemon in the future, an increasing lack of global cooperation will lead to economic instability, rising protectionism, and, implicitly, lower world economic growth. Collier (2007) is not very optimistic that the poor nations of sub-Saharan Africa can improve their internal security and governance enough to propel themselves onto the convergence path projected in the more optimistic global growth forecasts such as the one by Fouré et al. (2010). Several authors discuss whether the effects of climate change or crushing debt could spell an end for strong growth (Daly 1996; Heinberg 2011; Kotlikoff 2004; Speth and Zinn 2008).

In the IFs model, economic growth by sector (agriculture, manufacturing, energy, materials, services, and ICT) for each country is represented by a neoclassical growth formulation in which output is a log linear function of capital, labor, and technology. The IFs base case scenario contains an assumed rate of technological change, known as total factor productivity (TFP) growth, for the technology leader (the United States). This assumed rate can be changed in simulations by the model user and varies endogenously in model simulations based on other changes the model user can make.

Technological change for all other countries is assumed to be dependent on TFP growth in the leader, on a convergence factor that depends on how far each country is from the technological frontier, and on a number of factors that the literature (Barro and Sala-i-Martín 1995; Helpman 2004) has identified as being important for catch-up growth and technological change. In the IFs model the key factors affecting TFP growth are human capital (measured by years of education and life expectancy), social capital (measured by economic freedom and government effectiveness), and knowledge (measured by research and development expenditures and trade openness). All these variables are determined endogenously in the base case but are subject to intervention by the model user.

Which line of future thinking about world economic growth, optimistic or pessimistic, is more accurate? The spectrum of opinions is represented in our scenarios, although we do not present any scenario quite as gloomy as that of Meadows et al. (2004). We do consider a wide range of possible growth paths, based on different assumptions about innovation, governance, and policy. We consider where and how growth may occur, as well as the implications of growth and policy for the distributions of wealth and income. Weak growth in the non-OECD countries has led to vastly higher global inequality in the last 200 years; in all our scenarios, inequality between the OECD and the non-OECD countries shrinks even when inequality within a country rises. We also explore how different assumptions about energy and geopolitics affect economic growth.

Global Harmony or Disharmony

Characterizing the geopolitical element is not as simple as choosing between energy abundance and scarcity or between positive and negative world economic growth. The last 60 years were marked first by a prolonged period of bipolarity, which contained a threatening great-power rivalry but avoided a great-power war. International and some regional organizations also gained strength, in contrast to the failed attempt to create the League of Nations before World War II.

With the collapse of the Soviet Union in 1991, a period of almost two decades devoid of great-power rivalry allowed and encouraged the spread of commerce, industry, democracy, and global institutions. Armed clashes declined in magnitude and severity (Goldstein 2011; Marshall and Cole 2013; Pinker 2011), and world economic growth surged. We characterize this period between 1991 and 2010 as one of global harmony, perhaps because it was so much more harmonious than the previous 80 years, and because one can imagine a world so much less harmonious. What will happen in the next 40 years? Most of the discourse on this topic focuses on the rising power of China (and India) and the declining power of the United States (and Europe).

Like economic growth, violent conflict cannot be predicted precisely. There is a lack of convergence on the methods used to generate forecasts, and there are no systematic studies assessing the accuracy of the predictions. Some studies consider only one manifestation of political violence, and there is no consensus on the definitions of such violence, on the number of casualties it takes to define a war, or on how to rate the motivations and ultimate goals of the fighters.

There are several larger quantitative studies that do find similar general trends in civil conflict, however. Monty Marshall and his Political Instability Task Force at the Center for Systemic Peace in Vienna, Virginia, have conducted a multiyear study of the general condition of peace in the global system since the Cold War, charting the declining trend in armed conflict since 1946 (Marshall and Cole 2013) (see figure 1.2). Another report (Goldstone et al. 2010) demonstrated the ability to correctly predict the onset of instability two years in advance in 18 of 21 instances, or about 85 percent of the time.

According to a similarly large country study by the Center for the Study of Civil War at the Peace Research Institute Oslo of 416 armed conflicts since 1946, most were intra-state, 63 were inter-state and 21 were colonial wars of liberation (Binningsbø, Loyle, Gates, and Elster 2012). Moreover, Gates asserted in the *Economist* (2013) that victors will be fewer, replaced by negotiated endings. He further predicts an increase in the involvement of international organizations and outside regional organizations to resolve conflict but a decrease in outside interference in fueling conflict. Of course, negotiated settlements can also lead to more conflict, and the implications of a drastic global economic downturn, energy shortages, or unforeseen disturbances should be explored.

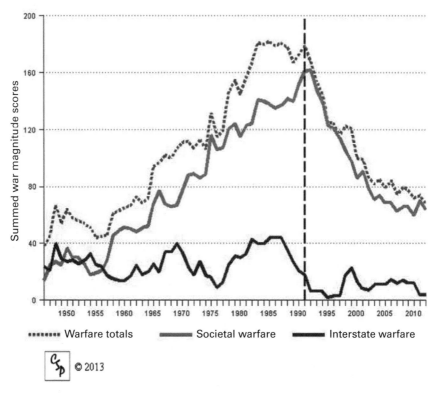

Figure 1.2
Global Trends in Armed Conflict, 1946–2012
Source: Marshall and Cole (2013).

Several realist theories address the relation between power and war. Hegemonic stability theory argues that the international system is likely to remain more stable when there is a single dominant power (Gilpin 1988; Kindleberger 1973; Webb and Krasner 1989). Balance of power theory, in contrast, claims that equality in power, including military might, is conducive to peace (Kegley and Wittkopf 2005).

Power transition theory focuses on the relative power of nation-states and warns that when a rising power approaches the power level of its regional or global leader and is dissatisfied with the existing system, the chances of war increase (Organski and Fimo 1968; Abdollian et al. 2000). Britain acquiesced to the rise of the United States after World War II, but Germany and Japan met armed resistance on a grand scale, and the Soviet Union fought and lost the 45-year Cold War with the United States.

Some analysts see nothing but danger from the rise of new great powers and the decline of the United States. Kugler (2006) warns that the rising power of China relative to the United States greatly increases the chances of a great-power war sometime in the next few decades. Mearsheimer (2001) points to a world of continuous great-power rivalry in the shadow of a great-power war. China is constrained now by American power, but Nasr (2013) believes that a world without strong and consistent American leadership is a frightening prospect. Bisley (2011) argues that China felt enormously strengthened by the Western financial crisis of 2008–2009 but failed to successfully assert itself through economic diplomacy (see also Drezner 2010) and came to feel trapped.

In this scenario, growth in mutual antagonism, not cooperation, defines the world system. Friction and conflict become the norm, and there is an increasing trend toward militarizing disputes. This is a situation that Bremmer and Roubini (2011) call "A G-Zero World," in which the major powers cannot sit down together and work out their differences amicably. Instead, "no country or bloc has the political or economic leverage—or the will—to drive a truly international agenda" (2).

With no way to forge agreements on trade, finance, and security, the world becomes increasingly mercantilist, shutting off growth opportunities for the poor countries and raising tensions on all fronts. Security becomes more of a concern for every country, and resources are diverted to military uses, producing less, not more, security. Bobbitt (2002) raises concerns about mercantilism. He asserts that the nation-state is losing out to three competing constitutional forms of the "market-state": the entrepreneurial market-state, the mercantile market-state, and the managerial market-state. There is no guarantee that the three forms of governance can coexist harmoniously and that the rise of mercantile market-states such as China and Russia will not pose a great danger to the international system.

In contrast, liberalism is present in scenarios in which democracy prevails and wars are prevented. Globalization accelerates the process of nation-states working through multinational corporations, nongovernmental organizations, and international governmental organizations. Ikenberry (2011) describes a future harmonious global order. In his vision, a peaceful power transition will take place as the relative power of the United States declines. The BRIC countries will not choose to overturn the existing liberal international system because they gain too much from it. Regionalism, militarism, and protectionism will not be economically or politically worth the effort.

Democratic governance will continue, from the third wave in Eastern Europe (Huntington 1991) to a fourth wave in the Arab world (Howard and Hussain 2013) and ultimately in China. American hegemony will disappear, but the liberal values and the global institutions—such as the United Nations, the International Monetary Fund, the World Bank, and the World Trade Organization—built under that hegemony will survive because it is in the interest of all the major players for the system to continue.

Constructivism suggests scenarios in which people are deterministic in changing the structures, processes, identities, and interests of world politics—in particular, the drive toward capitalism, appreciating the limits to growth, and adapting new patterns of interaction to address global challenges. Where values align, such as in the "responsibility to protect" (Evans 2008), nation-states will work together to end mass atrocities through humanitarian action or peace enforcement. War will become obsolete, according to Fettweis (2010), and only commercial and cultural competition will remain. The national interest of all nations will become so entwined with commercial interdependence that war will become economically unattractive. Nuclear proliferation will help avoid war, and instant global communication will make war even more remote. In this new harmonious world, the United States will not need much of a military because the world will be able to police itself.

At the nexus of energy, economics, and geopolitics is also the question of whether the struggle to acquire natural resources will result in greater disharmony. Klare (2001) strongly warns of future wars over resources, Victor (2008) minimizes the risks, and our scenarios embrace both views. In several of our scenarios, the rising production of conventional and unconventional sources in developing countries leads to instability rather than prosperity. Ross (2012), Sachs and Warner (1997), and Van der Ploeg (2011) all argue that countries with weak institutions, an inadequate rule of law, and an undiversified economy will find resource wealth a mixed blessing, at best. Only a few empirical studies have found the endowment of natural resources to be unambiguously positive (see, for example, Haber and Menaldo 2011; Herb 2005; Luong and Weinthal 2010).

The IFs model examines global harmony and disharmony by calculating conditional probabilities for social stability and international war. For social stability, the IFs model calculates the probability of regime failure for each country in each year.[3] Regime failure—resulting from revolutionary wars, ethnic wars, genocides, or politicides—is calculated as a probabilistic function of economic performance, trade openness, regime type, and overall social well-being, indicated by the infant mortality rate. These variables find the most theoretical and empirical support in the first four major reports of the Political Instability Task Force and its predecessor, the State Failure Task Force (Goldstone et al. 2005). Different assumptions about economic growth and political institutions are shown in our simulation results to generate large changes in the probability estimates for political instability.

The IFs model also calculates the probability of international war each year. Most of the probabilities are very small, but about a dozen countries—including China, Russia, and the United States—have a more than 3 percent initial probability of getting into a war in any given year. The probabilities are calculated based on two strands of research: the peace-through-trade argument, and power transition theory.

A tremendous amount of empirical research exists that mostly supports the idea of an inverse relationship between trade and war. Levy (2003, 127) argues, "While there are extensive debates over the proper research designs for investigating this question, and while some empirical studies find that trade is associated with international conflict, most studies conclude that trade is associated with peace, both at the dyadic and systemic levels."

The IFs model therefore combines the theoretical and empirical work of the peace-through-trade tradition with the work of the power transition scholars in an attempt to forecast the probability of war. In the model, Hughes, Hossain, and Irfan (2004b) consulted with scholars in both camps, particularly Edward Mansfield and Douglas Lemke, estimated the starting probabilities for each dyad based on the historical record, and then forecast future probabilities for dyadic militarized disputes and wars, based on the calibrated relationships they derived from the empirical literature.

Use of the power transition theory requires an empirical definition of *power*. Estimating national power has produced an enormous literature that has been summarized by Hoehn (2011), but it has produced no consensus beyond a general agreement that economic productive capability and military strength are important. The IFs model chooses to calculate comprehensive national power as the weighted sum of four components that are often cited in the literature: GDP, population, military spending, and technological prowess, each measured as a share of the world total. We equate comprehensive national power with geopolitical power in our scenarios. Reflecting the debate in the literature, the model gives the user the ability to choose a total of 18 additional concepts, including nuclear weapons and net energy balance, and the ability to weight any of the concepts as deemed important.

Will there be global harmony or disharmony? Disharmony can have more determinative horsepower than the other two drivers. At the same time, disharmony is likely to be fairly invariant, as argued by Marshall, Gurr, and Harff (2009), with a decrease in inter-state war. When we discuss disharmony, it is not always violent conflict (inter-state and intra-state); it can also be political upheaval like the Arab Spring, stagnation in international organizations because of various national interests, tension between bipolar hegemons, or a rise in anti-globalization movements. In these cases, poor economic growth and high energy prices can be the drivers of disharmony.

The Future in Eight Scenarios

Each of the eight scenarios, featured in table 1.2, begins with a different point in the post–financial crisis period, moves into the 2020s and the 2030s, and ends with the 2040s. The degrees of low or high energy prices, weak or strong economic growth, and global harmony or dis-harmony vary. There are four different energy price trends that we characterize as high and four that are low. Similarly, the average world economic growth, and how that growth is constituted by country,

Table 1.2
The Eight Scenarios

	Energy Prices	Economic Growth	Geopolitics
Scenario 1: Catching Up to America	Low	Strong	Global harmony
Scenario 2: Global Backtracking	Low	Weak	Global disharmony
Scenario 3: Peaceful Power Transition	High	Strong	Global harmony
Scenario 4: Regional Mercantilism	High	Weak	Global disharmony
Scenario 5: A New Bipolarity	High	Strong	Global disharmony
Scenario 6: Eco World	High	Weak	Global harmony
Scenario 7: Ambition Fuels Rivalry	Low	Strong	Global disharmony
Scenario 8: Natural Disasters Promote Unity	Low	Weak	Global harmony

Source: Authors.

differs by scenario, with four strong scenarios and four weak. Harmony and disharmony also vary by degree and by country and region, again with four harmonious scenarios and four disharmonious.

Chapter 2 presents the first scenario, Catching Up to America, in which low energy prices, strong economic growth, and global harmony allow non-OECD economies to grow strongly, driving a new global energy market. China's rise to become the largest economy strengthens its will to be the new hegemon, and there is no countervailing global power to contest it. China does not threaten the global order, however, and instead works within international organizations.

Chapter 3 presents the second scenario, Global Backtracking. This scenario is marked by low energy prices, weak economic growth, and global disharmony. Plagued by stalled reforms, the economies of the United States, the European Union, and China falter, driving down global growth and energy demand. Global instability ensues: Asian countries form a new alliance to counter an aggressive China; Iran emerges as the regional hegemon after war; Russia experiences a revolution; and, many African nations are mired in conflict. The international community fails to adequately address the underlying problems.

Chapter 4 presents the third scenario, Peaceful Power Transition, in which energy prices are high, economic growth is strong, and there is global harmony. The world economy recovers from the stagnation resulting in higher GDP growth than would be the case otherwise, and the BRICs (Brazil, Russia, India and China) are joined by a second echelon of emerging nation-states, the STICKs (South Africa, Turkey, Indonesia, Colombia, and Kazakhstan).[4] A combination of high energy demand and a decline in Middle East oil production leads to a large increase in the production of energy from renewable sources.

Chapter 5 presents the fourth scenario, Regional Mercantilism, resulting from high energy prices, weak economic growth, and global disharmony. As the United States' economy declines, the model of democratic capitalism is replaced by Chinese-style state capitalism, accompanied by growing protectionism, slowing trade growth, and more regional trade arrangements, none of which are very attractive to the others. Even as world economic growth slows, energy prices rise perilously because of faltering supplies.

Chapter 6 presents the fifth scenario, a New Bipolarity, resulting from high energy prices, strong economic growth, and global disharmony. In this scenario, the world economy recovers from the quagmire of 2008, and China asserts its growing power, but the United States employs trade measures and alliance diplomacy that contain China. A new tenuous bipolarity emerges as rising powers, hoping to gain economic benefits from both camps, are left disappointed. A reduction in Middle East oil supply is balanced by alternative energy sources, led by production in the United States.

Chapter 7 presents the sixth scenario, Eco World, which results from high energy prices, weak economic growth, and global harmony. In this scenario, the world economy continues to struggle, but drastic advances are made in global environmental cooperation. Aside from this, nations are focused inward, dealing with disruptive citizens unhappy with slow growth; in China the Communist Party collapses. The United States remains the sole superpower, albeit a more cooperative and less confrontational one.

Chapter 8 presents the seventh scenario, Ambition Fuels Rivalry, with low energy prices, strong economic growth, and global disharmony. Rapid technological change and improved economic governance propels growth in the OECD and non-OECD countries, particularly China, India, Brazil, and Turkey. This, combined with cheap energy, causes many countries to assert themselves internationally resulting in conflicts and, in the end, nations in the East and the West join one of two major blocs: the League of Democracies or the Shanghai Pact. Russia, Brazil, and Turkey and Iran are left to influence their respective regions.

Chapter 9 presents the eighth scenario, Natural Disasters Promote Unity, resulting from low energy prices, weak economic growth, and global harmony. A series of catastrophic natural disasters bring disparate countries together in humanitarian relief efforts, forging a strong international will to address human security above all else. With a few exceptions, low energy demand globally prevents large-scale investment in cleaner energy technology, and most countries choose to continue burning fossil fuels.

Chapter 10 summarizes the eight scenarios, discussing what we have learned from generating the scenarios and how the three variables affect one another in certain circumstances. Though not favoring any of the scenarios, we comment on which aspects of the scenarios we believe to be more plausible than others. We assign for each scenario a degree of low, medium, and high probability and explain why. We also discuss what, if anything, we believe to be missing from these scenarios. After all, our analysis could not cover every aspect of energy, economic, and geopolitical developments to 2050. We discuss the insights we had and the deductions we drew from conducting this exercise. We conclude by proposing how certain policy choices made by key actors in the international community push us in more or less plausible directions. Thus, rather than prescribing particular policies, we express concerns about how current decisions will affect the future.

2 Catching Up to America

SCENARIO 1: LOW ENERGY PRICES, STRONG ECONOMIC GROWTH, GLOBAL HARMONY

The first scenario is marked by low energy prices, strong economic growth, and global harmony. The OECD countries suffer low growth in 2010–2019, while Asian growth continues to surge. Rapid expansion of oil and gas production, coupled with slow OECD-country growth, results in subdued energy prices. The OECD economies eventually right themselves with a burst of technological innovation, some of which significantly reduces energy consumption and thus allows energy prices to remain low. An entirely new energy market is created globally that is more competitive and includes a variety of new energy sources.

By 2025, China has become by far the largest economy, with high per capita income, advanced technology, a powerful military, and the political will to be the new hegemon. This great and prolonged divergence in economic performance results in a geopolitical shift of profound dimension because there is little countervailing power or will to contest China's rise. After peacefully expanding its borders in most directions, China engages in a brief war with Russia over eastern Siberia.

This does not, however, stop the rise of a new period of hegemonic stability by the 2040s. China attempts to influence global affairs mainly through multilateral institutions and soft power. The Chinese renminbi eventually becomes a major reserve currency, held by all countries and used for trade invoicing by many. China does not assert itself aggressively beyond its Asian region and does not try to fundamentally alter the rules of the global economy.

The United Nations takes on a growing role in global affairs, and U.N. Security Council vetoes are rare. There is more international cooperation on issues such as climate change and global inequality.

The 2010s

Policy gridlock characterizes most OECD countries in 2010s. Part of the gridlock is a result of the intellectual debate between demand-side and supply-side economists. The demand-side economists, such as Paul Krugman, argue for more government spending to boost the economy; the supply-side economists, such as John Taylor, advocate lower business taxes and fewer regulatory burdens.

The stalemate is caused partly by the ideological battle between, on the one hand, angry unemployed youth and others who view globalization and technological change as a threat and, on the other hand, those trying to develop the economy through the process of creative destruction or revolutionary change from within. The stalemate is also caused by a systemic partisanship in American politics, mirrored by rising nationalism and polarization in Europe.

This policy gridlock prevents the determination of any meaningful long-term economic reforms to reverse growing indebtedness and reduce unemployment. North America and Europe suffer through a decade of low growth and mounting levels of government debt that threaten long-term growth.

Low growth in the OECD countries is a problem for Asia. China suffers a sharp economic slowdown because of OECD troubles and its own real estate bubble. Premier Xi Jinping fails in his first attempts to push through a set of reforms that threaten the power and wealth of much of the Communist Party elite. By the end of the decade, however, and after gradually purging many of his antagonists, Xi Jinping sets the economy on a renewed path of high growth.

The reform policies improve property rights in the countryside as well as in urban areas, free the banking system from the necessity to fund inefficient state-owned enterprises, and allow the exchange rate to rise significantly, fueling a burst in domestic demand. At the same time, China's huge investment in science and technical education starts to produce its own technology, leading to further advances in productivity growth. The new Chinese boom propels a strong rebound of economic growth in the rest of east Asia.

The leaders of some of China's neighbors—South Korea, Japan, the Philippines, Taiwan, and Vietnam—are caught in a precarious position. Their main market and primary protector, the United States, is limping, and their old antagonist, China, is surging. The Chinese economy has outgrown the U.S. economy in this decade by more than 7 percent per year.

Facing growing diplomatic pressure, these Southeast Asian leaders see little benefit in defying the Chinese, and they begin to offer new concessions on disputed islands, offshore energy exploration, and Chinese investment in their countries. This in turn weakens the U.S. "pivot to Asia" policy, and U.S. economic and military alliances lessen.

Multilateral arrangements in the region, such as the Asia Pacific Economic Cooperation, the primary economic forum supporting sustainable economic growth and prosperity in the Asia-Pacific region, gradually become dominated by a Chinese agenda. The Association of Southeast Asian Nations remains independent of China in membership but weakens as tensions within prevent the consensus-based approach from advancing agendas, since every member retains a veto. The U.S.-led Trans Pacific Partnership shrivels to a small rump group of nations, but many of its market-friendly concepts, particularly financial liberalization, become part of the new Chinese model.

The rapid expansion of unconventional oil and gas production, mostly in the non-OPEC states, coupled with slow OECD economic growth, result in subdued energy prices in this decade. Low oil prices lead to weak growth, dashed expectations, and smoldering tensions in the Middle East. The long U.S. interventions in Iraq and Afghanistan are terminated by 2015, but both countries remain violently unstable. The Taliban return to power over most of Afghanistan by 2020, but warlords in the north and southwest maintain continuous pressure on the regime, and human rights abuses escalate. The Islamic State of Iraq and the Levant (ISIL) continues to make incremental progress in holding swaths of land in Iraq and Syria.

Iraq is divided into two states. The Kurdish north establishes control over its own energy resources and builds a semi-fortified nation-state against ISIL with the help of foreign military assistance. The Shiite majority holds nominal control of parts of southern Iraq and Baghdad with the support of Iran, but the Sunni-led insurgency continues to prevent an orderly state-building effort. An agreement is reached with Iran on developing a peaceful nuclear energy program, and the conflict in Syria dissipates as regional proxies withdraw their military support for various factions, and instead support the Syrian government's war against ISIL.

The Deauville Partnership, established by the Group of 8 (G-8) countries in 2011, gradually starts to live up to its promising rhetoric. The newly renamed G-7 (after Russia's invasion of Crimea, Ukraine, leads to its expulsion in 2014) and Saudi Arabia, the United Arab Emirates, Kuwait, Qatar, Turkey, and multilateral financial institutions provide a significant amount of development financing and technical assistance to the North African countries. Domestic political tensions gradually ease in Egypt and its neighboring states, and governments prove more willing to accept outside assistance in strengthening their economic and political institutions.

The Arab Spring movement does not result in an overall democratic awakening or a burst of Arab constitutional liberalism, but it leads to more accountable governments, improves the tolerance of minority groups, and gradually reduces the threat of radical upheaval. New governments are elected in Egypt, Jordan, Libya, and Tunisia, and, along with the regime in Algeria, the countries' leadership consolidate power and gain increasing legitimacy by stimulating economic growth.

Most of sub-Saharan Africa and South America prosper as their countries increasingly shift their production to meet the needs of east Asian producers and consumers. As market orientation shifts from the Northern Hemisphere to the Eastern Hemisphere, so too does political orientation. U.S.-led pressure to enhance democratic institutions is delegitimized; rather, many more countries emphasize strong-man or one-party rule, such as that already prevalent in Venezuela, Bolivia, Ecuador, and Paraguay. This more authoritarian leadership seems to deliver better economic performance and more equitable growth than the institutional reform path prescribed by the Washington Consensus model.

In Africa, Burkino Faso, Ethiopia, Mozambique, Rwanda, Tanzania, and Uganda continue to reduce poverty levels while developing their economies. Stable and purposeful policy making is a primary reason for the growth, much of which comes from steps taken in the 1990s to control public finances and curb inflation. Improvements in governance also aid growth. There is less corruption, more efficient bureaucracy, and better regulation. Better governance leads to increased levels of foreign and domestic investment and stronger economic growth. Better governance also prompts the OECD and the BRIC countries

(Brazil, Russia, India, and China) to become more generous and more reliable with aid to African nations, further stimulating their growth. Burkino Faso, Tanzania, and Mozambique particularly stand out in their ability to use burgeoning resource wealth to build diversified economies, improve tax collection, and promote equality.

Mexico suffers in this decade. Hurt by slow growth in the United States and its own underperforming energy sector, it is unable to muster the resources or the political will to control the crime syndicates. The cartels are able to co-opt local and regional governments in much of the country, leaving the central government unable to have much effect outside the federal district. The national police and the military both tend to respond more to local leaders (and to their own economic self-interest) than to national policy.

The rise in power of the cartels intensifies fighting among the groups. The U.S. border region is severely affected by the disorder, which results in economic stagnation and increased militarization in Mexico. Disorder and political weakness impedes Mexico's ability to enact government de-regulation measures and open up its energy sector to greater foreign investment, limiting the expansion of hydrocarbon production during this period.

The 2020s and 2030s

Economic growth revives in the OECD countries in the 2020s. The battles between the groups advocating austerity versus stimulus fade as both sides are forced to give way. OECD governments adopt measures to raise taxes and reduce spending while also having to shift a higher proportion of resources to transfer payments. The European Union enacts a series of labor reforms that allow employers much more leeway in hiring, firing, working conditions, and wages. These moves go against deeply ingrained public support for social protection—15 years of very high unemployment have resigned the majority to change.

Despite the fiscal constraints, the United States and Europe resume growth, benefiting from a new wave of technological innovation that sparks rapid productivity growth in several key sectors, including electronics, aircraft manufacturing, and energy generation and efficiency. Both the United States and the European Union take steps to reduce the volatility of the financial sector. Explicit and implicit guarantees to the too-big-to-fail banks are reduced dramatically, which motivates these institutions to manage risk more carefully and focus more on productive investments. Massive fines on corrupt practices in the financial industry and lengthy jail terms for a few particularly bad actors help create better incentives. Financial tensions are reduced by a decline in the savings-investment imbalance in the United States and China, which had created acrimony in 2010s.

Great strides in energy efficiency in OECD countries result in a significant decrease in energy use, and this technology is transferred to the current big energy users, China and India. Led by U.S. government research funding, second-generation biofuels from nonfood sources are produced at competitive prices as hydrocarbons, allowing for the reduction of oil in transportation, including for the military and for commercial airlines (Closson 2013). The advances in energy technology help keep world energy prices in check.

The United States and Europe conclude a transatlantic trade agreement and greatly expand trade; much of the growth comes in the clean energy sector, including renewable energy but also safer nuclear technology, and in highly efficient appliances, cars, and other long-haul forms of transport. Stabilized financial markets and the booming energy economy have significant implications for other sectors of the U.S. economy, especially transportation and steel. For example, the low price of natural gas encourages significant amounts of previously outsourced manufacturing back to the United States. The technology boom and the fiscal and financial reforms propel real per capita income in the OECD nations by more than 2 percent per year in the 2020s and 2030s, greatly relieving the social tensions that undermined the appeal of the Western growth model in the 2010s.

The strides in energy efficiency and the rising oil and gas production from shale, deep water, and oil sands reduce the importance of the traditional producers of conventional oil and gas in the 2020s. The new energy boom is spurred by a host of new, smaller companies that are committed to innovation and willing to take risks. They enable the United States to take the lead in changing the way energy is bought and sold globally. A global liquid gas market replaces the previously three independent regional markets, stabilizing and lowering the price of natural gas.

As a result, Russia, among others, no longer has a monopoly on gas supplies to the European market with which it can exercise political leverage (Closson 2011). Russia, which at first seemed to be threatened by the new trends in the global energy market, gradually adapts to them, particularly after the United States and the European Union exact increasingly restrictive sanctions on cooperating with its oil and gas companies in response to its expropriation of Crimea and parts of eastern Ukraine in the 2010s. The government reduces its punitive taxes on energy production, unleashing a torrent of new investment. New gas and oil fields are opened in Siberia, including huge shale gas reserves. New pipeline capacity is added to supply more gas east to China and Japan, and south to India.

The surge in Russian economic growth and employment has a great positive effect on the country's morale, helping to lift its birth rate to self-sustaining levels and halt emigration. As markets grow, transportation lines are enhanced, trade surges, and living standards improve dramatically in the European portions of the former Soviet Union. The reorganization of the world energy markets and the ability of countries to adapt and find alternative sources of energy, means that Russia can no longer so easily punish its neighbors by energy and trade diplomacy (Closson, Hillebrand and Bervoets 2014).

By the mid-2020s, the Russian government decides instead to increase and normalize ties with the West, driven in part by low energy prices. Russia becomes a more cooperative member of the global community, abandoning its pursuit of a Eurasian Union in favor of joining the European Union. Even membership in the North Atlantic Treaty Organization (NATO) seems a possibility in exchange for its ceding influence in southeastern Ukraine; Russia badly needs NATO to reduce a growing Chinese threat on its eastern border.

Low energy prices and strong growth in China and the OECD countries mean that most other countries also prosper. All that is needed for robust growth in this global environment is a modicum of social stability and a system of governance that leans toward accountability and open markets. In addition to Russia, many of the big countries—including India, Indonesia, South Africa, and Turkey—do well in these decades.

Only a few nations miss out. Burma lapses into a harsh military autocracy that promotes patrimonial, not national, wealth. A few countries in central Africa remain mired in tribal and/or sectarian conflict. Bolivia, Paraguay, Jamaica, and Venezuela produce populist despots who pillage their own countries while scapegoating others, particularly the more democratic regional leaders, Colombia and Brazil, as well as the United States.

Despite the rise in non-OPEC production of fossil fuels and the gains in renewable energy technology, energy prices continue to rise in this scenario in response to the huge overall increase in energy demand. With rising prices and rising energy production, some Middle Eastern countries prosper, especially Qatar and the United Arab Emirates.

Saudi Arabia, however, struggles despite its energy riches. The kingdom's underemployed youth take to the streets, port and oil workers launch crippling strikes, and jihadists take up arms against the monarchy. Attacks on the energy sector become endemic and grow in intensity, further diminishing state revenue. The Saudi Arabian monarchy is overthrown by the mid-2020s after months of street protests. But rather than civilian rule being instituted, the army takes over. Thus the regime and its social structures remain largely unchanged; only the level of repression intensifies.

Some countries with great potential for an energy boom are slow to reverse protectionist nationalist resource policies. In Latin America, Argentina and Brazil are late in attracting private investors. It is not until the 2030s, when socialist and/or patrimonial governments are replaced by centrist technocrats, and their economies grow stronger and their institutions are more transparent, that their energy sectors are opened to outside investment and innovation. This leads to a significant increase in hydrocarbon production.

By 2030, China has grown in purchasing power parity (PPP) terms by more than 7.5 percent per year for 50 years. This rate is 1 or 2 percent faster per year than the rates of the previous growth leaders: South Korea (6.2 percent), Taiwan (6 percent), and Botswana (5.7 percent), achieved between 1951 and 2007 (Maddison 2001; World Bank 2011). China has several advantages over those countries, including more room for catch-up growth, a greater capacity for economies of scale, a lesser external threat environment, faster growth in the rest of the world, and less trade protectionism.

As China moves to a floating exchange rate and minimal capital controls, the use of the renminbi as an international currency for trade invoicing and reserves grows gradually. The rise in importance of the renminbi happens naturally and smoothly with the rise of the Chinese economy, and its rise is beneficial to the health of the world economy (Eichengreen 2011).

In these high-growth decades, China catches up to the United States in real GDP in 2024 (using 2005 PPP numbers).[1] By successfully liberalizing its economy in 2010–2019 and profiting from the environmentally friendly energy boom of the succeeding decades, China is on a path to a high standard of living, almost as high as that of Americans in 2010.

The United States and the rest of the OECD countries do not stand still, however, and their living standards also improve (see table 2.1).

As China's economic might rises, its neighbors grow more wary. Terrill (2005, 5) noted, "The expansionist claims of Beijing are transparent and unique among today's powerful nations." U.S. officials have anticipated this period with anxiety. Susan Shirk (2007, 5), the deputy assistant secretary of state for U.S. relations with China in the Clinton administration, feared China's rise and wrote the following:

Table 2.1
Scenario 1: Catching Up to America
Low Energy Prices, Strong Economic Growth, Global Harmony

Real GDP, billions of 2010$ at 2010 exchange rates

	2010	2020	2040	2050
USA	14,447	16,595	27,844	34,720
		1.4%	2.6%	2.2%
China	5,931	13,298	62,981	100,981
		8.4%	8.1%	4.8%
OECD	38,646	42,579	66,330	81,136
		1.0%	2.2%	2.0%
Non-OECD	24,944	42,588	148,561	238,449
		5.5%	6.4%	4.8%
World	63,590	85,167	214,891	319,585
		3.0%	4.7%	4.0%

Real GDP per capita, 1000s of 2005 PPP $

	2010	2020	2040	2050
USA	42.1	44.5	66.2	78.9
		0.6%	2.0%	1.8%
China	6.8	11.4	38.3	57.5
		5.2%	6.3%	4.1%
OECD	34.9	37.4	57.2	70.2
		0.7%	2.2%	2.1%
Non-OECD	6.0	8.0	17.5	24.3
		2.8%	4.0%	3.3%
World	9.9	11.6	21.9	29.2
		1.6%	3.2%	2.9%

Source: 2010 numbers from the World Bank's online "Development Indicators" as of August 2012. The percentages are the per-period average annual growth rates, which are determined by assumption. Consistency among countries and scenarios is maintained with the assistance of the IFs model, version 6.75.

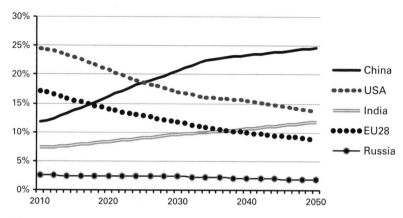

Figure 2.1
Share of World Geopolitical Power in Scenario 1
Source: Calculations with the IFs model.

History teaches us that rising powers are likely to provoke war. The ancient historian Thucydides identified the fear that a rising Athens inspired in other states as the cause of the Peloponnesian War. In the 20th century, rising powers Germany and Japan were the cause of two devastating world wars. Are China and America doomed to become enemies in the 21st century?

But up to 2020, despite persistent diplomatic spats about islands in the East China and South China Seas, the Chinese government mostly calms global fears by focusing on economic growth and domestic tranquillity. During the 2020s, China lacks sufficient power to significantly alter the shape of the geopolitical order.

As shown in figure 2.1, sometime around 2025, the United States and China reach parity in their share of geopolitical power. After this point, China surpasses the United States and continues a positive trajectory, reaching a 25 percent share of geopolitical power in 2050. The United States, in contrast, continues to decline to a little less than 15 percent of world power by 2050. During the power transition, the United States tries to maintain its supremacy while China relishes its rise in power. But they avoid fighting, mostly because since the mid-2010s, the U.S. political elite has understood the inevitability of China's ascent and U.S. limitations.

Nasr (2013, 2) wrote, "Gone is the exuberant American desire to lead the world. In its place is the image of a superpower tired of the world and in retreat. Hence, the role of the United States as the most influential global power continues to decline." As a result, as China expands into the areas it has long claimed, the United States only weakly speaks of the right of self-determination. Taiwan is folded into the Chinese empire; most of the Taiwanese people accept it happily and believe that the new relationship is essential to their continued progress. Japan is forced to cede control of all the previously disputed islands, as well as Okinawa, to China. The South China Sea peacefully becomes a zone of Chinese control. Only in Siberia does Chinese expansion of its economic zones meet serious armed resistance, from the Russian residents. However, Russia eventually cedes to Chinese economic influence in the region, striking deals for space and natural resources (Terrill 2005).

U.S. interests have altered as a result of the radically different domestic and global energy picture. Global energy production of fossil fuels soars, especially North American oil and natural gas (see table 2.2). A new market is created in which U.S. companies own the most patents and dominate the global energy mix, including, to a great extent, hydrocarbon production.

A global liquefied natural gas market is flourishing, enhanced by U.S. production, as well as production in the eastern Mediterranean and offshore in east Africa, with U.S. support. Shale gas production is also taken up by Europe after advances in technology that dispel public concerns about water contamination and environmental damage. Infrastructure, tax, and regulatory policies are enacted to support production. Even in Eastern Europe, including Ukraine, shale gas development booms.

The 2040s

The United States and Europe accept diminished geopolitical power and struggle to deal with maintaining prosperity in the face of demographic decline (in Europe) and an aging population (in the United States). More harmonious geopolitical relations allow European countries to further reduce their militaries and focus resources on internal problems. By the 2040s the European Union maintains its reputation as a premier research area, and advanced technology allows for an upsurge in local production that is more knowledge based and efficient.

Information technology, additive manufacturing (the industrial version of 3-D printing), robotics, nanotechnology, and biotechnology converge in ways previously unimagined. Major European cities maintain their reputations as progressive and livable, attracting millions of

Table 2.2
Energy Production

Billions of barrels of oil equivalents	2010	2020	2040	2050	Average annual percentage change, 2011–2050
World	89.1	98.7	143.6	179.9	1.8%
Liquids	29.3	30.9	43.0	45.5	1.1%
Gas	22.2	28.5	46.8	54.9	2.3%
Coal	26.6	29.4	39.4	46.0	1.4%
Nuclear	4.6	3.6	3.0	4.5	0.0%
Renewable sources	6.5	6.3	11.6	29.0	3.8%
Hydroelectric	5.4	5.6	6.5	7.5	0.8%
Other renewable sources	1.2	0.8	5.1	21.6	7.6%
World energy use/GDP ratio	100	84.9	56.5	50.9	–1.7%
World real price of energy (index: 2010 = 100)	100	124.7	146.4	157.5	1.1%
OPEC Middle East liquids	8.3	9.9	17.0	19.5	2.2%
Share of world liquids	28.3%	31.9%	39.5%	42.8%	
Share of world energy	9.3%	10.0%	11.8%	10.8%	
Other major liquids production					
USA	2.4	3.0	5.1	5.2	1.9%
Canada	1.2	1.4	3.3	5.3	3.8%
Russia	3.8	3.9	4.0	2.8	–0.7%
Major natural gas producers					
USA	4.0	5.0	6.3	7.9	1.7%
Canada	1.1	0.7	0.5	0.9	–0.3%
U.S. net energy imports as share of:					
Total energy use	23.5%	15.0%	7.4%	1.6%	
GDP (price adjusted)	1.9%	1.3%	0.6%	0.1%	
China net energy imports as share of:					
Total energy use	13.6%	5.1%	13.0%	5.7%	
GDP (price adjusted)	3.0%	1.0%	3.0%	0.7%	

Source: 2010 energy numbers from Energy Information Agency (2013) and the IFs model data bank. Energy growth rates by assumption. Other numbers by calculation with the IFs model.

the world's new elite to visit and perhaps stay. Labor reform and fiscal discipline imposed from Berlin helps to restore prosperity in southern Europe, but that region remains far poorer than Germany or the Nordic countries. Berlin continues to help shepherd the European Union through trying times, but more executive power gradually accrues to Brussels, and its competency and legitimacy soar (Manning 2013).

Defense cuts in the largest European militaries, as well as in the United States, seriously affect their ability to deploy and sustain forces for a long period. Instead, NATO reforms to more effectively address softer security issues, such as cyber security and transnational threats of narcotics, human trafficking, and disease. At the same time, smaller, more mobile and rapid units are created to respond quickly to man-made and natural disasters. NATO also reorients its previously ambitious geographical expansion to focus instead on the immediate environs of Europe. Previously reluctant European countries join NATO, including Finland, Ireland, Malta, Sweden, and Switzerland, and Russia signs an accession agreement.

The conflict between the West and the jihadists has dissipated; the West has largely withdrawn political interest from the Middle East, except for Israel, by 2040 (Friedman 2009). China and the United States retain strong economic interests in the region but avoid meddling in internal politics. It helps that both countries are far less reliant on Middle East hydrocarbons and no longer see a need to protect producers and transportation corridors.

The shifting of the balance of power from the United States to China does not alter the position of the jihadists or the Islamic world in general. Continuing sectarian and regional rivalries in the Middle East eliminate the possibility of constructing a significant unified fundamentalist state. Islamic fundamentalists have their own state to govern in Afghanistan, and that country provides a safe haven for discouraged jihadists from other lands. Moreover, Iraqi and Syrian security services manage to weaken ISIL forces by, first, isolating areas under strictly enforced Islamic laws and principles. This populace, walled off from the rest of society, suffers economically and psychologically. Security forces and disillusioned Islamists work with the security forces to route ISIL leaders, replacing them with more moderate leaders from the business sector.

Global economic growth spreads to the Middle East, and the subsequent political stability and dramatic drop in birth rates reduce the proclivity for youth to turn to violence. Likewise, the Israelis and the

Palestinians are able to reach an accord that leaves both parties able to focus on economic growth rather than conflict. The prospect of the rise of a regional superpower, such as Iran, remains low.

The rest of the world's regions benefit from the economic prosperity spurred on by the United States and China, as well as from affordable and available alternative energies and a peaceful hegemonic China. Most of Latin America prospers, gradually converging toward OECD levels of income. Argentina moves decisively away from populism and expands rapidly. Africa is mixed, with some countries developing institutions better suited to promoting prosperity and others continuing to wallow in sectarian and/or tribal strife. India and Pakistan gradually wind down their conflict; most of Kashmir is ceded peacefully to Pakistan because India realizes that the military costs of continued conflict are not worth the effort. Indian economic reform continues to produce significant rates of per capita economic growth in the 2040s, and India enters into the ranks of middle-income countries.

The United Nations takes on a growing role in global affairs, and UN Security Council vetoes are rare. The Security Council is reformulated: France and the United Kingdom agree to cede their individual seats for a European Union vote, and India gets the fifth permanent seat. The idea of moving the UN Secretariat to an Asian site is perennially discussed but not yet acted upon. New agendas for trade, finance, outer space, navigation, and the Arctic are determined by a group of experts and brought to the United Nations for discussion.

The G-20 gains in stature and takes on an increasingly powerful role in setting global agendas on economics and politics. Its membership reflects new geopolitical relationships, too: Italy, Argentina, and Saudi Arabia are out; Iran, Nigeria, and Ethiopia are in. Voting shares of the Bretton Woods institutions are once again reallocated to reflect a new global economic system. The World Trade Organization gains in prestige by finally negotiating a deal that trades agricultural support in the OECD countries for enhanced intellectual property protection and better treatment of foreign investors and service providers in the non-OECD countries. These negotiations are made easier by the fact that the OECD itself expands to 70 nations as living standards improve and the requirement for democratic governance weakens.

There is also more international cooperation on issues such as climate change. A strong natural gas market replaces coal in electricity generation to a significant extent. This, combined with affordable carbon-capture storage technology at coal plants, moves countries to accept strict reductions in carbon emissions in a new international protocol, two decades later than expected. This is operationalized in the form of smaller, regionally based carbon exchanges and projects on mitigating and adapting to climate change. China eases restrictions on exporting rare earth minerals, allowing Western technology firms to scale up the production of renewable energies.

The biggest challenge facing the international community is the availability of freshwater and adequate agricultural production. By 2040, freshwater availability cannot keep up with demand. As a result of demographic and economic development pressures, North Africa, the Middle East, and south Asia face major challenges coping with water problems. Water shortages become more acute, and water shared in basins by nations becomes a source of conflict. Although war does not occur in most cases, low-scale violence committed by a combination of activists, citizens, and opportunists puts a further strain on supply. The international community joins together to more effectively manage water resources, by funding infrastructure and wastewater reuse for irrigation and by enhancing efficiency through innovation to ensure that there is an adequate food supply.

As the United States and Russia reduce their nuclear warheads and missile delivery systems, China continues to increase its nuclear arsenal, claiming that it is building more warheads to convince its adversaries that it can retaliate effectively, deter a nuclear attack, and prevent nuclear coercion. China makes it known, however, that it does not intend to target a specific country in an offensive attack. By 2040, China has advanced delivery systems and reaches quality, but not quantity, of parity with the United States and Russia.

China has also expanded its production of military plutonium. The U.S., Chinese, and Russian presidents together pursue a platform of nuclear disarmament and are successful in concluding a 2050 agreement that eventually aims to rid the world of nuclear arms. Chinese pressure on North Korea results in the declaration of a nonnuclear region, and a peace agreement is concluded between the two Koreas.

Conclusion

This scenario posed the challenge of having strong economic growth and low energy prices even though strong growth tends to raise both demand and prices. We assumed that rapid technological advances will stimulate energy production and energy efficiency, thus keeping energy

Table 2.3
Catching Up to America

	Energy	Economy	Harmony
High/Strong		China matches the United States through progressive reforms. The United States is paralyzed by political gridlock but then benefits from technological advances.	An interconnected robust economy comforts the United States as China becomes the global superpower. The United Nations is very active.
Low/Weak	Energy supplies are abundant because of a global increase in unconventional production based on better technology.		

Source: Authors.

price inflation stable. Oil production in the Middle East also continues to rise, in this scenario.

Another challenge was the possibility that China might provoke the United States militarily as it reaches parity with it, according to power transition theory. We assumed that by the time China reaches near-parity with the United States, there will be little in the global order that it feels compelled to challenge. Moreover, we assumed that the United States will be satisfied enough with its economic and security situation that it will not resist China's rise. The international system will gradually adjust to support China's economic rise and expansion of influence throughout Asia.

We also assumed that that the interconnectedness of the global economy and the reduced demand by OECD countries for hydrocarbons means that only Russia, a fading global power, will temporarily pose a challenge to China's ambitions. Table 2.3 presents the combination of endogenous variables—low energy prices, strong economic growth, and harmony—and how we assumed they would interact to create a situation in which nations backtrack by 2050 to where they began around 2010.

3 Global Backtracking

SCENARIO 2: LOW ENERGY PRICES, WEAK ECONOMIC GROWTH, GLOBAL DISHARMONY

The second scenario is marked by low energy prices, weak economic growth, and global disharmony. The United States and the European Union falter because their macroeconomic policies never come to grips with unsustainable budget deficits caused by rising transfer payments in the face of declining working-age populations. Recurrent financial crises afflict the OECD countries and wreak havoc on the developing world. China is never able to establish the conditions of secure property rights, impartial rule of law, and transparent governance for modern economic growth.

The result is high volatility and low-trend economic growth in the world's biggest economies, which drives down growth abroad and has a debilitating effect on geopolitical stability. Illiberal trade policies are ramped up everywhere, which slows growth further and breeds ill-will and mistrust among nations. Weak economic growth leads to low energy demand, which, when combined with new supplies of conventional and unconventional energy sources, leads to a sharp drop in energy prices.

This is a tumultuous multipolar world. Oil producers in the Middle East resort to desperate policies to retain power, and Iran emerges as the regional power after a short but exceedingly violent regional war. After decades of economic decline and rising unrest, Russia experiences a revolution by disparate groups of aggrieved liberal parties. Asian countries form a new alliance to resist pressure from an aggressive China. Africa does not reap the expected rewards from oil production. Instead, poor governance leads to weak economic performance, and many African nations are mired in conflict over water resources and drought-induced famine. The international community fails to adequately address the underlying problems.

The 2010s

The world economy never recovers from the doldrums of 2008–2012. Higher deficit spending coupled with extreme monetary easing in the United States has a disastrous effect on the economy. The extra spending goes mainly to prop up incomes of favored political groups; the extra money creation pushes up asset prices to levels unrelated to profitability.

Rising tax rates and stifling new regulations on energy production and business activity cripple investment. Kotlikoff (2004) warned about the growing insolvency of the United States; he asserted that the main economic problem would be the growing amount of money required to meet the financial promises made to people, especially the elderly, that simply could not be covered by the earnings of the young. For a while, some leaders believe that the U.S. government can borrow the money from abroad to make good on these promises, print more money, or rely on technological progress to expand the economy.

In this scenario we follow the work of the pessimists who believe that the global economic system is in deep trouble. Malleret (2012) describes the global economic system of the 2010s as so complex, interdependent, and poorly governed that it becomes fundamentally unstable and creates random occurrences that have a propensity to propagate globally with disastrous effects. In his book *The Black Swan*, Taleb (2007) argues that Alan Greenspan and Ben Bernanke created high-tail risk with the accumulation of debt that would lead not to growth but rather to a financial blowup. Debt is the black swan of the future.

This disequilibrium leads to a second financial bubble that pops in the later part of the decade, unleashing a cataclysm much worse than the 2007–2008 series of crises. The United States enters a new and greater recession. Inflation soars, interest rates skyrocket, and foreigners, if they are willing to loan the United States money, demand to be paid back in their own currency. Financial credit rating agencies downgrade the United States, which further harms the country's credit worthiness and geopolitical might.

Europe's crisis comes even earlier. Reeling from years of low growth and high unemployment in the eurozone's southern periphery, no negotiated solution can be found to patch up the currency union. Attempts to create a banking union founder, and no agreement can be reached on creating some kind of safe eurozone asset that would allow governments to default without bringing down their national financial systems (O'Rourke and Taylor 2013). Germany pressures most of the troubled economies to accept austerity as the price of bridge loans, but years of these partial bailouts do nothing to solve the problem. With its own current account surplus approaching 10 percent of GDP, Germany refuses to stimulate demand at home as a way to help adjustment at the periphery.

Frustrated European citizens take to the streets, and austerity-minded governments are turned out of office. The southern periphery countries stop trying to restore budget discipline, Germany fails to provide any more support, and a wave of sovereign defaults brings down the banking systems of Greece and Spain. Soon all confidence in the ability of European debtors to repay their debts, at least in real terms, disappears. The money that can flee does so; investment stops, banks fail, and Greece, Cyprus, Spain, and Portugal abandon the euro and rush to print their own currency again, hoping to benefit from new national currencies uncoupled from the euro and an uncompromising German nationalist policy (Wolf 2013).

The eurozone breakup necessitates an incredibly complex redenomination of assets and liabilities, a mountain of litigation, a growing number of bank failures, and an eventual freezing of eurozone and even European Union–wide finance. The southern periphery countries are plunged into a severe depression, and Western Europe suffers low growth for a decade. The breakup further delays necessary pension, labor, and education reform. The turmoil in the European Union and the resulting proliferation of new financial regulations finally cause the United Kingdom to leave the European Union and seek closer ties with Canada and the United States.

There is trouble in Asia, too. After China's leadership transition takes place in 2012, the nation never quite regains its composure and self-confidence. Although the leadership plenum in 2013 abolishes penal work colonies, softens the one-child policy, and strengthens the market mechanisms, Chinese leaders question where they want to go and the position they wish to occupy in global affairs. Some argue that China should be a modern great power, a global leader, copying the best of what the United States was in the late 20th century but with Chinese characteristics (Huang 2008). Others argue that China should be a more traditional Chinese autocracy, focused on a narrow view of its own self-interest, at the risk of antagonizing others near and far.

In the end, China tries to do both, but the main feature of the new China is a continuing ruthless struggle among the ruling elite for power and money, which often turns bloody and fails to establish the conditions for China to become a modern prosperous economy. China becomes an incapacitated state (Pei 2006), unable to do much within its borders besides cling to sovereignty, and it exerts little influence outside its borders.

Parts of Latin America continue to struggle mightily in the early part of the 2010s to overcome the legacy of profligate populism and authoritarianism. At this time, Peru, Chile, Mexico, Colombia, and Brazil all enact significant reforms and make economic progress, even as Venezuela, Argentina, Bolivia, and Ecuador struggle politically and economically. With the onset of the new great recession in the later part of the decade, all hope of maintaining liberal policies in the face of stagnant world demand and rising unemployment vanishes.

New and more strident populist leaders take over in the Bolivarian Alliance for the Americas, including in Bolivia, Cuba, Dominica, Ecuador, Nicaragua, and Venezuela. The high-deficit, high-regulation, foreign investment–discouraging policies of Bolivia, Ecuador, and Venezuela in particular lead to sharp declines in economic growth. All countries rush to raise tariff walls against outsiders, including countries outside Latin America as well as neighboring countries in and out of the Bolivarian Alliance. Some pretense is made to keep regional trade flowing through the regional alliance Mercosur, but it quickly becomes apparent that the overwhelming impulse is to curb all imports that could possibly be produced at home.

Chile is one of the last holdouts. Both center-left and center-right governments have followed highly successful liberal market economy policies for 30 years, but by the later part of the decade, the Chilean government can no longer resist the pressure in the streets for more free education and health care, and the liberal consensus among the elites collapses. A new generation of political leaders comes on the scene, each promising more free goods and services than the others. This is a replay of the Bolivarian revolution in Venezuela and is indeed a replay of the populist revolutions that plagued Latin America for more than a century (Edwards 2010). The result is high inflation, capital flight, an overvalued currency, low growth, and rising tensions with neighbors.

Many sub-Saharan African countries (e.g., Angola, Benin, Botswana, Cameroon, Equatorial Guinea, Ethiopia, Ghana, Liberia, Mauritius, Namibia, Rwanda, Sierra Leone, Tanzania, and Zambia) grew strongly in the early part of this decade, recording real per capita growth averaging above 3 percent per year. This progress was mainly as a result of the global commodity boom inspired by the huge growth of the Chinese economy. As Chinese growth slows dramatically in the late part of the decade, however, commodity prices slump and African economic prospects slump with them. Most of the countries that saw high growth in the first decade of the 2000s used the opportunity to improve national cohesion and governance capability in the 2010s and are better able to weather the global downturn.

Many other African countries, however, are wracked by civil war or small-scale insurgencies. Marshall and Cole (2013) ranked 22 of them as highly fragile: suffering from poor security, a lack of government effectiveness and/or legitimacy, or outright war, in the case of Somalia, Democratic Republic of the Congo, Chad, Ethiopia, Central African Republic, and Nigeria. Most of these countries, with the exception of Chad and Ethiopia, do poorly in the boom times of the 2000s and continue to suffer in the 2010s. Even the oil exporters of Africa are hurt. The abundance of supplies in a time of declining demand leads to a sharp fall in global energy prices. Angola, Gabon, and Equatorial Guinea all suffer sharp reverses in economic growth, and Nigeria breaks apart as the Muslim and Christian areas give up all pretense of trying to live peacefully together.

The global economic downturn, coupled with the humiliation of the liberal democratic model in the United States and Europe, leaves India without either a strong market for its exports or a modernization model. Its government becomes incapable of making decisions, its infrastructure cracks, and its long-simmering insurgencies become bloody and widespread. In some cases, Pakistani-backed groups and their Indian sympathizers commit terrorist acts on critical sites in India. Full-blown low-intensity conflict erupts in Kashmir between the Muslims and the Hindus. The establishment of Al-Qaida branch in India also contributes to the increase in intra-religious conflict in the country. The Taliban resume control in Afghanistan, and Indian investments there are threatened.

The Philippines, Burma, Thailand, and Indonesia also slip into economic chaos and civil war. Long-standing grievances held by ethnic minority groups boil over into mass protests, which in turn result in a brutal crackdown by the government—more so in the case of Burma and the Philippines, less so in Indonesia and Thailand. In all cases, low-level violence continues, and no external organizations are willing to get involved to resolve the conflicts. China and the United States provide weapons and advice but do not interfere.

There is one bright spot in the Asian region. Australia, New Zealand, and Singapore realize they cannot prosper alone and forge a much closer three-way alliance known as SANZ, which supports a greater degree of international trade and provides some military security as well. Malaysia, Taiwan, South Korea, and Japan opt for an affiliate status in the new SANZ alliance in order to maintain some economic stability and provide a modicum of security from the Chinese threat. Instability in Asia, brought on by the economic downtown and intra-state conflicts in some member nations, weakens the influence of the Association of Southeast Asian Nations and the Asia Pacific Economic Cooperation, although the regional organizations continue to push forward their agendas for growth and trade. A trade agreement between the United States and the Trans Pacific Partnership is put on hold.

The growth of oil demand stalls because of the recession. New supplies of conventional and unconventional oil from North America and Iraq enter the market. Low world economic growth and the explosion of non-OPEC unconventional energy production lead to a collapse in energy prices that devastates the Middle East. Saudi Arabia, Kuwait, and Bahrain continue to boost social spending in the hope of keeping Arab Spring revolts at bay.

As oil prices continue to fall, social welfare programs become unsustainable, the people take to the streets, and the monarchies fall. They are replaced by Islamist regimes of various degrees of orthodoxy, but none are capable of providing economic growth or much stability. As the donor relationship between the oil-rich Gulf states and North Africa erodes, Egypt, Tunisia, and Libya further decline economically, and governments come and go with great frequency. Iraq and Syria are bogged down in interethnic warfare bolstered by radical Sunni insurgents under the banner of the Islamic State of Iraq and the Levant.

Russia too is staggered by the collapse in oil prices and European sanctions, but Vladimir Putin is able to maintain political control by a ruthless application of police power and canny doses of patronage. Caught between an ailing Russia and Europe, Eurasian states suffer from economic decline. In particular, Ukraine, mired in conflict with Russian backed separatists in its eastern and southern regions, suffers economic hardship. Russia racks up debt for gas supplies to dependent states of Eastern Europe, and prevents some states, such as Armenia, Georgia, Moldova, and Ukraine from redirecting their markets elsewhere, as debt is exchanged for goods.

The United Nations proves incapable of providing guidance or stability and is forced to cut back staff and engagement as most countries reduce their contributions. The Bretton Woods institutions of the World Bank and the International Monetary Fund, and later the World Trade Organization, are still active in attempting to make up for shortfalls in economic growth, but they too are harmed by dwindling legitimacy, donor contributions, and OECD will.

The 2020s and 2030s

The hegemonic leadership that the United States provided for 70 years was greatly weakened by the global financial crisis of 2007–2008 and has been further damaged by the second financial bubble that popped in the later years of the 2010s. By the early 2020s, U.S. hegemonic stability is gone. After many years of low growth, incoherent policy making, and sharp cutbacks in military spending, U.S. economic and political leadership is no longer potent or attractive to the rest of the world. "Leading from behind" becomes the mantra of a succession of presidents, but it is no longer clear who is leading.

France and the United Kingdom abandon their 1998 Saint Malo agreement to maintain a power-projecting independent force, and no other country is willing to expend much effort to undertake economic, security, or even humanitarian responsibilities beyond its own borders and beyond its own narrowly defined national interests. The European Union fails to budget for, and support the development of, a common security and defense policy covering defense and military issues. By this period it is also clearer that the eurozone breakup results in the European Union resembling the United Nations: a very weak confederation of countries that do not cede sovereignty to a central authority but that select the activities in which each is able or willing to participate. As a result, the Lisbon Treaty, which has formed the constitutional basis of the European Union since 2007, is revised to reflect the new reality, and the authority of the European Commission, its president, and the European Parliament are all greatly diminished or abolished.

A much more serious dispute breaks out in the Middle East in this period over oil. The world oil market, which has been struggling with oversupply since around 2017, is inundated with increasing production from the presalt fields off Brazil, new offshore production in west Africa, and around the Black Sea, and rapidly increasing production from shale and oil sands in Canada and the United States.

This, combined with growing competition to oil from natural gas in the transportation sector, put OPEC members (and Russia) under increasing pressure. OPEC repeatedly cuts quotas to try to keep prices up, but by the mid-2020s, quotas are well under capacity production figures for many countries, quota cheating is rampant, and animosity among the producers is great. Iran struggles with low oil prices and economic sanctions for more than a decade, and the crippled economy destroys the educated, Westernized middle class. Impoverished, much of this group flees, relinquishing an important check on the ambition of the mullahs.

Sensing weakness in the West and an opportunity to seize a greater share of the still substantial regional oil rents, Iran launches another Persian Gulf War. Krepinevich (2009, 23) outlined the scenario, albeit happening a decade earlier: "Iranian ballistic and cruise missile forces disperse. Mine seeding of the Strait of Hormuz commences. Iranian submarines begin their 'underwatch' patrols of the mine fields. Anti-ship missile batteries position themselves along the approaches to the strait."

Iran is interested in extortion, in pushing up the price of oil to its advantage. The mullahs demand that the U.S. military withdraw its already depleted forces from the region, that Saudi Arabia and the other Gulf states curtail their oil production, and that all ships passing through the Strait of Hormuz pay fees. The United States and Israel are encouraged by the Saudis and the other Gulf states to fight, but half of the American fleet is incapacitated in the first attempt to force the strait, and the fleet quits the fight altogether after Tel Aviv and Haifa are obliterated in separate nuclear attacks.

It does not seem worth it to the United States to fight to keep the strait open for the good of the world economy. A combination of lower demand, increased domestic production, and increased imports from North and South America mean that the United States imports little oil from the Middle East by the mid-2020s. Even an Iranian monopoly on Persian Gulf oil production cannot produce enough market power to seriously affect the world price of energy. The United States certainly does not have the will to attack Iran with nuclear weapons, the only plausible way to win this war.

The United States gives up, and Iran promises a further round of nuclear strikes if Israel does not submit. The Israelis choose to stop fighting, as many of their most ardent leaders are too disorganized to continue the fight at this time. Ultimately, Iran becomes the regional power at the expense of a few thousand Iranian lives and the lives of one million Israelis. Turkey manages to stay out of the conflict and becomes a beacon of normality and prosperity in a troubled region. Iran prefers to capitalize on its recent successes by pushing into Azerbaijan, but stern warnings from a heavily armed Turkey keep Iran at bay.

In this period, there are two factions in the European Union: a semi-prosperous north and a poorer south. Most of the southern countries left the eurozone in the 2010s, but the shock of inflation only makes their economic situation worse. Greece, in particular, does not have the ability to take advantage of the briefly competitive exchange rate, and it falls into steady decline. Spain, Portugal, and Italy are in only slightly better condition. Germany and the Nordic countries still have good governance, but their export-oriented economies are finding fewer and fewer places to export to. They have made some attempt to link up to the still vibrant SANZ alliance, but that market is too small to make much of a difference to northwestern Europe.

Neither the European Union nor the United States has the financial ability or the political will to invest in more renewable energy. Furthermore, with the cost of oil and gas still low, alternatives to hydrocarbons languish in the premarket phase. The cost of coal drops below natural gas in the European and Asian markets, resulting in an increase in coal generation. By this period, governments have stopped providing subsidies in various forms to alternative energies. With demand down in a sluggish global economy, countries do not see the need to address the call to enact another climate treaty after commitments under the Kyoto Protocol expire. The rush to deal with the threat of catastrophic climate change has been slowed by a whole decade of moderating global temperatures.

One country that succeeds peacefully in this era is Brazil. Unlike much of Latin America, the new Brazilian leadership does not totally renounce the liberal reforms of the previous governments, and it reaps a huge dose of momentum from increased energy production. Brazil does backtrack from trade liberalism, however, and by the 2020s it has achieved enough industrial scale and diversity to drive tariffs to prohibitive levels on Chinese, North American, and European goods.

Brazil forges extensive new trade agreements with other industrialized nations of the Southern Hemisphere (including South Africa and Angola), which allows for substantial and asymmetric gains from specialization and trade diversion.

Growing Islamic radicalism, coupled with growing economic hopelessness, leads to the collapse of the central government in Pakistan and a flood of youthful jihadists into an increasingly resentful and Hindu nationalistic India. A firestorm of suicide bombings is followed by mass reprisals, ethnic cleansing, and millions of refugees (Waslekar and Bhatt 2004). Pakistan collapses and breaks into half a dozen poor and violent regions. India survives, but as a repressive security state ruled by fervent Hindu nationalists who have lost the trust of their people and the confidence of foreign investors. Economic growth slows dramatically, and India remains very poor. India's geopolitical position as an emerging power weakens. Border conflicts with China and remnants of Pakistan over Kashmir intensify.

Russia also suffers from insurgency. A discouraged and shrinking Russian population is not eager to fight the Islamic insurgencies in the south, and the army withdraws. Islamists continue to provoke and terrorize the populations of Moscow and other big cities bordering the northern Caucasus. In response, a growing nationalist youth movement clashes with minorities. Russia becomes more violent, jailing, torturing, and killing dissidents. On the basis of human rights and the rule of law, Europe and the United States limit further financial and trade interactions with Russia, already sanctioned for several years following Russia's 2014 invasion of Ukraine.

The recent Persian Gulf War restores some luster to the Russian economy by driving up oil prices temporarily, but Russian technology is not able to exploit the nation's reserves of unconventional energy, and the big global energy companies with the necessary technology are not interested in investing while energy prices are low and the legal and security environment in Russia remains unpredictable. Putin retires from political life in 2024, and he handpicks a like-minded successor who rules for much of the 2030s.

China attempts to capitalize on the floundering and indebted U.S. economy and overstretched military by trying to dictate terms to its neighbors and to the United States. At the height of the U.S. economic crisis in 2008, Gao Xiqing, the head of the China Investment Corporation, reportedly said that the U.S. economy is "built on the support, the gratuitous support, of a lot of countries. So why don't you come over and ... I won't say *kowtow*, but at least *be nice* to the countries that lend you money" (Fallows 2008, 65).

Instead, the Chinese growth miracle gradually deflates, and China has a hard time convincing anybody to kowtow. In the 20 years after the 2007–2008 crisis, China experiences three boom-bust cycles, but each boom is shallower and shorter than the last. The Chinese chide the market-driven policy of the Washington Consensus model, and instead it touts the Beijing Consensus model, in which state-driven economic reform is anticipated to bring growth in the absence of political liberalization (Kennedy 2010; Naughton 2010; Ramo 2004). However, state capitalism soon runs into its own difficulties as authoritarian governance, crony capitalism, and an absence of secure property rights and the rule of law leave the country unable to progress to self-sustaining economic growth based on entrepreneurship and innovation.

As China slows, so does Africa. African leaders initially adopt the Beijing Consensus model, in part because it justifies authoritarian rule. However, the combination of authoritarian rule, slow rates of growth of demand for commodities, and less investment from China and the OECD countries means that sub-Saharan African economic growth rates fall, prompting a rise in internal instability and even cross-border wars.

Despite initially weathering the economic crisis in 2010s, Ethiopia breaks apart after years of a growing insurgency and dissatisfaction with unaccountable and ineffective governance. Kenya breaks apart under the pressure of massive migration from Somalia and Ethiopia. Rather than use its oil riches to further development, Ghana acquires enough arms to invade and take over Benin and Togo.

The 2040s

The world in 2040 is a far poorer place in this scenario, compared to the optimistic first scenario in chapter 2 (see table 3.1). Most OECD countries are poorer in 2040 than they were in 2020. World economic growth comes to a standstill in the 2040s. A few countries thrive, including Brazil, the Nordic countries, and the STICKs (South Africa, Turkey, Indonesia, Colombia, and Kazakhstan), but elsewhere demographic challenges, poor governance, civil instability, and warfare prevent much progress. The recurring bouts of financial instability, inflation, and regime uncertainty mean that investment is low and innovation is

Table 3.1
Scenario 2: Global Backtracking
Low Energy Prices, Weak Economic Growth, Global Disharmony

Real GDP, billions of 2010$ at 2010 exchange rates

	2010	2020	2040	2050
USA	14,447	16,065	15,954	15,967
		1.1%	0.0%	0.0%
China	5,931	10,971	21,607	23,272
		6.3%	3.4%	0.7%
OECD	38,646	40,349	35,844	33,952
		0.4%	−.6%	−.5%
Non-OECD	24,944	37,460	62,622	69,442
		4.2%	2.6%	1.0%
World	63,590	77,809	98,466	103,394
		2.0%	1.2%	0.5%

Real GDP per capita, 1000s of 2005 PPP $

	2010	2020	2040	2050
USA	42.1	43.0	38.3	37.0
		0.2%	−0.6%	−0.4%
China	6.8	9.9	15.5	16.8
		3.8%	2.3%	0.8%
OECD	34.9	35.4	31.1	29.3
		0.1%	−0.6%	−0.6%
Non-OECD	6.0	7.2	8.8	8.9
		1.8%	1.0%	0.1%
World	9.9	10.7	11.2	11.0
		0.8%	0.2%	−0.2%

Source: See table 2.1.

minimal in most countries. National economic policies discourage competition and reduce cross-border trade.

The United States tries to join the SANZ alliance in 2040 and to align itself with Brazil in a bid to restart global trade, but its extreme financial instability and aggressive rhetoric make it an unattractive partner to the Southern Hemisphere nations. The demographic challenges in the United States and Europe—too few workers to support the income and health programs for too many old people—mean that there is no surplus for investment in physical capital, education, or research.

The Chinese export model is ruined by the collapse of international trade. China faces an even worse demographic challenge than Europe, and its authoritarian development model is ill-suited to a slow-growth environment. China is convulsed with internal disorder as rival regional leaders seek various degrees of autonomy from the government, which struggles with civil disturbances ranging from peaceful demonstrations to full-fledged insurgencies.

After 2040, there is an attempt by the president of Russia to purge the Kremlin of the oligarchs who gained their riches from Russia's natural resources in the post-Soviet era. The economy is struggling, oil exports are declining, and although natural gas export volume is high, the price is low. Russia is unable to develop either a high-tech manufacturing industry or an innovation center. China outbids Russian companies in acquiring foreign energy assets and rights to exploration. China surpasses Russia in arms manufacturing and related global trade and begins to approach Russia's long-range nuclear warhead missile capability.

Russia uses a heavy hand to maintain order in its sphere of influence. In central Asia, Kazakhstan and Turkmenistan are able to maintain independence because of their energy wealth and non-Russian transportation routes, but almost all the rest of the former Soviet republics slip back into a close embrace with Russia, which they depend on for credit, markets, and worker remittances. The only exceptions are Azerbaijan and Georgia in the southern Caucasus.

Toward the end of this period, Russian workers without job security, members of the intelligentsia, disunited liberal political parties, and nationalists are finally able to unite in massive protests across Russia over poor economic conditions, oppressive authoritarian leadership, and immigration from neighboring states. After a year of tumultuous protests, the leader steps down and democratic elections are held. A liberal party comes into power. Treisman (2011, 158) prognosticated as follows:

A fall in economic growth would slow the evolution of Russian society toward greater modernity and autonomy (the big picture), yet would likely provoke more vocal opposition, splits within the ruling elite, and perhaps a turnover in the leadership (the close-up view).... What happened next would depend— other things being equal—on whether the economy continued to decline or began to recover.

Great-power politics shrivel to regional politics as governments everywhere focus on holding together their own countries in the face of dashed expectations and mass discontent. Iran dominates the Middle East, focusing more and more on ideological purity (and the covert high lifestyle of its elites). Iraq, Syria, Lebanon, Saudi Arabia, and the smaller Gulf states fall under the sway of a nuclear-armed and aggressive Iran; Jordan, Oman, and the North African states do not. Israel, focused on rebuilding with the support of the United States, strategically avoids engaging in regional politics for some time. Iran dictates the region's energy production decisions, but the contribution of the region to world energy is so diminished by the 2040s that its decisions have little effect on world prices. The region is increasingly disconnected from the world. India is subdivided into three new states, and parts of its northeast are absorbed by China.

No Latin American country or alliance has much influence outside its region or enough military potential to be a threat. Brazil influences most of South America on trade and foreign policy. Its power is based on providing markets, credit, and energy as well as nuclear weapons. Bolivia launches a strike against Chile that temporarily gives it sovereignty over a route to the sea, but the much richer and stronger Chile eventually gathers its forces and returns the borders to their 20th-century status quo.

As U.S. power wanes, Brazil gains regional respect and influence. Reveling in its (relative) economic success and growing geopolitical power (at least in the South Atlantic region), Brazil volunteers its capital city, Brasilia, to host the UN General Assembly. After years of mutual antagonism between the United States and the United Nations, the United States downgrades its participation in, and contributions to, the activities of the United Nations. Brasilia provides the funds to build a new UN complex. In return, Brazil becomes one of the new permanent members on the revamped Security Council.

Conclusion

This scenario posed the challenge of a key driver shifting during the decades. In the 2010s, the assumption that slowing energy demand caused by a global economic downturn was responsible for lower energy prices seemed compelling. This situation then generated a host of self-serving and desperate policies that bred mistrust among nations. By the 2020s, the big thread in this story was global disharmony, which in turn slowed economic growth and lowered energy prices further.

Table 3.2
Global Backtracking

	Energy	Economy	Harmony
High/Strong			
Low/Weak	Slowing demand is linked to weak growth and unconventional production.	Faulty policies lead to a sustained global crash.	Low growth promotes civil unrest. Iran is empowered to strike Israel and dominate the region.

Source: Authors.

Table 3.2 presents the combination of endogenous variables—low energy prices, weak economic growth, and global disharmony—and how we assumed they would interact to create a situation in which nations backtracked by 2050 to where they had begun in 2010.

4 Peaceful Power Transition

SCENARIO 3: HIGH ENERGY PRICES, STRONG ECONOMIC GROWTH, GLOBAL HARMONY

The third scenario is marked by high energy prices, strong economic growth, and global harmony. In this scenario the world economy recovers from the stagnation in 2008–2012, and energy prices are pushed up sharply. Countries are assumed to follow policies that enhance property rights, improve the rule of law, and increase trade openness. All these assumptions generate higher GDP growth than would be the case otherwise. China continues to have very high growth but finds that accommodating the existing global regime makes more sense for it economically and politically than challenging the existing order. Since energy prices are higher, China's growth is not quite as strong as in scenario 1, but China's relative rise in geopolitical power is still very large.

The United States and the European Union remain strong and prosperous and find a way to get along peacefully with a rising China. Buoyed by peace and prosperity among these big three economies, many countries in several regions continue on a gradual path toward convergence with the OECD. The BRICs (Brazil, Russia, India, and China) are joined by a second echelon of emerging states, the STICKs (South Africa, Turkey, Indonesia, Colombia, and Kazakhstan).

Technological breakthroughs in new forms of energy result in global energy markets divorced from oil trade. As a result, when Middle Eastern oil producers suffer a terminal decline in energy output and face growing domestic turmoil, outside powers do little. Energy prices remain high because of growing demand from strengthening economies. Competition for water sources from a growing agricultural sector also keeps energy prices high.

The 2010s

Higher deficit spending in the United States finally pushes the American economy into a sustained recovery. In this recovery, Keynesian principles such as those advocated by Summers and DeLong (2012) and Krugman (2012) win the policy debate and are successfully implemented in the United States. These include aggressive deficit spending to counter deficiencies in demand. In Europe, austerity-minded governments are turned out of office, and increased deficit spending eventually prompts a return to sustained growth even when unemployment remains much higher than desired, particularly in the south. Workers from southern and eastern Europe benefit from changes in labor regulations that allow for easier migration within the European Union.

China's economy grows strongly throughout this decade. Much of this success is accounted for by growth in the domestic market as well as by China's aggressive push beyond its borders. China's vast spending on infrastructure starts to pay off in terms of spreading prosperity beyond the narrow coastal zone. From the highly inefficient command economy of Mao's era to the free market reforms of Deng Xiaoping, the Chinese government has refined state capitalism to a highly productive system. China is able to manage its rapid development by backing its state-owned enterprises and providing significant advantages to key private enterprises, including cheap financing, protection of domestic markets, and assistance in the acquisition of foreign intellectual capital.

China's premier companies are endowed with three crucial competitive advantages: lavish government subsidies, full backing by the state in their foreign endeavors, and the ability to act where Western companies fear (or are forbidden by their governments) to act (Bremmer 2010). Whereas in 2011 only six Chinese companies ranked among the global top 100 (*Fortune* 2011), mostly involved in energy and utilities, by the end of this decade, 20 companies make the Fortune 100, with industrial, finance, transportation, and insurance companies making the list.

After the withdrawal of the majority of U.S. troops from Afghanistan in 2014, the residual American force is able to work with the Afghan security forces to stabilize the situation internally and along the border with Pakistan. The United States is no longer using drones in this zone, the Pakistani political system stabilizes (relative to the recent past of military coups and assassinations), and the Indians and Pakistanis cooperate with Western nations in ensuring that the Taliban do not regain power in Afghanistan. As a result, India and Pakistan can now turn inward to focus on the development of their rural sectors and to enhance their human security. Indian-Pakistani relations stabilize, but no solution is reached on Kashmir. Both New Delhi and Islamabad still loudly maintain that the other is a primary threat to regional security.

Brazil and Mexico both take off in 2010s. Growth in Brazil is sustained through a combination of strong external demand for its prodigious natural resources and conservative macroeconomic management (Brainard and Martinez-Diaz 2009). Brazil, for the most part, resists the temptation to reduce foreign access to its domestic market. Unable to hide behind a tariff and quota wall, Brazil's private companies respond by improving productivity and seeking out new Latin American and global markets. The government helps by rewriting labor and social legislation to boost jobs while strengthening the social safety net and by keeping inflation under control. Brazil also rapidly expands educational opportunities, thus providing the human capital to take the country to a higher development level in the future.

Mexico profits by China's increasing wages and declining competitiveness. By the end of this decade, Mexico has once again become the low-wage production base for the United States. Improved transportation links and smoother border crossings help significantly. Even as Mexico's domestic economy improves, however, both drug-related violence and low-level insurgencies continue. By the end of the decade, the government reaches an understanding with criminal syndicates on their place in the drug trade, which was the case before the turn of the century.

As Brazil and Mexico strengthen, Chile continues to prosper, and other Latin American countries follow—particularly Argentina, Colombia, and Peru. The Bolivarian movement, headed by President Hugo Chávez of Venezuela and spreading to Ecuador and Bolivia, is curtailed by the untimely death of its leader and the failure of subsequent leadership to stop a downward spiral of the Venezuelan economy. Presidents of the Bolivarian Alliance countries are elected based on their promise to follow the Mexican model: adopting liberal policies and opening trade relations with the United States and Europe to expand their economies. More free trade agreements are concluded between the Bolivarian Alliance countries and OECD economies.

The U.S. interventions in Afghanistan and Iraq in 2001 and 2003, respectively, fail to bring stability to the Middle East. Instability in Iraq, exacerbated by the rise of radical Sunni group ISIL, and continuing tensions over Iran's nuclear program keep oil production far below its potential. A growing Sunni-Shiite divide within nations and between them, spearheaded by Saudi Arabia and Iran taking opposite sides on regional security issues, further disturbs the market. Unconventional oil and gas, especially from North America, initially helps the situation, but not enough to keep real energy prices from rising. In turn, the rise in energy prices props up autocratic regimes in the Middle East, most of whom continue to repress their own people and some of whom continue to support global extremist groups.

The revolutionary awakening that occurs during the Arab Spring of 2011 is temporary, followed by the election of authoritarian leaders who support conservative military-security institutions or of Islamist parties that adopt a fundamentalist interpretation of Islam in social and economic governance. The only exception is Tunisia, where a coalition of disparate parties manages to maintain a tenuous balance among them. The Arab Spring also creates an opportunity for extremist groups to reorganize after their losses in Afghanistan and Pakistan. Recruitment and training is expanded in Yemen, Libya, and Egypt.

A return to growth in the OECD countries along with continued strong growth in East Asia results in high demand and high prices for African minerals and agricultural products. Export demand leads to strong economic growth in this decade, but these easy earnings allow certain African governments to avoid institution-building reforms that could set the stage for diversified and sustainable long-term growth. Without reforms, these African goverments remain susceptible to corruption and to the uneven distribution of rents from resources that occur when patronage networks dominate the economic sector.

Ethnic and religious rivalries and the predominance of warlords leading separatist movements continue to take a heavy toll in sub-Saharan Africa. There are a few exceptions, however. The countries that are not as resource dependent—such as Ethiopia, Rwanda, and Senegal—are thriving, and the formerly violent states of Angola, Chad, Eritrea, Liberia, and Sierra Leone are relatively calm. However, the devastating impact of the Ebola virus outbreak grips African countries, including Guinea, Liberia, Nigeria, and Sierra Leone, killing tens of thousands. After a period of time the international community is able to contain the outbreak and lower the mortality rate from the disease.

China's strong growth and falling competitiveness in low-wage industries boosts growth in the poorer Southeast Asian countries, particularly Cambodia, Laos, and Vietnam. China's aggressive claims to sovereignty up to nearly the shorelines of most of its Pacific neighbors, however, create a good deal of ill-will in the region. Japan and most of the members of the Association of Southeast Asian Nations seek closer ties and more security assurances from the United States. The "pivot to Asia" policy of the United States continues, and by the end of the decade, 60 percent of U.S. military assets are shifted to Asia. China also continues to build up its naval forces and to aggressively harass fishing vessels and energy exploration operations in the East China and South China Seas.

Tensions gradually ease by the end of the decade. The animosity caused by China's bullish foreign policy, and the accompanying reduction in trade and investment opportunities caused by the sovereignty disputes, does not seem to be worth the effort. China and Japan conclude an "incidents at sea" agreement, such as that between the United States and the Soviet Union. This puts into place conflict resolution mechanisms even if the fundamental sovereignty issues are not yet resolved. The United States takes a neutral position on the sovereignty claims but encourages peaceful and cooperative development of the region's resources. Deep water oil exploration by U.S. companies begins, but it is less successful than anticipated.

The recovery from the great recession, the survival of the euro, and the dependence of China and the other BRICs on global trade all converge to strengthen multilateral institutions. However, within the UN Security Council, the status quo of agreeing to disagree continues between China and Russia, on the one hand, and the Americans and the Europeans on the other. This creates a continued stalemate on resolving intra-state conflicts, since China and Russia insist on respecting the sovereignty of other nations (except for the former Soviet Union states, for Russia) as the preeminent consideration in engaging with them. As China's influence grows, so too does its global view of non-intervention in the internal affairs of other countries. The international agenda of protecting the human rights of people globally, or the Responsibility to Protect, therefore, remains primarily the concern of Western nations. The transatlantic alliance increasingly relies on NATO and other regionally based security organizations such as the Organization of African States to address security issues, further sidelining the United Nations.

The 2020s and 2030s

Economic growth in the OECD countries is propelled by a wave of innovation in electronics, composite materials, health care, and energy production and efficiency. Initial government-supported research and development result in strong private revenue increases. Eventually, hundreds of billions of dollars are cut from government energy subsidy programs and from U.S. military spending. The United States and most European countries gradually regain their prominent global fiscal positions. The long-term fears about debts and entitlement programs are still present, but the potential crisis is put off for a few decades by buoyant economic growth (see table 4.1).

Whereas the 2010s were marked by catch-up growth and a commodity-price boom in many of the non-OECD countries, the next two decades are marked by a radical restructuring of the world economy resulting from technology-led productivity growth and a shift in capital flow toward the non-OECD countries. A significant number of countries also modernize their political and economic institutions, setting the stage for a burst in growth. Many other factors, such as technological change and human capital development, affect growth trends in each country. An entirely new energy market is created globally; it is much more competitive and includes a host of new energies: electric vehicles, natural gas vehicles, hydrogen vehicles, battery storage, smart grids, distributed generation, and off-grid technology. As a result of concluding a free trade agreement, the United States and Europe triple trade, much of it in the clean energy sector.

The highly politicized world of oil markets is transformed by these more competitive and less polarizing sources of energy. The use of social media technologies and communication to regulate these new energy markets makes them more democratized, more diverse, and more competitive. Some of the traditional oil states transition away from oil revenues by boosting renewable energy investments and gaining recognition as centers of global finance and science and technology innovation, supported by the establishment of foreign universities.

Russia is no longer able to use energy as a weapon, not just in Western Europe but also, more important, in Eurasia. As a result, the European Union and NATO expand into the former Soviet space, enlarging markets and stabilizing the region. Membership requires resolving the status of separatist regions in the Caucasus, Moldova, and Ukraine.

Table 4.1
Scenario 3: Peaceful Power Transition
High Energy Prices, Strong Economic Growth, Global Harmony

Real GDP, billions of $, at 2010 exchange rates

	2010	2020	2040	2050
USA	14,447	17,577	26,726	31,497
		2.0%	2.1%	1.7%
China	5,931	12,380	42,194	53,899
		7.6%	6.3%	2.5%
OECD	38,646	44,065	58,282	66,294
		1.3%	1.4%	1.3%
Non-OECD	24,944	40,979	120,405	180,878
		5.1%	5.5%	4.2%
World	63,590	85,044	178,688	247,172
		2.9%	3.8%	3.3%

Real GDP per capita, 1000s of 2005 PPP $

	2010	2020	2040	2050
USA	42.1	47.1	63.5	71.7
		1.1%	1.5%	1.2%
China	6.8	10.6	25.9	31.1
		4.6%	4.5%	1.9%
OECD	34.9	38.7	50.6	57.8
		1.0%	1.3%	1.3%
Non-OECD	6.0	7.7	14.7	19.2
		2.5%	3.3%	2.7%
World	9.9	11.5	18.6	23.3
		1.6%	2.4%	2.2%

Source: See table 2.1.

As energy markets grow, transportation lines are enhanced, the reliability of electricity increases, and the citizens of these countries now enjoy OECD-equivalent standards. Some countries with great potential for an energy boom are slow to reverse nationalist protectionist resource policies. In Latin America, Argentina and Venezuela are late in attracting private investors. It is not until the 2030s, when socialist, patrimonial governments are replaced by centrist technocrats, that their sectors are opened.

Strong world demand and a gradual real appreciation of the Chinese renminbi help Mexican industry continue to strengthen in the 2020s.

By the end of the 2010s, Mexico had become a favored production platform for the global automotive industry. Plants for Volkswagen, Nissan, and Ford generate far more in Mexican export earnings than the oil or tourism industries do. This, in turn, changes the importance to the ruling party of the revenue from the state-owned oil and gas company, which leads to privatization of the sector and, with it, more Western drilling technology to increase production, including shale gas.

Booming Mexican employment dries up the pool of disaffected youth, reducing the attractiveness of the drug trade and social violence in general. The two dominant parties, the National Action Party and the Institutional Revolutionary Party, trade the presidency on an almost regular cycle.

Brazil, India, and China are successful at capturing a fair share of this global redistribution of capital. They continue on their projected path of increasing institutional efficiency. Their central governments maintain macroeconomic stability, their deficits remain modest, and inflation remains under control. The rule of law is strengthened in these countries, which encourages entrepreneurship and reduces the ability of the elites to control markets and financing. Government spending on education improves the quality of the workforce, which boosts productivity and growth and also improves income equality and social stability. India, in particular, emphasizes regional cooperation and reaches out to its neighbors, deepening trade treaties and heavily investing in regional rail, highway, and energy pipeline links (Waslekar and Bhatt 2004).

Economic success also spreads to the second tier of developing countries known as the STICKs: South Africa, Turkey, Indonesia, Colombia, and Kazakhstan. By following the path of market-friendly economic reforms and incentive-creating institutional reforms, these five countries begin to absorb a large inflow of foreign direct investment. They increase their capital-to-labor ratio and acquire new technologies and new industries as multinational corporations seek to escape the confines of the slower-growing OECD countries. They take advantage of their geographical locations near or on the way to bigger markets, combined with relative stability and a growing skilled labor force, to develop more successfully than others.

Gradual political change solidifies growth in Mexico, the BRICs, and the STICKs. As more people grow up in conditions of economic security, societies choose to move away from authoritarian governments

(Inglehart and Baker 2000). It seemed unlikely in 2010 that China's Communist Party would ever relax its grip enough to allow the development of the inclusive kind of political and economic institutions that Acemoglu and Robinson (2012) contend are critical to sustainable development. Nor did it seem likely that Kazakhstan would break out of decades-long fluctuations between authoritarianism and reform, or that Turkey would reverse the rule of the Justice and Development Party (AKP) dominance over government and return to the path of secular-driven reform. But now China, Kazakhstan, Turkey, and many other countries reach a tipping point, where the years of good economic growth and increasing exposure to information about life and politics in the rich countries create a large enough mass of people to successfully demand democracy, human rights, and accountable government.

In this new regime, market-based competition replaces the system in many countries in which opportunities, contracts, and finance are dependent on favors from governmental officials. More inclusive economic and political institutions encourage a greater broadening of the economic base and shift the focus of ambitious men and women from receiving sinecures or favors from the government to founding new businesses and opening new markets. Multinational corporations respond to the new openness, but indigenous entrepreneurship is even more important in propelling these countries onto a higher growth path. Trade and capital flow across borders, and the movement of labor and companies is an important part of the growth dynamic of the 2020s and 2030s.

This intensified globalization necessitates improvements in the international institutions. The World Trade Organization (WTO) is revived after a troubled period in the 2010s. Trade liberalization and market access improves, the dispute-resolution mechanism gains greater credibility, and new areas of services and investment increasingly fall under international jurisdiction. The countries that participate most fully in the WTO process and that most faithfully comply with WTO treaty obligations gain a disproportionate share of the technology and capital that becomes available in these decades.

While unconventional energy production continues to expand globally, it gradually becomes apparent that Saudi Arabia's oil reserves are, as some have long suspected, grossly exaggerated (Archibald 2012). There is also a lack of success in transferring unconventional production technology to the Persian Gulf, for political reasons more than institutional ones. Oil production from Saudi Arabia and Kuwait begins to plummet in the 2020s. Oil and other energy prices fluctuate sharply over the course of the business cycle, but the trend rate of energy price rise is roughly 2 percent a year more than other prices. The share of unconventional oil and gas, as well as renewable energies, goes up dramatically in the 2020s, but not fast enough to keep energy prices from rising sharply.

Saudi Arabia's declining oil production, even in the face of high oil prices, means that its promises of income to its growing population cannot be kept. By the mid-2020s, per capita income in the kingdom starts to decline. This leads to the overthrow of the monarchy and years of internal strife as the radical Islamists, the military, and royal loyalists vie for control of the fractured state.

The Middle East as a whole, however, maintains a tense stability. Both Iraq and Iran are able to generate huge incomes from oil and gas production, which they use partly to expand their economies and partly to enlarge their militaries. They maintain a balance of power that prevents either from trying too hard to expand its influence over the faltering states in the region. The shift in focus in Iran from geopolitics to modernization and building the economy, along with the crash in Saudi finances, means that there is much less money and energy fueling radicalism outside the region. Political tensions in the Persian Gulf also decline as interest in the region from the United States, the European Union, and China wanes; new sources of energy and increases in energy efficiency make the Persian Gulf much less important to the global energy picture (see figure 4.1).

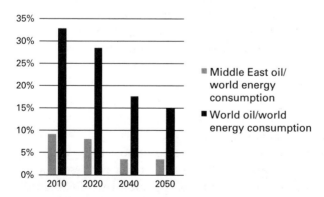

Figure 4.1
Oil's Declining Share in World Energy Consumption
Source: 2010 from Energy Information Agency (2013), later years by assumption.

Russia is the major exception to the global trend toward liberal governance. Vladimir Putin is succeeded by another former member of the security services whose views about the power of the state and the perquisites of the ruler are no different. Like Putin, he focuses his economic policies on solidifying state control over the energy sector for the purposes of extracting the majority of state revenue. This Russian development model is challenged in the 2020s by three major factors.

First, the rise of shale gas production in North America and Europe makes natural gas into a normally traded commodity, ending Russia's near monopoly-provider status in Europe. Second, Russia's domestic oil production, like Saudi Arabia's, begins a precipitous decline. Third, the international oil companies whose capital and technology could have at least slowed the production decline in Russia refuse to participate in any meaningful way in Russian projects, as a result of increasing Western sanctions on Russia as its military expands into parts of Eurasia, beginning with Ukraine in the 2010s, and moving into Moldova in the early 2020s. Economic growth is slowed and eventually turns negative as energy production declines outpace energy price rises.

Thus, Russia as a geopolitical entity diminishes, maintaining some importance only to Eurasia, where it retains territory taken by force in Ukraine in 2014. Even in Eurasia Russia loses influence, because many countries are able to gradually increase their economic independence from it by strengthening ties with their European neighbors and with China.

The 2040s

World economic growth slows in the 2040s as the available gains from technological catch-up diminish and a drag is felt from high energy prices. But the 2040s still enjoy high world growth rates compared to almost any other decade in recorded history. Growth is driven by a combination of factors: high levels of research and development spending in the OECD countries keep technological innovation at a high pace, the BRICs and the STICKs contribute a growing body of new growth-propelling knowledge, and the continuing trend toward institutional reform in most of the rest of world helps the global spread of a high-income lifestyle. The institutional reforms implemented by many countries in the 2030s pay off by 2050. By 2040, the non-OECD countries have far surpassed the OECD countries in aggregate economic output. The income gap between the Northern and Southern Hemispheres is still large, but far smaller than it was in 2010.

China adopts a far more cooperative stance by 2040, allowing the United States to gain economically from a new security environment and joint investment. Eager to cut its defense budget, the United States responds to Chinese moderation by reducing its military posture in the eastern Pacific, resulting in lower military budget allocations. Chinese and Western competition for resources and markets in Africa produces some serious political disagreements, but as China increasingly adapts to market behavioral norms, tensions diminish. There is more cooperation in energy exploration between U.S. and Chinese companies globally, and more mutual investment in third countries. China eventually lets the renminbi float freely against other currencies, and financial and trade imbalances are corrected. Much more global trade is invoiced in the renminbi, which becomes widely held as a reserve currency.

By 2050, most of Latin America and about half of the African countries join the push toward inclusive institutions and accountable governments. There are still occasional coups, populist revivals, and insurgencies in both hemispheres, but many fewer than before, and the detrimental policy steps backward are shallower and shorter-lived than they were previously. Global poverty diminishes greatly, and the huge disparity between incomes in the Northern and Southern Hemispheres falls sharply (see table 4.2). The number of people living in absolute poverty, as defined by the World Bank (GDP per capita less

Table 4.2
World Poverty and Inequality

	$2.50 a day		$1.25 a day	
	2010	2050	2010	2050
Millions of people living in poverty*	2,942	824	1,215	310
Share of world population	42.7%	9.1%	17.6%	3.3%
Average per capita income, OECD income as multiple of non-OECD income	5.8	3.0		

Notes: *At $2.50 and $1.25 a day per person standards, 2005 purchasing power parity dollars.
Source: 2010 poverty numbers from the World Bank's data, at www.povcal.net. Other figures have been estimated with the assistance of the IFs model, version 6.75.

than $1.25 per day per person, 2005 purchasing power parity dollars), decreases from more than 1.2 billion in 2010 to fewer than 310 million in 2050.

Nevertheless, about one-third of the 186 countries tracked in this project have still not transitioned by 2050 to the level of institutional development associated with achieving a high standard of living. Many of these countries, mostly in Africa and the Middle East, lack a strong centralized authority and continually suffer from insurgencies or intra-state rival-group warfare. Some remain constrained by entrenched autocrats or by rotating groups of elites retaining power, as in Russia, most of central Asia, and a few countries in the Middle East and Latin America. In these countries a noncompetitive bureaucratic elite manages to direct the power of the state mostly to its own uses. The non-OECD countries as a group greatly improve their governance by 2050 but still lag behind the OECD countries.

The decrease in regional nations' support for radical Islamist groups, combined with Western assistance to a determined Iraqi government, finally result in a viable federal Iraqi state. As a result, Iraq has done better than most countries in the Middle East. The nation has grown rich from energy and—in Kurdistan, at least—from entrepreneurial activity. Iran's nuclear capability has not been of much geopolitical use; too many of its neighbors have equivalent weapons or can call on allies that do. More important, Iraq has a large and efficient army that serves as the primary check on Iranian ambitions. Iran has grown much richer and still supports radicalism and terrorism abroad, but the appeal of this kind of behavior is much lower in the more prosperous world that exists by 2050. Israel and Palestine are now two sovereign states, hostile but economically intertwined. They suffer occasional internecine violence, but relations are tolerable if not smooth.

Resource constraints at the nexus of food, energy, and water play a bigger role in the 2040s, and given the high energy intensity of water purification technologies, trouble arises mainly over water, not hydrocarbons or other mineral resources. Strong world growth has pushed energy demand up sharply, but gains in energy efficiency, more efficient production of unconventional oil and gas, a new capacity in nuclear generation, and the growing use of renewable fuels means greater diversification of sources of energy and greater energy security for almost all countries.

The sharp increase in demand, however, and the increased use of higher-cost renewable energies, has led to rising energy prices.

Moreover, producing new energies and generating energy for an increasingly prosperous global population is more water-intensive. Despite efforts to create more sustainable energy that uses less water, the increase in demand for energy means that overall water use increases.

More intensive water use in the energy sector also competes with water use in agricultural production. Population growth slows, but the world population by 2050 is still 2.3 billion more than it was in 2010, an increase of 33 percent. Because this population surge is accompanied by rising wealth, people on average are eating more food per capita and food of higher quality. In this high-income and high-population growth scenario, the Food and Agricultural Organization of the United Nations estimates that global food production will have to rise about 40 percent from 2010 to 2050 (Alexadratos 2011).

This significant rise in food production is achieved with technological and policy changes. The growing tendency to adhere to the market-based rules of the WTO helps to achieve the necessary production gains, including the avoidance of export bans (Msangi and Rosegrant 2011), and to discourage domestic policies that encourage consumption over production. These practices keep global food prices in check and help to prevent local shortages. Nevertheless, as with energy, the sheer increase in demand means that more water is used to produce food.

Overall, water resources by 2050 are still adequate to meet rising demand (Bruinsma 2011), but more countries face very severe water shortages, particularly those countries that have not changed their agricultural and urbanization practices. China and countries in the Middle East and North Africa are most at risk. China is able to directly and indirectly reallocate its available water supplies, partly by transporting water from the south to the north, but also by shifting more production from rice to corn. China and Vietnam are able to peacefully share the water resources that were contentious before.

Likewise, greater cooperation in the Nile basin and in the Tigris-Euphrates area makes it possible to avoid potentially destabilizing conflicts over critical resources. Western and northern states in India (especially Gujarat, Rajasthan, and Punjab) face severe water crises (Waslekar and Bhatt 2004), but a strengthened central government facilitates internal migration as well as the better utilization of existing resources to keep suffering to a minimum. Recycling water becomes more widespread in Asian cities.

Table 4.3
Energy Production

Billions of barrels of oil equivalents	2010	2020	2040	2050	Average annual percent change, 2011–2050
World	89.1	102.6	135.6	148.9	1.3%
Liquids	29.3	29.3	23.9	22.5	−0.7%
Gas	22.2	28.1	40.4	42.2	1.6%
Coal	26.6	29.6	37.5	38.5	0.9%
Nuclear	4.6	5.9	8.3	10.6	2.1%
Renewable sources	6.5	9.7	25.5	35.0	4.3%
Hydro	5.4	6.5	7.2	7.9	0.9%
Other renewable sources	1.2	3.2	18.4	27.2	8.2%
World energy use/GDP ratio	100	88.6	62.9	52.9	−1.6%
World real price of energy (index: 2010 = 100)	100	113.9	157.4	276	2.6%
OPEC Middle East liquids	8.3	8.5	4.8	5.2	−1.2%
Share of world liquids	28.3%	28.8%	20.0%	23.0%	
Share of world energy	9.3%	8.2%	3.5%	3.5%	
Other major liquids production					
USA	2.4	2.7	3.4	3.4	0.8%
Canada	1.2	1.5	2.9	3.4	2.7%
Russia	3.8	3.6	1.7	1.1	−3.0%
Major natural gas producers					
USA	4.0	5.9	6.5	6.3	1.1%
Canada	1.1	1.9	1.5	1.1	0.2%
U.S. net energy imports as share of:					
Total energy use	23.5%	10.6%	−4.5%	−7.1%	
GDP (price adjusted)	1.9%	0.8%	−0.4%	−0.8%	
China net energy imports as share of:					
Total energy use	13.6%	14.6%	5.5%	0.5%	
GDP (price adjusted)	3.0%	3.0%	1.1%	0.2%	

Source: See table 2.2.

Great-power politics are transformed. China is the world's biggest economy and is still growing faster than its great-power rivals. It remains poorer than the United States on a per capita basis, but it is rich by 2010 standards and is able to afford the world's best in military technology. China is now the hegemon, but peacefully so. It has some success developing oil and gas resources in the South China and East China Seas and shale gas in western China.

China still imports considerable amounts of energy, but it is far more energy secure by the 2040s (see table 4.3). China demands internal stability, global respect and deference, and a greatly shrunken U.S. presence in the western Pacific. It gets all of these by 2050, which reduces its desire to militarily challenge the United States. China's economic power also allows it to hold great influence in most of Africa.

China's rise in power and influence leads to a more harmonious world because China has gotten ahead by adapting its institutions and norms in mostly nonthreatening ways that have allowed the United States to peacefully adjust to the new global reality. The Chinese—like most people living in prosperous, peaceful, and stable nations—are eager to maintain that status (Inglehart and Baker, 2000). Interdependence has helped make China great, but it has made other states powerful, too, and these states (mostly) play by the rules of peaceful competition to satisfy their national needs.

Table 4.4
Probability of a Country Having at Least One War in a Given Year

	2015	2050	Number of War Years* 2015–2040
China	5.9%	5.8%	5
United States	10.5%	8.0%	10
India	4.4%	4.3%	7
Russia	10.4%	6.8%	13
Japan	2.2%	1.4%	0
Israel	5.4%	3.6%	7
Iran	7.0%	4.6%	3
Turkey	5.2%	3.6%	4

Note: *Wars are defined as any militarized inter-state dispute with at least 1,000 deaths. The count includes some years with multiple wars. The probabilities of war are calculated in all scenarios, but wars are not allowed to happen in order to keep the model simulations deterministic.
Source: Calculations with the IFs model.

The rest of the BRICs, the STICKs, Mexico, and a still rich European Union help to promote global harmony by balancing China. Although China is the predominant power by 2050, it still only accounts for less than 25 percent of world output, and its economy is far more dependent on others for trade, investment, and technology than the U.S. economy ever was.

War has not become obsolete, but it has become somewhat less likely. The probability of China going to war with the United States rose slightly in the late 2020s but never became very high. China's probability of going to war with any country decreases, from 6.5 percent in 2015 to 6.3 percent by 2050 (see table 4.4). This is not a large decrease, but it is preferable to the results in the four disharmonious scenarios, all of which show a rise in the probability of war.

Conclusion

This scenario led with the economy, with the key aspect of it being a science and technology boom, particularly in the energy sector, that transformed the world by 2050. As with scenario 1, a major challenge we faced was how to transition to a benevolent hegemonic China without war. In the first scenario, the Chinese economy and Chinese power so dramatically outpaced that of the United States that resistance seemed futile. In this scenario, however, with a somewhat weaker economy, China calculated that it was to its advantage to act within the existing norms and institutions. As China became increasingly rich and

Table 4.5
Peaceful Power Transition

	Energy	Economy	Harmony
High/Strong	A strong economy drives demand beyond supply, despite new energies. The competition of energy and food for water raises prices further.	Keynesian principles result in strong growth. Technological breakthroughs transform the energy sector.	Liberal institutional reforms strengthen the non-OECD countries. A modern diversified energy market lessens tension among the powers over oil. China is the hegemon by 2050.
Low/Weak			

Source: Authors.

stable, it decided that potential flash points like Taiwan or the South China Sea could be dealt with diplomatically.

Another major challenge we faced was why energy prices remained high while a major technological revolution in energy increased supply. We assumed that the new technology did not come cheaply. The world transitioned to renewable energy sources in this scenario, but they cost more than extracting oil. Table 4.5 presents the endogenous variables— high energy prices, strong economic growth, and global harmony—and how we assumed they would interact to create a peaceful power transition by 2050.

5   Regional Mercantilism

SCENARIO 4: HIGH ENERGY PRICES, WEAK ECONOMIC GROWTH, GLOBAL DISHARMONY

The fourth scenario is marked by high energy prices, weak economic growth, and global disharmony. Economic weakness in the United States and the government's failure to come to grips with its long-term problems results in a gradually diminishing respect for its model of democratic capitalism and a diminishing role for the dollar as a reserve currency. The leading alternative, Chinese-style state capitalism, has its own set of problems, but at least it offers populist leaders a politically attractive rallying point. The push for state capitalism engenders a move away from competition and globalization and weakens the prestige of the multilateral institutions that U.S. and European leaders worked so hard to build.

This scenario sees a long period of growing protectionism, slowing trade growth, and more regional trade arrangements. Even as world economic growth slows, energy prices rise perilously because of faltering supplies. The shale revolution fizzles because of technological and environmental problems, Middle East oil production peaks, new oil production areas in Africa are hampered by political instability, and renewable energy is available only at very high prices. Some of the regional powers—in particular, Brazil, South Africa, Indonesia, and Iran—do relatively well, but they are not able to exert much influence beyond their immediate neighborhoods. All powers turn inward to confront heightened domestic conflict brought on by low economic growth and rising income inequality. The result is a multipolar world defined by regional groupings in competition, none of which are very attractive to the others as examples for escaping weak growth.

The 2010s

In the United States, partisan divisions over fiscal policy, budgetary allocations, and the preferred scope of regulatory guidance create a deep-seated uncertainty that discourages investment, entrepreneurship, and job creation. Europe faces similar policy problems but finds its affairs complicated by a growing movement by some countries to loosen the level of bureaucratic control that Brussels gained through the Lisbon Treaty (see chapter 3). The euro remains intact, but it is a cause of growing discontent among the weaker nations, which feel aggrieved by the currency's perceived harmful effects on their competitiveness.

Economic growth in the United States and Europe does not recover in this decade. Another deep recession hits both regions in the later years, and the monetary authorities are at last forced to tighten policy in order to ensure continued demand for the still-increasing supply of government bonds. In the United States in particular, but also in Europe, the capacity to produce competitive consumer goods gradually erodes. A decade of low investment and hesitant competition has encouraged companies to focus more on cost cutting than on exploring new opportunities.

Europe is further hobbled by the European Union's imposition of extremely high taxes on fossil fuel use and a decline in nuclear power generation. Paris's push to raise income tax rates on the rich is followed by many other European Union members, which leads to substantial migration of high-income and highly talented people. These policies burden European industry in this decade and set the stage for dislocation in the 2020s.

The United States is increasingly weighed down by the unsustainable growth in transfer payments for retirement, universal health care, and support for the indigent. Domestic political strife increases, the business climate worsens, and the attraction for foreign investment in the U.S. economy wanes.

Energy prices in this decade are volatile, making the financial situation of countries all the more unpredictable. The production of oil and gas by independent producers is rising in the Americas and in Africa but is not yet enough to prevent prices from rising. Uncertainties in the Middle East about the unrest begun in the Arab Spring of 2011, the violence in Iraq following the U.S. withdrawal, the civil conflict in

Syria, and increased tensions over freedom of navigation through the Strait of Hormuz contribute to volatile pricing.

Weaker growth in OECD countries is compensated initially by strong growth in the BRICs. India profits from major upgrades to its transportation and power infrastructure and tries to use its relative economic strength to expand its regional political influence. China's economic growth remains strong relative to the OECD countries, but it gradually decelerates in the face of growing protectionist measures from the United States and Europe. Brazilian growth spurts from a combination of slowed energy exploration and development, agricultural exports, and infrastructure investment.

Russian growth is sustained by high oil prices in this decade. Instead of trying to create a more sustainable economic platform, however, the Russian government focuses its clout on trying to re-create a broader and more economically subservient sphere of influence in Eurasia. In the face of renewed recession in the OECD countries, growth in the BRICs is not enough to sustain economic growth in the rest of the world.

As global economic conditions worsen, internal security deteriorates in many countries and international tensions rise. Street protests, disgruntled elites, and opportunistic military leaders combine forces (or battle one another) to overthrow weakly democratic regimes in a number of African, Latin American, and Asian countries. The drug wars intensify in Mexico and the Andes, conflicts rage in central Africa over resources, and piracy intensifies in the Indian Ocean.

In Europe, Japan, South Korea, and the United States, growing public dissent enhances the power of transnational advocacy networks. Domestic political movements supporting those disenfranchised by the global economic downturn create transnational networks of like-minded organizations. Their demands involve an inchoate mixture of pleas for social justice, environmental protection, and a retreat from globalization. This activism achieves few explicit policy reforms, but it does weaken the legitimacy of the establishment, making it even harder to come to grips with the structural problems plaguing the system. The political legitimacy and the financial power of large multinational corporations are also weakened in this low-growth environment.

Nations still remain attached to multilateral institutions in the middle of this decade, using the G-20, the International Monetary

Fund, and the World Trade Organization (WTO) to try to maintain a functioning integrated global system. The great powers shrug off concerns over internet spying and territorial disputes in the Asian coastal regions, and there are no significant conflicts involving China, the United States, or India.

Regional organizations, however, take on an increasingly important role, as exemplified by NATO's renewed vigilance in the wake of Russia's seizure of Crimea, counterterrorism efforts by the Shanghai Cooperation Organization, the Arab League's success in brokering the departure of Bashar al-Assad from Syria, Mercosur's expansion in South America, and the African Union's multiplicity of peacekeeping operations. The United States and Europe are able to launch their Transatlantic Trade and Investment Partnership agreement in the later part of the decade, but it has little effect on transatlantic trade before 2020. The U.S.-led Trans Pacific Partnership (TPP) is also established, with a great deal of fanfare, by 2020. These two new regional trade deals help push the WTO toward irrelevancy, and the world's major economies press forward with exclusive deals among like-minded states.

In this decade, the United States records almost no increase in average real per capita income (table 5.1). Economic growth in the United States in the 1930s was about the same, but this time the starting level of income is much higher, and a more developed welfare state means that no one suffers to the point of starvation. Nevertheless, attitudes gradually shift internally to focus on domestic concerns, and the U.S. commitment to liberal internationalism wanes. Foreign aid budgets are not increased, and some programs are cut altogether.

The 2020s and 2030s

In the early 2020s, the developed economies move toward a new level of regional mercantilism. After more than a decade of sluggish growth in the OECD nations, growing populist sentiment encourages governments everywhere to heighten trade barriers. The two new U.S. free trade agreements with Europe and Asia are a perfect way to divert trade from nonpreferred partners by using a variety of new and strengthened nontariff barriers, especially those dealing with health, labor, and environmental issues as well as government procurement and treatment of foreign investment. Protectionist measures have widespread popular support, but they are also supported by a rising tide of professional economic literature that questions the benefits of

Table 5.1
Scenario 4: Regional Mercantilism
High Energy Prices, Weak Economic Growth, Global Discord

Real GDP, billions of $ at 2010 exchange rates

	2010	2020	2040	2050
USA	14,447	15,943	19,983	21,187
		1.0%	1.1%	0.6%
China	5,931	11,319	24,535	25,328
		6.7%	3.9%	0.3%
OECD	38,646	41,244	44,779	45,036
		0.7%	0.4%	0.1%
Non-OECD	24,944	37,992	70,716	80,305
		4.3%	3.2%	1.3%
World	63,590	79,236	115,495	125,341
		2.2%	1.9%	0.8%

Real GDP per capita, 1000s of 2005 PPP $

	2010	2020	2040	2050
USA	42.1	42.7	47.8	48.7
		0.1%	0.6%	0.2%
China	6.8	10.1	16.8	17.5
		4.0%	2.6%	0.4%
OECD	34.9	36.2	39.0	39.6
		0.4%	0.4%	0.1%
Non-OECD	6.0	7.3	9.6	9.9
		1.9%	1.4%	0.3%
World	9.9	10.9	12.8	13.0
		1.0%	0.8%	0.2%

Source: See table 2.1.

unfettered free trade (Gomory and Baumol 2001; Krugman 2008; Samuelson 2004).

The TPP attracts many fewer members than originally hoped for, and it arouses a great deal of opposition in the far Pacific as well as from groups in the United States. Only a few highly developed Eastern Hemisphere countries end up joining the TPP, including Australia, New Zealand, Japan, South Korea, Singapore, and Malaysia. China remains suspicious that the TPP is more about the U.S. geopolitical ambition to contain China's rise than about expanding trade (Song and Wen 2012).

In the early 2020s, China devises an aggressive policy combining lavish offers of aid and investment with not-so-veiled threats of diminished access to the Chinese market to deter countries from joining the U.S.-led group. As a result, Indonesia, Thailand, the Philippines, Vietnam, Laos, Burma, Cambodia, and Bangladesh cast their lot with China in an enhanced Asian free trade area, called the Asian League. Late in the decade, trade cooperation between the United States and Europe withers. The United States chooses to intensify its trade and financial relationship with its Pacific partners even if it means reconstructing some of the barriers to transatlantic integration.

Countries everywhere begin to raise barriers to those outside their regional blocs, hoping to stimulate their own production and employment. The Russian-led Eurasian Union, an enhanced African Union led by South Africa, Mercosur, and a new Islamic free trade area all grow in importance. Governments provide capital to new domestic industries, create favorable tax regimens, and encourage the establishment of monopolies in local and nearby markets. In classic mercantilist fashion, they assist local industry by imposing tariffs, quotas, and prohibitions on the import of goods that compete with those of local manufacturers. Governments also discourage the export of tools and capital equipment and the emigration of skilled labor that would allow foreign countries to compete in the production of high-value manufactured goods. The blocs ultimately divert trade from normal efficiency-driven channels.

The OECD countries and China fare better than the rest of the world at the protectionist game. The TPP and the intensified trade barriers imposed by the European Union mostly involve trade between countries at a high stage of development, so closer ties mean more intraindustry trade with countries with similar wage structures. This allows most OECD countries to continue to profit from some of the principles of comparative advantage and economies of scale without suffering from the dislocations associated with building new interindustry trade with low-income countries that have much different factor endowments. The rise of protectionism does not spur growth or employment, but in most cases it does succeed in enriching the bureaucrats and companies that can best influence the rules and channel government spending in their favor.

China initially benefits from new regional trading relationships. Its overwhelming size allows it to impose unequal trading relationships on its neighbors, reserving the high-technology dynamic sectors for itself and foisting the raw materials and low-skills industries on its partners.

In this period, the growth of regional protectionism diminishes global growth. Competition is reduced, and trade and investment are diverted from market-driven channels. The newly empowered regional blocs in Latin America, Africa, and the Middle East make little economic sense: they ensure that competition and foreign investment can no longer challenge outmoded and inefficient domestic industries. But the regional associations do give a new sense of purpose and legitimacy to the politicians as well as new sources of wealth and security to the protected industrialists and merchants. The regional leaders Brazil and South Africa gain in power and neighborhood respect.

Exports, housing growth, foreign direct investment, and natural resource production sustain some economies, particularly in Latin America. Buoyed by a young and still-growing population, Latin America continues to develop through 2030. The leaders manage to weather the first global financial crisis as the region's major nations lessen their dependence on exports to the United States and China. Building on Mercosur, the region emphasizes exports of energy and raw materials and tries to reduce imports of manufactured goods, in a replay of its failed import substitution policy of the 1950s. New leaders in Venezuela adopt more peaceful relations with Colombia and the United States, privatize aspects of the oil industry, and disavow any intent to spread the Bolivarian revolution. Drug warfare in the region and unrest from indigenous groups, however, put a serious burden on the economy and the social order. Brazil's leaders consider aspects of economic liberalism for several decades, but the appeal of state capitalism eventually proves too great to resist.

Facing a declining population, astronomically high energy prices (from high taxes in addition to high market prices), and soaring health and retirement payments, Europe does not grow at all during these 20 years. The United States is in a somewhat better demographic position, but the shift toward protectionism incapacitates the government, as all parties turn their attention to jockeying for protectionist favors. Faced with less foreign competition, U.S. firms raise prices, reduce quality, and cut back on research. Employment rises, but real wages do not, and living standards decline for most Americans. Inequality, as measured by the Gini coefficient, rises in the United States (in contrast to stable or slightly falling inequality in the high-growth scenarios) because slower technological improvement results in relatively fewer high-skilled workers.

The slow growth of demand in the OECD countries, diminished market access, the economic costs of trade diversion related to regional trade, and the high cost of imported energy all combine to drag down Chinese growth. U.S. and European companies with large investments in China reduce their exposure as China further tightens legal and regulatory requirements on foreign operators, making it increasingly hard for them to turn a profit. The retreat from foreign investment further stifles global growth. China watches unhappily as its central role in global manufacturing gradually dissipates while rising OECD protection returns a growing amount of low-skilled manufacturing activity to the West and prevents the export of any new high-tech industry. No significant new production-sharing deals for aircraft, renewable energy technology, or biotech products are signed after 2020.

Global prices for manufactured goods rise as a natural response to the trade diversion. Foreign investors who have considered China a good production base now see China's rising wage structure and its reduced access to global markets as a reason to move operations offshore. India benefits from this global realignment. Its improving infrastructure, low wages, and positive political relations with the West all help it to gain world market share at China's expense. China, buffeted on all sides by this shift toward global protectionism, becomes increasingly resentful of the OECD and India and becomes increasingly insular in its foreign policy.

Although global economic growth is relatively weak in this period, energy prices are high because of falling global oil production in most areas. Domestic consumption rises among producers in the Persian Gulf, Russia, and North America and limits supplies to the global market. Rapidly growing populations in the non-energy producing non-OECD countries puts further pressure on energy use for transportation, food production, and water treatment and distribution.

Latin American energy exporters reach a peak in easy oil production in the early 2020s. The mostly nationalized oil companies lack the technical expertise, capital, and management skills to maintain production in their old fields or to start production in challenging new areas offshore or in shale deposits. Venezuela's exploitation of its massive reserves of heavy oil grinds to a halt as the government starves the state-owned company of capital and a growing insurgency disrupts the production and transport of oil out of, and logistical support into, the country. Brazil and Mexico are unable to attract significant foreign investment and increase production of conventional and unconventional sources, despite new regulation meant to enhance industry performance. Table 5.2 summarizes the trends in energy production.

New oil discoveries in Africa are a mixed blessing. States that have a diversified economy, mature governing institutions, an active civil society, and private ownership of a significant percentage of the oil and gas sector remain stable and grow strong. States that retain tight control over the development of resources and have corrupt governance and a lack of accountability are unable to translate resource wealth into growth. Ghana is a good example of success, whereas Gambia succumbs to the resource curse.

Multinational corporations, including the big Chinese oil companies, are still welcome in many parts of Africa, but government eagerness to capture the bulk of energy revenues and insurgencies in the oil-producing areas keep production far below the potential. Nigeria's energy production is sporadically interrupted by sectarian violence. Oil exports from South Sudan trail off to almost nothing as violence in the production areas and sabotage and contract disputes with Sudan disrupt flows to the coast. In the rural areas of Kenya, Mozambique, and Equatorial Guinea, separatists and bandits discourage investment and production, while in the cities African nationalist movements protest Chinese and other foreign involvement in the economy.

Energy production in the Middle East declines sharply. Oil production declines in most of the Gulf states. Their reserves were vastly overstated for decades to intimidate potential competitors and to enhance their political clout within OPEC. Iraq still has a large amount of untapped potential, but a failure to reach agreement between the Shiite, Sunni, and Kurdish communities inhibits much-needed investment and results in sabotage to production sites and disruption of transportation routes. Iran is the one bright spot in the world oil picture. The Iranians successfully detonate a nuclear test device in the 2020s, and there simply seems to be no point in trying to keep Iran and its oil reserves out of global commerce. A flood of foreign capital, especially from China, pours into Iran, and oil production and exports rise steadily through the 2020s.

Natural gas, considered to be a bridge fuel between carbon-intensive coal and oil to cleaner technology, falls short in global production in

Table 5.2
Energy Production

Billions of barrels of oil equivalents	2010	2020	2040	2050	Annual average percent change, 2011–2050
World	89.1	99.6	102.5	89.0	0.0%
Liquids	29.3	31.9	25.4	16.7	−1.4%
Gas	22.2	22.9	28.7	23.5	0.1%
Coal	26.6	30.5	23.9	19.6	−0.8%
Nuclear	4.6	5.3	5.8	5.3	0.4%
Renewable sources	6.5	9.1	18.8	24.0	3.3%
Hydro	5.4	6.6	6.9	6.7	0.5%
Other renewable sources	1.2	2.4	11.8	17.2	7.0%
World real price of energy (index: 2010 = 100)	100	91.2	68.8	56.0	−1.4%
World price of Oil (index: 2010 = 100)	100	118.5	152.4	257.6	2.4%
OPEC Middle East liquids	8.3	10.3	8.5	6.0	−0.8%
Share of world liquids	28.3%	30.1%	31.0%	30.7%	
Share of world energy	9.3%	8.6%	6.5%	4.8%	
Other major liquids production					
USA	2.4	2.4	2.1	1.5	−1.2%
Canada	1.2	1.3	1.0	0.6	−1.8%
Russia	3.8	4.7	3.5	2.5	−1.0%
Major natural gas producers					
USA	4.0	5.1	4.7	2.5	−1.2%
Canada	1.1	0.8	0.3	0.2	−4.6%
U.S. net energy imports as share of:					
Total energy use	23.5%	20.0%	14.0%	29.5%	
GDP (price adjusted)	1.9%	1.7%	1.1%	3.3%	
China net energy imports as share of:					
Total energy use	13.6%	7.2%	28.9%	21.4%	
GDP (price adjusted)	3.0%	1.5%	5.2%	5.3%	

Source: See table 2.2.

this period. There is not as much gas as the geologists had estimated; what is there is harder to recover, and much of the gas is in areas short on water or on the political will to exploit. Controversies over hydraulic fracturing of the shale during drilling, especially fears about chemicals contaminating water supplies and an increased risk of earthquakes, limit full-scale drilling for unconventional resources except in parts of North America.

Shale gas production never even gets started in Europe because it is blocked by that region's strong consensus against increasing the use of carbon-based fuels, environmental concerns about hydraulic fracturing, and the political clout of the renewable energy industry. Russia also fails to exploit its massive potential in shale gas. The logistical and geological challenges of exploiting gas in eastern Siberia, and the inability of the Russian government to create a reasonable incentive structure for investment, limit production. China's shale gas reserves also prove difficult to exploit because of water shortages and geology. As a result of these widespread difficulties, the natural gas trade gas remains regional rather than global, which keeps prices too high to replace other fuels on a large scale.

In the United States, a partial switch to natural gas and rising regulatory restrictions on emissions reduce coal demand. Coal-fired electricity generation plummets in the United States, but increased exports to China and India sustain the U.S. coal mining industry during this period. Plans for new nuclear power plant construction, meant to begin on a large scale in the United States in the 2020s, remain on hold as a result of the reassessment of plant design following the 2011 disaster at the Fukushima nuclear power plant in Japan.

International agreements to limit carbon-based fuel use are not realized. Global governmental and nongovernmental meetings press for climate change mitigation measures but fail to bridge the differences between China and the United States on mandatory emissions allowances. Implementation of cap-and-trade systems and taxes on carbon emissions falter outside Europe and in certain U.S. regions. The United States does not adopt federal renewable energy standards, and some other OECD countries drop subsidies to stimulate funds for renewable energy development.

Efficiency standards, apart from those in some U.S. states and in the European Union, do not advance. Subsidies remain for big oil companies in the United States. As a result, global energy prices continue to fluctuate widely with the business cycle and with random, conflict-related, production shortfalls, but on average the price of energy relative to other goods and services rises over 2 percent a year, ignoring increases in taxes and transport costs.

The ongoing weakness of the U.S. economy and the diminished need for imported energy to drive it combine to reduce U.S. interest and activity in global affairs. Similarly, China's new focus on its Asian sphere of influence for trade and energy lessens tension between the great powers. Their interests do not seem to conflict as much in the geopolitical and geoeconomic environment of 2030. China's energy imports rise sharply in these decades, but given China's rise in relative power and the lessening of the U.S. presence in the Middle East and in the waters between east Africa and Japan, the Chinese government feels reasonably confident about its energy supply.

However, while great-power tensions ease and the number of major inter-state conflicts decline globally, low-intensity conflict increases. The security vacuum left by the larger powers and the dissatisfaction accompanying falling living standards result in increasing numbers of nonstate armed groups. This results in persistent conflict and an increase in insurgencies by ideological, ethnic, and profit-inspired groups and networks.

For example, in the North Caucasus, separatists attract the support of externally funded and trained Islamist groups that have long wanted to create a trans-Caucasian caliphate. Frustrated from losses fighting in Iraq and Syria for over a decade, Islamists gravitate to the Caucasus to fight Russian forces. Elsewhere, nonreligious terrorism, such as political activist groups or those representing ethnic grievances, increase their activity. The theft of globally traded goods through piracy and cyber attacks significantly disrupts trade and financial management as well as utilities operations, particularly in OECD countries. Increasing violence accompanies a rise in arms and the drug trade. In some Latin American areas, rebel groups, insurgents, and racial tensions increase.

The dynamics within the Middle East change significantly. The region breaks into different camps, based on religion, politics, and economic ties. The Sunni-Shiite divide continues to widen, and the Gulf states and Iran fund opposite sides in several countries. Iran weakens the role of its presidency and strengthens theocratic rule. With the aid of Russia and China, the end of economic sanctions, and increasing oil and gas revenues, Iran increases its regional power considerably while lessening its worries about Western intervention. Arab Spring movements usher in mostly Sunni-led Islamist governments that suppress minority rights and result in a continuous cycle of street protests against the regimes, civil conflict, and suppression by security forces. At the end of Prime Minister Recep Tayyip Erdogan's leadership, Turkey turns inward, reconciles its Islamist and secular factions, ceases to be a big player in the Middle East, and joins the European Union by 2030.

Most Asian countries resent Chinese bullying over territorial claims and trade disputes. But Washington's attempts to push these nations into unequal trade and investment relationships, along with a reduced U.S. military presence in the region, leave most of the poorer Asian nations and Taiwan with little choice but to accept Chinese dominance. China organizes its newly created Asian League, hoping to create a self-contained economic unit that is able to satisfy resource needs.

Nevertheless, by 2040 China is still importing substantial amounts of oil from the Middle East and Africa and coal from the United States. The renminbi is the currency of convenience for intraleague trade and finance. As China flexes its muscles in the Asian region and U.S. power continues to wane, even original TPP members South Korea and Malaysia are drawn into the Chinese orbit. The North Korean regime retains Chinese aid and is able to exist several more decades.

The 2040s

In the 2040s, countries move further away from the globalization of trade and finance and embrace the power and security they enjoy in separate regional power structures. Four strong regional groupings exist: the Asian League, the TPP, the EU2050 (an expanded version of the European Union), and Greater India. They all possess large populations and economies, geographic coherence, and a great degree of economic self-sufficiency. Four other groups—the Eurasian Union, Mercosur, the Islamic Brotherhood, and the African Union—are generally smaller and poorer than the first four groups, but, most important, they are not self-sufficient in either resources or advanced manufactured goods and thus must approach the major powers as supplicants. The remaining countries are either failed states or small island states that have negotiated some sort of agreement short of full membership with one of the eight large groups. Table 5.3 gives an indication of the demographic and economic size of the blocs.

Table 5.3
Scenario 4: Regional Blocs in 2050

	No. of countries	People, billions	Share of geopolitical power	GDP, trillions of $, 2010 $	GDP per capita, 1000s of 2005 PPP $	Average annual GDP per capita growth, 2041–2050
Asian League	22	2.73	26.0	33.2	11.9	0.1%
Trans-Pacific Partnership	25	0.97	26.4	35.5	32.6	0.2%
EU2050	41	0.65	13.3	20.8	27.6	0.1%
Greater India	4	1.68	13.5	13.9	10.0	2.4%
Islamic Brotherhood	17	0.59	5.0	4.0	8.5	–1.1%
African Union	31	1.03	5.4	4.5	4.8	1.6%
Mercosur	9	0.36	4.0	8.9	17.2	0.6%
Eurasian Union	11	0.25	2.5	2.9	12.1	–0.5%
Others	26	1.01	3.9	1.7	2.6	0.6%

Source: See table 2.1. For composition of the blocs, see appendix B.

The United States leads the TPP in alliance with Canada, Mexico, Japan, Australia, New Zealand, Colombia, and Chile. It has lost Malaysia and South Korea to the Asian League, but it has gained adherents in Central America and on the Pacific coast of South America. The United Kingdom considers the idea of withdrawing from the European Union and joining its English-speaking friends in the TPP but has not yet acted. A newly democratizing Cuba, however, has chosen to join the group.

Each country in the TPP remains sovereign in many ways and has a say in regional affairs, but the United States is firmly in control of foreign policy, defense, and trade relations within and outside the region. Besides including a few small island states, the TPP consists of 25 countries by 2050—it has about 10 percent of the world population, 28 percent of world GDP, and by far the highest standard of living. The TPP is almost completely self-sufficient in energy, food, raw materials, and all but a few manufactured goods that are produced elsewhere behind high walls—physical and cyber—that protect their trade secrets. The TPP possesses a vast internal market of affluent consumers, and since its geopolitical ambitions are limited to independence and security, its military requirements are small.

However, like most of the other blocs, the TPP is hindered by a slowly growing and rapidly aging population that depends heavily on income transfers from the young to the elderly. This demographic challenge, along with the lack of competition engendered by protectionism and the rigging of markets to protect jobs and to enrich the politically connected, sap much of the economic dynamism from the capitalist system. A per capita annual growth rate of about 0.5 percent per year is the new normal—about one-quarter of the rate the United States achieved in the last half of the 20th century.

The Asian League dominates the East by 2050. Its 22 countries contain about 29 percent of the world population and 27 percent of the world's annual economic output. China is far larger than any other member of the Asian League, and China's Central Committee dominates policy making for the group, for industry and trade, and for foreign and security matters. The bloc as a whole is still poor compared to the TPP or to the EU2050; its GDP per capita is only about 40 percent of the TPP's.

With most of its Pacific flank secured by reliable client states, China is tempted to expand its sphere of influence toward Japan, India, and the Russian Far East. So far, however, the difficulties of dealing with its own demographic challenges and the threat of nuclear retaliation for any attempts at border rearrangement have forced China to keep its ambitions in check. U.S. tariff walls and overall economic retreat from Chinese economic influence set the Chinese back in the 2020s and 2030s and remains a source of deep resentment. But in the deglobalized world of the 2040s, in which China is secure and dominant in the East, the United States is only a minor annoyance.

The European Union expands to 41 countries by 2050. The addition of Turkey, Morocco, Israel, and the remaining Balkan countries add another 100 million people to the association and give it a more stable buffer zone with the Arab world. The new members bring down the average per capita income of the European Union considerably, but they also give the region a small surge of growth for a few years in the 2040s as countries adjust to take advantage of new opportunities and markets.

The income divide between northwest Europe and its old and new eastern and southern members grows very large by 2050 and is a source of rankling discontent. The newer members believe that the richer countries should provide more aid, but Germany and the Nordic countries are already hard-pressed to fund their pension schemes because of their declining working-age population. One obvious solution—facilitating increased migration from the poorer regions of Europe—is still a step too far for most of the northern populace.

The European Union's heavy bet on renewable energy in the early decades of the century starts to pay off in the 2040s. High investment and the increasing efficiency of solar, wind, and wave energy, and even a new generation of small and safe nuclear power generators, greatly reduce the need for imported carbon-based fuels. Europe's hope to be the world leader and giant exporter of these technologies has failed, however. High trade barriers keep European products out of the TPP and the Asian League, and the aggressive theft of intellectual property has widely disseminated European advances.

Europe maintains a small amount of trade with the other blocs and tries to maintain amicable relations in all geopolitical directions. One of the region's major income streams is tourism, and the region avoids any policy moves that might dampen the flow of moneyed outsiders. Europe maintains a small nuclear deterrent force, managed by France, but it sees little threat from other trade blocs. Instead, it relies on the still large Turkish army, which it now subsidizes, to keep Iranian ambitions in check.

India is a giant region all by itself, but it finds few partners willing to join its association. By 2050, Greater India includes only Sri Lanka, Mauritius, and the Seychelles. Pakistan, a bitter rival of both Iran and India, prefers Chinese dominance, and so does Bangladesh. Growing world trade barriers keep Indian growth far below what it might have been in a globalized world (see scenarios 1 and 3). Rail and pipeline routes from Iran and the other Caspian Sea energy producers never materialize because of poor relations with Pakistan.

India's energy problems are another significant hindrance on growth, until renewable fuel sources become more widely available in the 2040s. Despite these difficulties, the Indian government manages to create an industrial strategy that works fairly well to gradually modernize the economy. It also works hard to keep some trade channels alive with the EU2050 and the TPP trade blocs to ensure access to the advanced capital goods that it cannot produce itself at affordable cost. India is forced to continue to spend a large proportion of its resources on defense. A nuclear deterrent is helpful, but by 2050 the Indian government feels increasingly threatened by China and its client states.

Despite the age-old hostility between Shiites and Sunnis, Iran gradually assumes regional hegemony from Afghanistan to Libya. Saudi Arabia's power withers in the 2030s as its oil production shrinks and its U.S. support dissolves. Iran's energy revenues rebound, and it uses its growing economic clout and its unified and focused state to gradually create a regional bloc—the Islamic Brotherhood—that defers to the Iranian government's preferences on trade, energy, and foreign relations. Iran's success in withstanding U.S. pressure and its eventual success in demonstrating its status as a member of the nuclear club raise its prestige enormously in the Islamic world. Israel's absorption into the European Union as well as its nuclear deterrent keeps it safe. This membership comes with a guarantee of Israel's support to revive the economy of the West Bank and Gaza Strip by facilitating greater trade and aid.

The African Union is the third largest bloc in terms of population, but it is by far the economically weakest and the most politically unstable bloc. As the largest, richest, and most politically stable state, South Africa naturally assumes leadership of the bloc. South Africa and its southern neighbors—especially Mozambique, Zambia, and Zimbabwe—manage respectable economic growth rates in the 2040s. The rest of sub-Saharan Africa, whether members of the African Union or not, still suffer from internecine violence and far too little effective governance. The more successful southern states end the decade considering whether it would be useful to reduce economic and political ties with the poorer regions in order to join with Brazil and Mercosur in a new South Atlantic association.

By the 2040s, Mercosur is actively courting the Africans. Though relatively wealthy, the South American bloc is much smaller in population than the four strong blocs and lacks military or geopolitical stature. Worse, its potential as an energy powerhouse fails because the offshore deposits are rendered too expensive to produce. Brazil finds that its restrictive trade policies, successful at first in stimulating manufacturing, are now stifling competition and economic progress. In the end, Brazil's initial grandiose plans for creating a rival superstate in the Americas are dashed by the success of the much larger TPP. Because Brazil is restless and uncomfortable with its second-tier status, it explores economic union with the richer parts of Africa and embarks on ambitious state-building projects in the Andes.

The Eurasian Union is led by another fading regional power: Russia. Although it succeeds in bringing much of Ukraine and most of the rest of the former Soviet Union into its fold, Russia never adapts the policies of either democratic capitalism or state capitalism. Instead it continues to focus on predatory resource nationalism, a policy that works well on a short-term basis to enrich the political leaders but that is economically unsustainable. Rather than focusing on trying to develop a new and more productive economic model—a hard task in a small trade bloc in a nonglobalized world—Russia is forced in the 2040s to maintain large military forces in the Far East to ensure that Chinese forces do not take advantage of its weakness.

Both China and Russia reinforce their exclusive economic zones, raising tensions on issues of oil and gas exploration as well as shipping and fisheries. In a move that exacerbates tensions, Japan and China test Russia's resolve to keep access closed to the Okhotsk Sea. This period ends uneasily, as China is further emboldened to make claims to the South China Sea.

Finally, as the high Arctic opens to greater transit and exploration, Russia stakes more claims to the Arctic seabed as part of its continental shelf and permanently stations its submarines and surface ships there. The United States, Canada, Denmark, and Norway push back diplomatically but fail to unite on forceful countermeasures. The continued long U.S. absence from the UN Convention on the Law of the Sea prevents the U.S. exercise of a veto against further Russian claims.

Table 5.4
Regional Mercantilism

	Energy	Economy	Harmony
High/Strong			
Low/Weak	Low production, expensive renewable energy, and contention in oil regions make the supply inadequate.	The global economy weakens, and there is no successful model for growth. World trade shrivels.	Regional trade blocs make for contentious multilateralism. Intra-state instability increases with economic decline. Transnational threats of piracy and terrorism increase.

Source: Authors.

Conclusion

This scenario, as opposed to the idealist scenario 3, contained all negative variables: high energy prices, weak economic growth, and global disharmony. We assumed that this combination was most suitable for regional mercantilism. Although this scenario shares an international system defined by multipolarity with scenario 2, in this case the disharmony was centered on conflict among contentious blocs engaged in trade wars rather than on traditional inter-state conflicts. It is a stark reminder of how regional mercantilism can harm global economics and politics. The retreat into state capitalism and mercantilism produced few economic gains and left many of the major players dissatisfied. In this scenario, the nexus of economics and geopolitics were the main drivers, and energy production suffered as a result. Table 5.4 presents the combination of endogenous variables and how we assumed they would interact to create regional mercantilism by 2050.

6   A New Bipolarity

SCENARIO 5: HIGH ENERGY PRICES, STRONG ECONOMIC GROWTH, GLOBAL DISHARMONY

In the fifth scenario, the world economy recovers from the quagmire of 2008, which has pushed up energy prices sharply. China continues to have very high growth, which tempts it to assert its newfound power against its neighbors and its great-power rival, the United States. However, the United States employs trade measures and diplomacy that contain China's power. Thus, there is a new bipolarity in which there is no superpower, and both the United States and China struggle for influence over other nations. It is a tenuous bipolarity, since the emerging powers focus on economic benefits from both camps and refrain from joining either superpower in a security arrangement.

However, the scenario falls short of multipolarity because no other great power emerges. The disharmony occurs mostly within developing countries, which continue to supply the richer countries but whose citizens do not reap the rewards. It gradually becomes apparent that oil reserves in Saudi Arabia and Kuwait were vastly overstated; production slides, which creates further pressure on prices. Production in Iraq and Iran never meets expectations because of continued turmoil and sanctions, respectively.

A reduced world oil supply has minimal effects on world economic growth, because for several decades the OECD countries and the emerging economies have adjusted by phasing in more natural gas supplies, building more nuclear plants, and making renewable sources more cost-effective. The United States becomes significantly more energy secure in this scenario as it moves away from reliance on oil and into new energy technology markets that it dominates. At the same time, higher energy prices enable more production from higher-cost nontraditional hydrocarbon sources in North America, which raises export capacity.

The 2010s

In the OECD countries, the business cycle eventually rights itself as pent-up demand and the need to compensate for deferred maintenance and depreciation outweigh the caution and balance-sheet concerns that restrained demand for so long. Growth recovers to a more normal rate of about 2 percent per year per capita. Administrations in both Europe and North America have considerable success in reining in government deficit spending through a combination of entitlement and tax reforms. In this recovery, the principles advocated by Taylor (2011, 2012)—fiscal consolidation, structural reforms, and a rule-based monetary policy— win the policy debate and are implemented by governments in North America and Europe.

China suffers a brief pause as its housing market adjusts to an over-supply, but then it regains a strong upward trajectory. Export growth slows, but higher wages and a higher real exchange rate lead to growing domestic demand, which helps Chinese industry restructure away from exports and leads to greater consumer satisfaction and more domestic tranquillity. China continues to rely heavily on its model of state-directed capitalism, providing cheap credit and strategic direction to a widening set of industries.

Most of the other large non-OECD countries—specifically, Brazil, India, Indonesia, South Africa, and Turkey—also resume high-growth trajectories in this period, but they refrain from raising their military budgets or projecting their power. Likewise, many of the poorer non-OECD countries, particularly those not torn by domestic strife, are pulled along by high demand in the big countries.

Energy demand grows sharply in this decade. Increased production of unconventional oil in North America and new production from east and west Africa keep world prices in check for a while. However, slowing production in Saudi Arabia and Kuwait, and instability in Iraq due to ISIL's attacks, heighten a concern about rising energy prices in the future. Rumors intensify that Saudi Arabia is facing sig-nificant difficulty in fulfilling its OPEC quota. Production in Iran and Libya remains well below potential because of sanctions in Iran and internal strife in both countries. By the end of the decade, declining production in the North Sea and the Middle East starts to conflict with the great rise in demand in east and south Asia, and energy prices start to rise.

With the upswing of the business cycle, the talk of U.S. economic decline subsides, and the capitalist model regains some credibility (see table 6.1). China, which had begun to assert itself more forcefully after the 2008-2009 financial crisis, downplays its unhappiness with a U.S.-centered system. Cooperation over trade, water rights, and energy resources improve on China's periphery. But the underlying fears about China's long-term ambitions—to reduce the U.S. presence and influence in Asia, to be able to guarantee (by force, if necessary) its

Table 6.1
Scenario 5: A New Bipolarity
High Energy Prices, Strong Economic Growth, Global Disharmony

Real GDP, billions of $ at 2010 exchange rates

	2010	2020	2040	2050
USA	14,447	17,352	28,067	34,471
		1.8%	2.4%	2.1%
China	5,931	12,635	36,062	44,470
		7.9%	5.4%	2.1%
OECD	38,646	43,091	56,505	64,538
		1.1%	1.4%	1.3%
Non-OECD	24,944	40,875	103,560	142,457
		5.1%	4.8%	3.2%
World	63,590	83,966	160,065	206,995
		2.8%	3.3%	2.6%

Real GDP per capita, 1000s of 2005 PPP $

	2010	2020	2040	2050
USA	42.1	46.5	66.7	78.3
		1.0%	1.8%	1.6%
China	6.8	10.8	22.1	25.7
		4.7%	3.6%	1.5%
OECD	34.9	37.9	49.3	56.7
		0.8%	1.3%	1.4%
Non-OECD	6.0	7.7	12.7	15.2
		2.4%	2.6%	1.8%
World	9.9	11.4	16.8	19.6
		1.5%	1.9%	1.6%

Source: See table 2.1.

access to markets and resources, and to alter world institutions more to its ideology of authoritarianism and noninterference in sovereign affairs—do not go away. India and most Southeast Asian nations, fearful of China's ambitions, increase military spending and strengthen military ties within the region and with the United States.

China's economic policy choices in this period set the stage for a further period of rapid growth but fundamentally undermine the global trading system and the geopolitical regime that supported it. China's indigenous innovation policy, supported by a mercantilist trade policy and a revitalized system of state-owned enterprises, leads to a profound geopolitical shift. China's goal is to use state power to create national champion companies in seven strategic industries that will create their own technology rather than rely on Western knowledge.

Instead of trying to achieve this goal by investment, education, and research, the Chinese government ramps up its efforts to copy foreign-owned technology (using bribery, intelligence assets, and computer hacking). It also uses export controls and limits on market access to encourage foreign firms to expand operations in China, to conduct more research there, and to allow Chinese partners to share more fully in the fruits of the imported knowledge (Looney 2011). China's efforts are particularly damaging on a short-term basis for U.S. and European companies that are dependent on minerals, including rare earth elements, for the production of renewable energy technology and sensitive military weapons systems.

China's military modernization continues at a rapid pace, and by 2020 China is spending $400 billion a year on its military. China spent about $125 billion on its military in 2010 and that spending grows about 12 percent a year in real terms; this implies a defense budget of about 3 percent of GDP by 2020. U.S. military spending stagnates in this decade because of budget restraints and the winding down of the wars in Iraq and Afghanistan. By 2020 the two great powers are spending about the same amount on their militaries. The United States is not able to respond to this as effectively as it wishes; its "pivot to Asia" policy is compromised by fiscal restraints and by continuing troubles with radical Islam.

The pivot is also postponed during this period due to Russia's aggression in Ukraine. Shared concerns among NATO allies as to further Russian expansion west results in a build-up of Western forces in Central European states bordering Russia, including Estonia and

Poland. The gradual increase in the number and type of sanctions against Russia temporarily harms its export markets, including for energy. In retaliation, Russia spends even more on defense spending, scales up military exercises in its northern and eastern regions, and successfully tests intercontinental nuclear missiles.

After the majority of U.S. and allied troops leave Afghanistan in 2015, a many-sided tangle of conflict remains. Pakistan's security forces, with the complicity of the Pakistani government, back the Taliban forces, which put in place a new central government in Afghanistan that is sympathetic to Pakistan. Pakistan and the Taliban demand that India reduce its role in Afghanistan, but India and Iran continue to provide arms and financial support to groups that oppose the Pakistani-aligned factions.

The Chinese back Pakistan's efforts with arms supplies and aid. The conflict in Afghanistan between rival factions remains at low intensity during this period and does not escalate into a full-blown civil war (Giustozzi 2013). Meanwhile, rising instability is enough to deter state-building efforts, inhibit economic growth, and reverse social gains made in the early part of the decade by women and civil society groups.

Despite its failure to stabilize Afghanistan, the United States continues its efforts to counter the growing militarization of radical Islamist elements in North Africa, sub-Saharan Africa, the Arabian Peninsula, and Iraq. Al-Qaida is revitalized during this period, and threats to the United States increase. Turmoil inspired by Al-Qaida in the Maghreb (AQIM) plagues Chad, Mali, Mauritania, and Niger. The Tuareg in Mali, Boko Haram in Nigeria, and the more radical forces in Libya, Syria, and the Sinai are infiltrated by AQIM. Al-Shabab spreads violence from Somalia into Uganda. Radical elements of the Muslim Brotherhood in Gaza, Jordan, Egypt, Libya, and Tunisia continue using violence in an effort to gain or retain a hold on power. Civil war ensues in Iraq and Syria as the Islamic Caliphate is declared by ISIL and a coalition of nations tries to crush it. It becomes increasingly difficult to distinguish local grievances, transnational terrorist networks, and corrupt local regimes.

The 2020s and 2030s

China's rise and the mercantilist policies it uses to achieve its rise leads to increasingly negative responses from the OECD and non-OECD countries. The idea that trade leads to growth and will keep the United

States on top gradually erodes. The long-standing U.S. consensus supporting free trade rests to some extent on history. The memories of the disastrous fall in world trade and world economic growth, in part as the result of the imposition of tariffs in the 1930s, and the gains from trade the United States reaped during its more recent period of hegemonic power remain strong. However, the historical arguments weaken as the relative position of the United States diminishes.

In addition to historical antecedents, real world events weaken the theory of comparative advantage. Samuelson (2004) demonstrates theoretically that growth in the rest of the world can hurt a country if it takes place in sectors that compete with its native exports, where it has a comparative advantage. Relative and even absolute per capita GDP can fall in such a situation. Despite a backlash from other economists, such as Bhagwati (2009) and Hufbauer and Schott (2009), the idea gradually gains traction, both among politicians and a broad segment of the voting public. Perhaps trade still boosts growth, but it appears to come more and more at the expense of the American worker and the strength of the middle class, the backbone of the economy.

The U.S.-China Economic and Security Review Commission (2011) has longed pushed for stronger action to encourage China to live up to its WTO obligations. In 2020 the Review Commission morphs from a congressionally mandated study group to an executive office within the White House to manage counter-Chinese policies. The U.S. government decides to unilaterally declare that China's undervalued exchange rate is an illegal export subsidy and imposes staggering countervailing duties aimed at a strategically selected set of industries to boost the retention and export of critical skills at home.

New legislation is passed to hamper American companies from moving research and development and sensitive manufacturing operations offshore. Some industries deemed vital to the U.S. defense industrial base are taken over by the government when threatened by Chinese acquisition, and others are subsidized to enable them to compete with heavily subsidized Chinese state-operated enterprises.

The U.S. backlash against Chinese mercantilism inevitably causes new trade disputes with third countries. It is hard to protect American industry from Chinese competition without protecting it from all competition. Claims and counterclaims proliferate at the WTO even as new barriers are erected by most countries. The WTO attempts to stem the tide of protectionism, but there is no longer a protrade consensus, respect for judicial findings from the Dispute Settlement Body, or enforcement of WTO decisions.

Rising energy prices spark intense efforts worldwide to find alternative energy sources and new ways to economize on available energy. During this period, world conventional oil production slows, except in parts of east and west Africa. Unconventional oil and gas production continue to rise, however, in response to high demand and increasing prices. High energy prices also encourage a series of technological breakthroughs, especially in solar power, hydrogen, and fuel cells and in technologies that improve energy efficiency. Energy from renewable sources rises rapidly (see table 6.2), and technology breakthroughs in energy spread to the rest of the economy.

OECD economic growth accelerates in the early 2020s, as countries adjust to higher energy prices, through a boom in investment to replace obsolete energy-using equipment and through a wave of technical innovation to facilitate the transition to a future less dependent on fossil fuels. The revolution in energy technology leads to a widespread, growth-enhancing technological boom that begins in the United States and Europe. The United States becomes significantly more energy secure with the development of unconventional sources of energy and a gradual switch to nonoil transportation, including biofuels, natural gas, hydrogen, and electric vehicles. The productivity surge in addition to budgetary restraints push the U.S. and the EU debt problems into the background.

The weakening of the old, U.S.-led trade regime and the backlash by the United States against China's mercantilist trade policies slows China's growth below the more optimistic projections of scenario 1. China nevertheless becomes much richer by 2040, with GDP per capita (in PPP terms) rising to about half the level that the United States enjoyed in 2010, while GDP (in constant market dollar terms) rises to 130 percent of the 2040 U.S. level. This is good growth by world historical standards, but not by the standards the Chinese set for themselves. The absolute gap between American and Chinese living standards (as measured by GDP per capita in PPP terms) has actually grown larger (as was shown in table 6.1). This failure to live up to its own high expectations, the perceived resistance by the OECD countries to China's rise, the still formidable distance from Western living standards, and a perceived parity in military capabilities all result in a more fractious geopolitical environment as bipolarity takes hold.

Table 6.2
Energy Production

Billions of barrels of oil equivalents	2010	2020	2040	2050	Average annual percent change, 2011–2050
World	89.1	105.8	138.1	147.5	1.3%
Liquids	29.3	31.4	27.8	22.1	–0.7%
Gas	22.2	28.3	44.5	41.8	1.6%
Coal	26.6	32.2	33.5	30.3	0.3%
Nuclear	4.6	4.7	6.6	7.2	1.1%
Renewable sources	6.5	9.2	25.8	46.0	5.0%
Hydro	5.4	6.7	7.4	7.7	0.9%
Other renewable sources	1.2	2.5	18.3	38.3	9.2%
World real price of energy (index: 2010 = 100)	100.0	92.3	71.0	61.9	–1.2%
World price of oil (index: 2010 = 100)	100.0	129.3	197.6	297.0	2.8%
OPEC Middle East liquids	8.3	9.2	6.9	5.4	–1.1%
Share of world liquids	28.3%	29.3%	24.9%	24.2%	
Share of world energy	9.3%	8.7%	5.0%	3.6%	
Other major liquids production					
USA	2.4	3.5	5.5	5.1	1.8%
Canada	1.2	1.6	2.1	1.5	0.6%
Russia	3.8	3.4	1.6	1.3	–2.6%
Major natural gas producers					
USA	4.0	6.0	8.0	6.9	1.7%
Canada	1.1	1.6	1.3	0.9	–0.7%
U.S. net energy imports as share of:					
Total energy use	23.5%	15.9%	–9.9%	–6.7%	
GDP (price adjusted)	1.9%	1.5%	–1.1%	–1.0%	
China net energy imports as share of:					
Total energy use	13.6%	8.2%	20.0%	6.5%	
GDP (price adjusted)	3.0%	1.9%	5.1%	2.1%	

Source: See table 2.2.

Despite good overall world economic growth, many of the poorest nations are still torn by domestic instability, corruption, and ineffective government policies. Inequality increases in many countries and between them and the OECD countries. Most of the weakest countries are in Africa (such as Niger, Somalia, and Guinea Bissau) but also in Latin America (Nicaragua and El Salvador).

China's increasing demand for oil, gas, coal, copper, and other minerals makes it more aggressive in Africa. China gains more rights to minerals, wins more contracts, extracts more natural resources, and builds more infrastructure to facilitate trade. China's multidecade expansion into Africa, Asia, and Latin America for natural resource extraction, investment, and agricultural production appears to the locals to be similar to the activities of the previous colonial powers—most recently the United States. China is just another rich country taking advantage of the local people, part of the oppressive global system that is holding them back—but also, perhaps, a source of aid and patronage.

Water problems are explosive when combined with poverty, social tensions, environmental degradation, ineffectual leadership, and weak political institutions. The water stress placed on the globe from increased GDP, the withdrawal of water exceeding replenishment, and an increasing population creates severe tension among groups, both within nations and across borders. With this comes an increase in demand for agricultural production, which requires more water but also competes with the energy sector for the same water. With high energy prices, desalination and recycling—which could both offer more freshwater—is too expensive for most countries. There is also an increase in the consumption of water by expanding industrial complexes.

All this means a greater stress on the environment. In some poor countries, the prices of most environmentally stressed foods rise sharply. The people most prone to water stress (and thus water conflict) live along the Nile, Tigris and Euphrates, Mekong, Jordan, Indus, Brahmaputra, and Amu Darya Rivers.

Egypt and Ethiopia are unable to resolve their dispute over the use of Nile River water after the completion of the Grand Renaissance Dam. Electricity generated by the dam does not reap the necessary payback because of the diversion of supply and illegal sales. The Ethiopian government tries to cover this up by generating out-of-season electricity, which uses up precious water reserves and results in insufficient Nile flows into Egypt. The Egyptian military intervenes to reverse this disruption. When the Ethiopian military repels this effort, Egypt responds by sponsoring rebel forces, some of whom have been fighting in the Sinai and are radical Islamists. This proves to be too much for the Ethiopians, who have been fighting similar groups in Somalia for some time, and full-scale war erupts.

The African Union appears incapable of resolving the dispute. The Chinese and the Americans back different proxy groups in the dispute. Similarly, in Libya there is low-scale conflict among groups vying for the right to control aqueduct water that passes through the southern desert to the coastal area in the north. These groups are armed ethnic tribes that are controlled by regional authorities and that rule their fiefdoms in the desert. The weak Libyan government in Tripoli is unable to counter their control and disruption of the water supply.

Russia is sustained by energy exports, but it is weakened by domestic trends: continued authoritarian governance; the lack of rule of law that will encourage modern and nonresource-based economic growth; and, dwindling societal expectations that might have led them to reverse their sharp decline in population. By 2040, Russia's population has shrunk a further 18 million people, to 125 million. Its dreams of reconstituting its empire based on energy supplies and energy transportation routes are thwarted by the explosion in the world supply of natural gas from nontraditional sources.

Russia's leverage over Western Europe is significantly weakened by the development of shale gas resources in the United States and in Europe. Russia's design to control the weak central Asian states also diminishes because of the redirection of these nations' oil and gas, including current and new production, east to China, southeast to Pakistan and India, and west to Turkey. Nevertheless, Russia does manage to build a new pipeline to China, which provides more than a quarter of its gas supply.

Russia is aggravated by the failure of the United States and Europe to accept it into the orbit of some variation of a Greater Europe, which it has suggested since the beginning of the century. Most of all, Russia resents that NATO will not work with it on a joint missile defense system stationed in Central Europe to counter a threat that, according to NATO, is imminent from Iran (Trenin 2012). After Russia's takeover of Crimea and its efforts at subversion in the rest of Ukraine, the United States strengthens its ties with Kiev and renews its efforts to establish a functioning global missile defense system with Europe as a primary subsystem. As a result, strategic tension between Russia and NATO increases, particularly after NATO concludes membership action plans with Azerbaijan, Georgia, Moldova, and Ukraine.

Russia reacts angrily to NATO by further expanding its strategic nuclear force. Russian officials threaten to target the missile defense system. Security is tightened in Europe and the United States against a Russian attack. Nervous NATO members in Central Europe seek a confirmation of the guarantee that NATO forces will protect them. Russia, understanding that its position in Europe is weak, once again conducts military operations in the former Soviet republics of Georgia, Moldova, and Ukraine in the name of protecting ethnic Russian enclaves.

NATO does not send troops, but it does send arms and military advisors. Ultimately, through a combination of force and aid, Russia is able to diminish U.S. and European influence in Eurasia. It ends this era with efforts to enhance economic ties through an expansion of the Eurasian Economic Community. It also strengthens the security arm of the Commonwealth of Independent States. Europe is divided between countries that are more reliant on Russian trade and countries that are less so. This results in the weakening of the Organization for Security and Cooperation in Europe.

Afghanistan becomes increasingly unstable as much of the territory once again falls into the hands of forces opposed to the weak central government. Conflict spills over into other central Asian nations; militants from Uzbekistan and Tajikistan join the fight, and refugees seek shelter among their northern neighbors (Giustozzi 2013).

China and Pakistan disagree over the Pakistanis training Uyghur insurgent groups in Afghanistan. The Saudis disagree with Pakistan over the ruling party's increasing infiltration by Shiites and their efforts to strengthen relations with Iran. The struggle in Afghanistan becomes a proxy war between Pakistan and India as well as between the United States and China, and terrorist groups conduct a stream of coordinated attacks on popular Hindu establishments. Kashmir flares up again with renewed terrorist attacks and regular cross-border skirmishes.

By 2035, the provocation from Pakistani-based militants has become intolerable, and the Indian air force launches major attacks on key Pakistani military installations. The attack has multiple goals, not the least of which is to appease the war fever of the long-suffering Indian people. Another hope is to force the Pakistani government to realize it has no choice but to clamp down on the extremists if it expects to escape further hostilities with India. The conflict stops well short of all-out war, and Pakistan promises to curb the terrorists in return for some compensation for the Indian-inflicted damages. The deal might satisfy the two governments, but it leaves a deep scar on Pakistani politics and political stability.

Near the end of this period, the United States and other outside powers reduce their interest and military presence in the Middle East as oil supplies dwindle in importance in the new energy-technology economy. Middle East powers, desperate for oil and gas revenues to fuel their demographically challenged and chronically dissatisfied populations, eagerly sell all the energy their national oil companies can bring to market. Saudi Arabia and Kuwait finally make it official that their oil reserves have been vastly overstated for decades, and their oil exports and export revenue go into terminal decline.

Large-scale unconventional resource development in the Middle East is unrealized because source rock cannot be fully exploited. Economic growth slows dramatically, and government transfer payments are impossible to maintain. Iranian oil production and natural gas exports remain unrealized as the breakdown in NATO-Russian relations impairs diplomatic negotiation among the five permanent members of the UN Security Council plus Germany.

A succession of coups, countercoups, and civil wars occurs in these decades in the Middle East—from Tunisia and Egypt to Lebanon and Syria to Saudi Arabia, Kuwait, and Yemen—but the persistent internal violence does not spark serious cross-border conflict and does not motivate great-power intervention. One exception is the Kurds in Syria, Iraq, and Iran who declare—at first, independently, and later, together— —a sovereign state of Kurdistan, separate from the three titular states. The initial declarations are reacted to by the three nations with threats, police action, and, in the case of Syria, fighting. However, all three nations are weak, and by 2040 Kurdistan is functioning as a quasi-independent entity. The other exception is ISIL, who remain entrenched in Sunni-dominated areas of Iraq, but are increasingly isolated by better trained and equipped Iraqi forces. Eventually society turns on the brutal ISIL leaders and sides with the Iraqi government.

The United States has become more like China, eschewing intervention in other nations' internal struggles. The returns, in terms of energy security, are also no longer worth the effort. China and the United States do, however, share a common interest in containing the turmoil within the region. New leadership takes command in Saudi Arabia and Kuwait, and both governments loudly proclaim their defiance of Iran but privately accommodate themselves to the policy dictates of the mullahs as long as Iran helps to keep Shiite unrest in check in the Gulf states, and constitutes a major part in assisting the Iraqi forces in isolating ISIL forces within Iraq. New power in the Persian Gulf resides with Qatar and the United Arab Emirates, since they produce the majority of hydrocarbons and also excel in using the new energy technology being developed in the West.

Exponential growth in China's global influence, along with a more moderate positioning of India and many of the larger and stronger non-OECD countries, builds resistance to the global leadership of the United States and the OECD in general. Respect and cooperation for the international financial institutions disappears, and regional organizations are strengthened in east Asia, Latin America, sub-Saharan Africa, and the Middle East. Since global growth remains strong and security concerns are mostly intra-state, the regional organizations exist mainly to coordinate efforts to castigate the OECD countries (and, increasingly, China) in order to defuse political pressures from continuing domestic difficulties. The organizations do little to facilitate trade or resolve regional disputes.

China's power and its sense of grievance grow. It has grown to almost match the economic prowess of the United States and the European Union, and it has surpassed all other emerging powers, yet it lacks the respect a great power deserves, such as that given the Soviet Union during the Cold War. Chinese leaders are particularly perturbed that American leaders have not acceded to their strength and recognized them as a global equal. The United States continues to prosper and contend for global leadership. Nevertheless, U.S. rhetoric is toned down from the Bush-era rhetoric of the national security strategy instructing the Chinese government on how it should rule its people:

Ultimately, China's leaders must see that they cannot let their population increasingly experience the freedoms to buy, sell, and produce while denying them the rights to assemble, speak, and worship. Only by allowing the Chinese people to enjoy these basic freedoms and universal rights can China honor its own constitution and international commitments and reach its full potential. Our strategy seeks to encourage China to make the right strategic choices for its people while we hedge against other possibilities. (Bush 2006, 42)

The U.S. government reduces its human rights hectoring, but it also deploys a whole new trade-containment strategy, curbing access to American markets, investment, and technology. The Chinese find they cannot respond with the debt weapon; they lose hundreds of billions of dollars of paper wealth as the dollar slides against the renminbi, and forced sales would only cost it more. The Chinese are hardly powerless, however. They continue to push for the use of the renminbi and other currencies in international trade, trying to reduce the dollar's privilege.

China's continuing economic success increases Beijing's prestige and helps it to challenge U.S. influence abroad. China and Russia together gradually erode American control of the global internet. This is supported by a majority of the world's emerging economies in response to intrusive U.S. spyware capabilities with foreign governments and firms. China's wealth and soft-power activism also help it to influence U.S. government policy choices of American corporations that are still dependent on Chinese trade and investment ties.

China's economic success lends prestige to its authoritarian model of political and economic governance, to some extent rolling back the global wave of democratization that peaked in the first decade of the 2000s. This less democratic style of governance claims some notable economic success stories, such as Brazil and Nigeria, and relies on accelerated levels of energy production at high prices. But in most of the poorer non-OECD countries, this backlash against democracy and market-based resource allocation simply leads to more corruption, more rent-seeking behavior by favored elites, and weak economic growth. It also increases social strife and leads to popular protests that further destabilize these nations.

China's state-directed mercantilist trade policies and the U.S. countermeasures lead to a reduction in bilateral trade. Trade continues where absolute advantage dictates it, but the United States believes that on balance, the potential gains from comparative advantage trade are not possible, given China's stage of development and its policies. In order to keep a modern manufacturing sector both to provide reliable military equipment and to reap dynamic gains from technological advances, the United States limits more of its trade to its OECD partners and to a select group of ideologically friendly non-OECD countries.

As a result, China's economy suffers from a gradual reduction in trade with the OECD. However, strong growth continues because its domestic market has grown so large and its technological capacity has expanded. Most of the smaller countries on China's periphery—including Vietnam, Burma, Cambodia, Nepal, Bangladesh, and Thailand—

join a close China-dominated regional trade, development, and mutual aid society. Malaysia, Indonesia, and Singapore, however, struggle to remain independent.

The 2040s

By the fifth decade of the 21st century, the global geopolitical and economic landscape is far different from the world of 2010. Hegemony is long gone, and a new balance of power has been achieved. China's economic growth and political ambitions allow the country to become a full equal to the United States in a new bipolar system. Southeast Asia has become close to the old-fashioned tributary states that China desires. However, several lesser powers in China's orbit resist joining either bloc.

On China's southern flank, India remains hostile and wary; a series of border skirmishes and China's support for indigenous insurgents in the state of Arunachal Pradesh keeps tensions high enough to lead to outright war at any point. Australia and New Zealand develop strong economic ties with their Asian neighbors but retain an affinity with the United States and Europe. Likewise, Japan, South Korea, Taiwan, and the Philippines retain ties to the United States yet benefit greatly from Chinese trade. This peculiar nature of bipolarity is partly influenced by the lack of appealing soft power emanating from China. Autarky, state-led capitalism, and the lack of an attractive cultural and political model limit Chinese appeal.

Rapid technological advances in renewable energy allow some advanced countries to increase energy production in response to rising prices. The United States increases energy exports and significantly decreases energy imports. The long-term economic growth of the United States increases slightly; the restructuring and growth of the energy industry more than compensates for the adjustment costs of replacing capital that has been rendered inefficient by the gradually rising prices.

The relatively smooth transition to renewable energy allows continued strong growth in the rest of the OECD and removes energy security as a source of geopolitical tension, at least for the United States. A substantial long-term increase in the real price of energy ultimately has a minimal effect on the long-term economic growth of the energy importers. GDP growth effects, even from very large shocks in the oil price, dissipate after a few years as demand falls because of conservation efforts and as alternate supplies come to the market (Huntington 2007).

Nascent attempts to promote African unity have been shattered by the new great-power rivalry. China's efforts to lock up mineral and even agricultural resources in Africa, however, has spurred a new great-power rivalry, and the United States vigorously competes with money, arms, and troops for influence and markets in the region. As a result, the continent becomes divided again; most of the Anglophone countries line up with the United States as they struggle to build democracy and create modern diversified economies.

Most of the other countries are ensnared in tightening bonds with China. The weaker and less democratic a nation is (and the more natural resources it has), the more likely it is to be in the Chinese camp. These countries come to expect some infrastructure aid and largesse for friendly officials, but they also get an increasing number of Chinese workers, military bases, and troops. China establishes a massive naval base at Mogadishu, Somalia, and its Indian Ocean fleet patrols in strength from Mozambique to Singapore.

Toward the end of this period, Chinese economic growth slows, which affects the power balance. Its state capitalism model stalls. China fails to keep up with, or is purposely left out of, technology advances made in the OECD. China's state-directed companies are deprived of meaningful competition with their Western counterparts, and state-directed capital goes to too many unproductive activities. U.S. policy moves to insulate the United States from China's rise is part of the problem, but most of the trouble lies in China's economic model itself and in its demographic burden. The Chinese growth slowdown, combined with the rise in growth in the United States related to the surge in energy-related technological developments, reverses the power transition that took place in the mid-2020s (see figure 6.1). China was briefly on top in the 2030s, but the new growth dynamics (the United States growing faster than China) causes a new crossover point in 2040. Bipolarity remains to 2050, but it is questionable what will happen beyond that point in time.

These dual power transitions suggest a period of great tension and possible war between the rival great powers. The IFs model estimates a doubling of the risk of a U.S.-China war, but the estimated risk is still quite low, and no great-power war is assumed. As China's economy slows and the United States continues to enjoy productivity-enhancing growth, the two great powers are hostile but evenly matched.

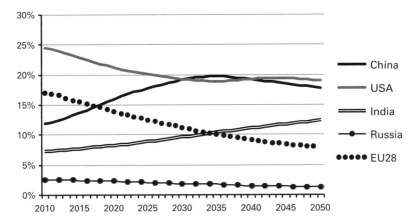

Figure 6.1
Share of World Geopolitical Power in Scenario 5
Source: Calculation with the IFs model.

The United States remains committed to promoting democracy and human rights, but that quest is no longer as important to it as it was at the turn of the century. Economic security and distribution issues rise far higher on the priority list. China achieves a far stronger geopolitical position by 2050, but not as great a one as it had expected. The government seeks to expand its influence and weaken the leadership of the United States in every way possible short of outright war. But to make further serious inroads on U.S. power, China must find a way to rekindle growth.

Great-power tensions erupt in numerous shooting or near-shooting events in geographically disparate proxy disputes in Africa and Asia, but the level of tension never reaches the level of discord between the two superpowers during the Cold War. The new great-power struggle is more one of honor and prestige, values, and economic statecraft. A new but tenuous balance of power dominates world geopolitics.

Conclusion

The three key drivers in this scenario—high energy prices, strong economic growth, and global disharmony—related to one another in interesting ways. The declining production of conventional fossil fuels led to high energy prices and a technology revolution in energy. Technology spillovers from the energy sector led to high economic growth, which spurred high energy demand and still higher energy prices. At

Table 6.3
A New Bipolarity

	Energy	Economy	Harmony
High/Strong	Oil production is curbed in Middle East and fails to keep up with rising demand. The energy technology revolution gears up.	Growth returns to OECD countries. Chinese industry restructures away from exports; domestic demand grows, along with the satisfaction level. High demand pulls non-OECD countries along.	
Low/Weak			The United States is bogged down in the Middle East. China builds up its military and expands its influence in Asia and Africa. China's growth wanes. A contentious bipolarity results by 2050.

Source: Authors.

the same time, long-simmering dissatisfaction in the West over unequal gains from trade with China resulted in extensive new trade barriers that separated countries politically as well as economically.

China paid the biggest price for the trade meltdown, and its growth and geopolitical power waned in the 2040s. The scenario ended in a new bipolar arrangement between the United States and China by 2050, replacing the U.S.-Soviet bipolarity of the Cold War. China approached the U.S. level of comprehensive national power, but many of its aspirations remained unmet. Table 6.3 presents the combination of endogenous variables and how we assumed they would interact to create a new bipolarity by 2050.

7 Eco World

SCENARIO 6: HIGH ENERGY PRICES, WEAK ECONOMIC GROWTH, GLOBAL HARMONY

In the sixth scenario, the world economy continues to struggle, but drastic changes are made in global environmental policies. The United States and the European Union have only weak recoveries from the travails of 2008–2013, and China is unable to transition to a sustainable high-growth path. Energy production of fossil fuels runs into geological and political barriers, and energy prices rise despite weak economic growth. There is a consensus, at least among the OECD countries, that the fossil fuel–driven global economy is environmentally unsustainable and that much higher fuel taxes are the correct way to proceed, even if it means lower economic growth. Stringent new environmental regulations and huge new taxpayer-supplied funds spur new research, innovation, and a large-scale move away from coal and oil. There is a significant decrease in carbon emissions, aided by new international agreements on efficiency standards and technology adaptation, as well as prolonged slow growth.

Countries that wish to catch up to the OECD nations have no choice but to adapt to this new eco world, given the high energy prices and weak overall growth. In China, civic activism and a stolid leadership result in the demise of Communist Party rule. After a series of water crises, the international community finds ways to ensure that the water-food-energy nexus is balanced. Aside from cooperating on environmental issues, nations are focused inward, dealing with disruptive citizens who are unhappy with slow growth. A few conflicts that happen on the margins are swiftly resolved, and major offensive military operations are mostly absent from this scenario. The United States remains the sole superpower, albeit a more cooperative and less confrontational one.

The 2010s

This scenario starts off like scenario 2: Very weak growth in the United States because of structural problems and policy mistakes hinders entrepreneurial activity and the pace of technological change and innovation. Several southern European countries withdraw from the eurozone's common currency arrangement and eventually withdraw from the European Union itself as a result of domestic political pressures and runaway inflation. The Chinese growth rate slows dramatically as the easy gains from first-stage transformation are exhausted, and the shift to widespread modern economic growth is difficult to achieve. The Chinese model of state-sponsored capitalism attracts many adherents but produces little growth in Latin America or Africa.

Lower global energy production and a more benign geopolitical atmosphere take this scenario in a very different direction from scenario 2, however. The United States recovers from the doldrums of the economic recession through Keynesian spending that spurs domestic consumption and rekindles the housing market. The energy boom spurs the recovery, but new success in green technology also helps. The stock market and the dollar continue to rise in value, and the dollar remains the dominant reserve currency throughout this period.

The recovery dispels the notion that the BRICs, particularly China, might outpace the United States. American companies are back on top, with the private sector outperforming state-dominated behemoths such as China's National Petroleum Company, Gazprom, Rosneft, and Petrobas. In the BRICs, scandals related to corruption, poor protection of property rights, and declines in commodity prices hurt returns and push away investors. Likewise, the euro crisis has a debilitating effect on many of Europe's top performing companies, but like the United States, Europe continues to develop its green technology sector. By the end of this decade, almost all the world's top 10 performing companies, and well over half of the top 100, are American.

Energy efficiency gains and green technology drive the new economy. Pressure mounts in the United States to further increase the corporate average fuel economy mileage requirements, known as the CAFE standards. The amount of energy used per unit of GDP continues to decrease sharply in the United States, and the amount of renewable sources of energy increases. But carbon emissions still remain uncomfortably high, and international efforts to reduce them intensify. There is a concerted effort by citizens of the OECD countries to discourage their governments and the international financial institutions from coal-related investments. A strong grassroots movement in the United States succeeds in blocking construction of the Keystone Pipeline XL, and Canadian opposition to production from the Alberta oil sands slows development. Likewise, the hydraulic fracturing used for oil sands meets fierce opposition from environmentalists after surface water contamination is proved in several major lawsuits against U.S. companies.

Most non-OECD countries decline to follow the example of the United States. Rapid increases in the automobile fleets in China and elsewhere, and continuing construction of new coal-fired power plants, lead to increased greenhouse gas emissions. Nonetheless, pressure from the West, a growing public awareness of the dangers from climate change, and a series of ecological disasters gradually lead to a new consensus. Local groups rise up, particularly in south Asia, and civil action is taken to block coal import facilities, hamper the construction of new coal power plants, and discourage the use of hydraulic fracturing to produce oil and natural gas. As these projects face determined resistance, the calculations in favor of fossil fuel investment and use change.

The United States and Europe cooperate in national climate security policy through the passing of a free trade agreement, known as the Transatlantic Trade and Investment Partnership (TTIP). It creates the world's largest free trade pact. In its initial state, the TTIP is focused largely on financial harmonization, trade in services, and investment issues, but by the time the negotiations are completed it also includes significant new mechanisms to reduce climate emissions. After its initial resistance, the United States embraces the European Union's effort to impose carbon taxes on commercial air traffic. This move penalizes Asian airlines flying to Europe or North America by forcing them to also participate in the scheme or lose access to most of the OECD airspace.

The TTIP also imposes sharply reduced carbon quotas on industry, which leads to the revival of carbon trading schemes on both continents. A direct carbon tax is still not politically feasible through this decade, but support for it mounts every year. The OECD countries try to add carbon reduction schemes to WTO negotiations, but that effort also seems a step too far at this time.

In the 2010s, the United States grants more export applications to increase gas exports, but this raises the price of gas within the country.

For a time, this makes the price of gas comparable to nuclear generation. Several new nuclear power plants begin construction in the United States and in Europe, and Berlin backs away from its pledge to eliminate its nuclear program. French and American companies actively engage in international construction projects and in setting new efficiency and safety standards for nuclear plants in China, India, Russia, and South Korea.

The environmental movement succeeds in raising public awareness over the linked problems of economic growth, dwindling resources, and climate change. Global agreements, however, are hard to achieve. The UN Framework on Climate Change Convention's effort to replace the Kyoto Protocol with a binding treaty after 2015 breaks down. After almost three decades of global climate change negotiations, no countries remain under mandated reductions of carbon emissions in 2015.

Instead, a group of mostly Western countries offers nationally determined commitments that are nonbinding but under review through a voluntary reporting mechanism. Dissension ensues after 2015 between the countries that have made commitments and those that have not, between those with mandates and those without, and between the rich and the poor countries. Without formally binding commitments, the OECD countries, though growing more environmentally conscious, lack the collective will to commit hundreds of billions of dollars longterm for the developing countries to adapt to, and mitigate, the effects of climate change.

Despite the difficulty of taking multilateral action, nongovernmental groups, high-profile activists, and citizens pressure governments at the state and national levels to address these issues. Groups of states, provinces, and countries coalesce around common causes, such as smog in China, the contaminated water supply in India, and the rationing of water usage in key river basins in the Middle East, Africa, and central Asia.

These localized efforts affect people more directly and sooner than broader environmental programs do, which encourages the populations to press for even more environmentally friendly actions. There is a renewed focus on expanding climate technology and energy production technology—both within the five or more countries that dominate the patent regime and to newer research areas in the BRICs. A practical approach is taken to conclude several smaller legal agreements based on shared concerns: the 1987 Montreal Protocol concluded by 46 states on substances that deplete the ozone layer, complemented by the

2013 UN agreement to phase out the use of mercury, succeed in limiting harmful emissions.

The International Renewable Energy Agency (IRENA), an intergovernmental organization based in Abu Dhabi, gains in stature and effectiveness by bringing together governments and companies to share information and develop action plans. IRENA is particularly successful in helping small countries work together to expand renewable energy development. In one case, a dozen Pacific Island nations—none of them large enough to attract sufficient resources on their own—work together to generate enough grants and low-interest loans to construct a series of large solar-powered desalination plants. Cooperative work also proceeds in setting new standards for water use in the energy sector and in agricultural production in a large number of non-OECD countries. These measures have a positive effect on the environment and also act as a confidence-building measure for countries with outstanding riparian water rights disputes.

Doubts about the accuracy of the climate models (Curry and Webster 2011) are resolved by the end of the decade and reported in the sixth assessment report of the International Panel on Climate Change (IPCC). A true scientific consensus is achieved on the climate's sensitivity to greenhouse gas emissions. This consensus allows the construction of generally agreed-upon economic models to better estimate the total cost (market cost plus social cost) of environmentally damaging activities. These new total-cost accounting models serve as a more rational basis for public policy decision making and help reduce political resistance to climate change legislation.

Equally important, the total-cost accounting measures channel environmental spending into the most efficient uses. The United States and Europe are the first to adopt total-cost accounting, and they jointly create common standards for power generation. As a result, best business practices in the energy sector are adopted around the world. The new accounting models are applied to automobiles, building standards, agricultural production, and water usage. Allied militaries also revamp their energy use and turn as often as possible to adding biofuels and algae to fuel (Closson 2013).

Markets and regulations also play a part in this decade. Tightened emission standards and an improved carbon trading scheme mean that more efficient, less costly solutions are found for environmental problems. More companies actively seek to gain competitive advantage by early adoption and by seeking out direct government subsidies and research grants. A number of additional players become engaged in the effort, including insurance companies, small businesses, finance ministers, defense establishments, and the maritime industry.

Conflict plagues the Middle East and Eastern Europe, but a coalition of willing states strengthens their resolve to work together in addressing both threats. In the Middle East, Egypt and the Gulf states take a leading role in repelling the ISIL threat from taking power in Baghdad and further spreading beyond a smaller region bordering Syria and Iraq. In Ukraine, Russia, harmed by sanctions and dwindling hydrocarbon revenues, accepts a cease-fire, withdraws its support for the separatists, and gradually Ukraine regains sovereignty over its east.

The 2020s and 2030s

The expected global boom in shale oil and gas fades by the early 2020s. These energy resources are more difficult to extract geologically than anticipated, which leads to lower recovery rates and more environmental problems. Controversies related to the contamination of drinking water from the hydraulic fracturing process of shale oil and gas lead to a halting of exploration in critical parts of the United States.

In the United States and particularly in Europe, an increase in seismic activity and the growing fear of earthquakes also disturbs the public. These difficulties generate overwhelming political opposition, particularly from the governments backed by environmental groups, and production is cut significantly in the United States and Canada (see table 7.1). As a result, shale production never takes off in Europe, Russia, Latin America, or China.

In the wake of an unrealized shale boom, other sectors gain a foothold in the energy mix. Pumped storage gets a huge boost from tax credits that secure private-sector equity and debt financing to expand the industry. As a result, grid-connected systems are able to store energy, which makes it cheaper to produce and sell renewable energy. The market decides that there is vast potential in renewable sources worldwide, and big and small companies retrofit with renewable energy. Distributed generation is favored by city and district utilities and replaces single vertically integrated statewide companies.

Installations of wind and solar power also expand exponentially in the OECD countries, but since these resources produce only very high-priced energy, energy prices became a significant hindrance to eco-

Table 7.1
Energy Production

Billions of barrels of oil equivalents	2010	2020	2040	2050	Average annual percent change, 2011–2050
World	89.1	100.4	101.1	87.0	–0.1%
Liquids	29.3	32.5	23.9	16.0	–1.5%
Gas	22.2	24.8	23.4	18.0	–0.5%
Coal	26.6	28.3	22.7	16.1	–1.2%
Nuclear	4.6	4.3	3.0	2.1	–1.9%
Renewable sources	6.5	10.4	28.2	34.7	4.3%
Hydro	5.4	6.8	6.9	6.5	0.5%
Other renewable sources	1.2	3.6	21.3	28.2	8.3%
World energy use/GDP ratio	100	91.7	72.6	60.5	–1.2%
World real price of energy (index: 2010 = 100)	100	132.5	151.2	332.9	3.1%
OPEC Middle East liquids	8.3	8.3	6.3	4.3	–1.7%
Share of world liquids	28.3%	25.6%	26.1%	26.6%	
Share of world energy	9.3%	8.3%	6.2%	4.9%	
Other major liquids production					
USA	2.4	2.7	2.2	1.6	–1.0%
Canada	1.2	1.3	0.8	0.4	–2.4%
Russia	3.8	5.6	3.3	2.4	–1.1%
Major natural gas producers					
USA	4.0	5.1	3.7	2.8	–0.9%
Canada	1.1	0.8	0.4	0.2	–4.4%
U.S. net energy imports as share of:					
Total energy use	23.5%	25.4%	–3.6%	–18.6%	
GDP (price adjusted)	1.9%	2.5%	-0.3%	–2.8%	
Chinese net energy imports as share of:					
Total energy use	13.6%	11.1%	14.1%	9.6%	
GDP (price adjusted)	3.0%	2.6%	2.6%	3.2%	

Source: See table 2.2.

nomic growth and, for most countries, a serious balance-of-payments issue.

Amid global pleas for increased oil production, Saudi Arabia and the other OPEC states announce, to everyone's disappointment, that they have reached peak production capacity in 2025. Further exploration of oil reserves in the Arctic region reveals that the prior estimates of producible reserves at market prices were vastly overstated, and this limits the global alternatives to OPEC stores. Offshore exploration is too expensive and too difficult for most state-owned companies in Russia and Latin America, which remain unwilling to liberalize enough to allow significant foreign investment and management. Promising finds in Africa fall prey to low investment, rapacious governments, and local disputes about sharing rents.

In the 2020s, the OECD countries, starting with Europe, adopt new policies that accept static growth for the sake of the environment. The U.S. government adopts a carbon tax, which is deemed to be a good fiscal and energy policy. A high carbon tax is initiated to change behavior but also as a way to fund the growing financial burdens associated with a rapidly aging population. The high tax is made easier for U.S. manufacturers to accept by a new bilateral agreement with China to limit carbon emissions in both countries.

This new U.S.-China agreement, in turn, strengthens the European-American carbon trading system, which expands to include Australia, New Zealand, and Japan. Countries that resist falling in line with these OECD-led policies find themselves facing countervailing duties on their exports to the carbon-taxing countries. Instead of taking advantage of high energy prices in the OECD countries to expand production, exports, and jobs, the trade sanctions imposed by the OECD dangerously cut into non-OECD market access. Although the intensified environmental policies stir up a great deal of rancor, most countries soon fall in line with them, or at least sign agreements that will gradually bring the countries into compliance.

World economic growth was low in the 2010s; only 1.1 percent per year in real per capita GDP, compared to 2.2 percent per year in 2000–2009. But the low growth of the 2010s was caused mainly by financial market shocks and policy incoherence. Economic growth in the 2020s and 2030s is even lower (see table 7.2), partly because of low fossil fuel availability and high energy prices, but mainly because of explicit policy choices by national governments to sacrifice current consumption for long-term sustainability.

Table 7.2
Scenario 6: Eco World
High Energy Prices, Weak Economic Growth, Global Harmony

Real GDP, billions of $ at 2010 exchange rates

	2010	2020	2040	2050
USA	14,447	16,502	17,572	18,666
		1.3%	0.3%	0.6%
China	5,931	11,475	25,711	25,969
		6.8%	4.1%	0.1%
OECD	38,646	41,765	41,652	41,986
		0.8%	0.0%	0.1%
Non-OECD	24,944	37,862	67,691	73,028
		4.3%	2.9%	0.8%
World	63,590	79,627	109,342	115,014
		2.3%	1.6%	0.5%

Real GDP per capita, 1000s of 2005 PPP $

	2010	2020	2040	2050
USA	42.1	44.2	42.1	43.1
		0.5%	−0.2%	0.2%
China	6.8	10.1	17.3	17.8
		4.0%	2.7%	0.3%
OECD	34.9	36.7	36.2	36.9
		0.5%	−0.1%	0.2%
Non-OECD	6.0	7.3	9.4	9.6
		1.9%	1.3%	0.2%
World	9.9	11.0	12.5	12.6
		1.1%	0.6%	0.1%

Source: See table 2.1.

The new higher energy prices stimulate research and investment, leading to new discoveries and innovation in both energy production and energy efficiency. Some technologically nimble countries—including the United States, France, Germany, Taiwan, Singapore, and South Korea—gain competitive advantage in this new economic environment. But these countries and most others are also hurt by high energy prices, which make a great deal of capital stock obsolete and force massive industrial retrenchment. Some new sectors expand, but most suffer from high energy prices and stifling regulation. In the OECD countries and China, greatly increased government revenues from carbon taxes go mainly to increased transfer payments for retirement pensions and mandated health care, not to research or industrial restructuring.

The non-OECD energy importers are hurt particularly badly by these developments in energy markets and energy policy. They face high import bills for fossil fuels and high costs for new imported renewable technology. They also suffer from lower exports and lower export prices for their traditional exports to the OECD countries and China, which all seem to be willingly embracing low growth.

The Iranian theocracy has been replaced by a military junta that is more focused on its own economic perquisites than on theology or jihadism. With the help of Chinese and Russian energy companies, the new Iranian military leadership reorganizes the energy industry to produce substantial rents for itself, but it does so in an economically rational way that boosts oil and gas production from a very low level and uses its homegrown nuclear industry to free up more fossil fuels for exports.

Turkey is also doing relatively well. A program of gradual economic reform—curbing monopolies, freeing up the banking system, reducing the power of rent-seeking bureaucrats, and acting as a safe haven for other people's money in troubled times—enables the Turkish government to continue on a convergence path with the European Union. The huge and modern Turkish military acts as a check on Iranian ambitions—the United States no longer cares much about Middle Eastern politics, in part because of its significantly decreased oil imports.

In Latin America, Brazil and Mexico have both kept their economies moving ahead. Brazil has a difficult time deciding which economic model to follow: the eco-friendly yet industry-hampering model, the top-down Chinese model, or a more free market approach. Finally opting for the free market approach in this period, Brazil passes new energy legislation and begins incentivizing the multinational oil companies to bring their capital and expertise to develop the country's prodigious offshore resources. With declining OPEC production and rising oil prices, Brazil does well, despite international political efforts to reduce fossil fuel use.

At the same time, the global sustainability movement has a big effect on Brazil's nonenergy policy decisions and on economic growth. Although Brazil's manufacturing sector has some great successes in energy-efficient engines and aircraft, efforts to exploit the national agricultural, mineral, and forestry resources are much more restrained. The Brazilian government still dreams of moving vast amounts of water from rivers in the north to the arid lands farther south, but that dream will have to wait until more financial resources become available.

Mexico too reforms its energy legislation and is able to take advantage of high global prices. The weakening of the U.S. economy hurts Mexican exports and remittances, but it is something of a blessing as well. Mexico is forced to take more responsibility for its own internal weaknesses; it takes steps to reduce bureaucratic inefficiency and to break up its monopolies in telecommunications, construction, transportation, and banking.

With a more welcoming physical and legal infrastructure, Mexico attracts more U.S. and Canadian companies eager to manufacture in a stable, low-wage country close to home. Mexico is also blessed with more favorable workplace demographics; the ratio of working-age people to those over sixty-five years of age is much higher than in its neighbors to the north (and in China; see table 7.3). A wave of indigenous entrepreneurial activity takes over in Mexico, both to support the new foreign operations and to develop Mexico's own unexploited opportunities.

Most non-OECD countries, whether led by despots or democratic governments, are not happy with the growth-retarding measures undertaken by the great economic powers. Apart from making scathing denunciations in the press and at the United Nations, however, the non-OECD countries have few options but to comply with the effort to reduce fossil fuel use. China's own demographic and environmental challenges ensure compliance and thus the grudging acceptance of the rest of the world.

Some of the rising energy producers in sub-Saharan Africa—such as Ghana, Mozambique, and Tanzania—continue to have good economic growth, but most of the other countries are badly hurt by rising energy prices and slow growth in the major northern markets. Nigeria

Table 7.3
Ratio of Working-Age Population to Elderly*

	2010	2020	2030	2040	2050
Mexico	10.7	8.2	6.1	4.2	3.3
USA	5.1	3.9	3.1	2.9	2.9
Canada	4.9	3.6	2.6	2.5	2.4
China	8.8	6.0	4.2	2.8	2.5

Note: *Population ages 15–65 divided by population over 65.
Source: Calculations with the IFs model.

fractures into two separate and warring states, and oil production fluctuates wildly in the Niger delta as rival bands fight among themselves and with the government for resource control.

Growth slows in much of Southeast Asia as well. Continuous political turmoil in many countries is the result of high energy prices and slow growth, which lead to confusion over which economic and political model to follow. Eventually, new military-led governments take over in Thailand, Indonesia, Laos, Burma, and Cambodia. The new regimes can at least preserve internal order, but in economics, predation rather than growth dominates. The new rulers manage to enrich themselves while their economies stagnate.

India makes a virtue out of necessity and embraces high-energy-price policies that curb energy demand. A neo-Gandhian movement assures people that a low-growth, non–energy intensive lifestyle is morally superior, more consistent with Hindu values (Pachauri 2004). India records the lowest economic growth of any major country in this period. As India renounces economic growth and geopolitics in favor of environmentalism and spirituality, its neighbors encroach on its borders. The seven states of northeast India fall under Chinese domination, and Kashmir reverts to Pakistani control.

The transatlantic auto industry under the TTIP falls under stringent new efficiency and emissions standards. Since the new regulations apply to Asian transplant companies operating in the United States and the European Union, the TTIP standards spill over into South Korea and Japan as well. These new cars are initially more expensive than the older, less efficient models. The higher cost forces more people to use improved mass transit systems that emit less carbon per person per mile. Many people lament the loss of personal freedom associated with the shrinkage of the private automobile fleet, but their voices are vastly outnumbered by those who support the shift. Over time, people begin to appreciate the improvements in health from less carbon emission and more walking and biking in lieu of driving.

As electricity rates rise in the United States, customers demand competition and spark a boom in distributed generation. More renewable energy comes onto the market in competition with natural gas, which frees up gas for export. Renewable energy and distributed generation bring energy to more households, first in the United States and Europe, then worldwide by the transfer of technology. Innovations in financial instruments encourage investment in renewable energy retrofitting of existing homes.

Smart grids allow for power to be bidirectional, with plants and homes producing energy. The use of photovoltaic panels becomes common in residential housing globally as commercial technologies improve and costs come down. Europe and China cooperate in urban power generation plants for solar, wind, and algae. As a result, power generation equipment is downsized and is available in stores everywhere so that communities can provide their own electricity and heat.

Climate variability exacerbates the growing global insufficiency of freshwater. Water management technologies do not mature enough to offer solutions. In the early 2020s, many countries experience water problems—shortages, poor water quality, changes to the ecosystem, or floods—that risk instability and state failure, increase regional tensions, and distract the countries from working with the United States on important policy objectives.

After shortages lead to humanitarian crises in parts of Africa and Asia, a global effort sponsored by the G-20 is created to find adaptive management solutions. In particular, inefficient agricultural use of water in the less developed countries becomes a major concern. Where river water is controlled by upstream nations with unresolved water rights, tensions rise. However, rather than conflict increasing, more water-sharing agreements are concluded (National Intelligence Council 2012b).

In the 2020s, the United States reaches its emission target of 20 percent below 2005 levels through presidential directives under existing laws limiting coal production, new carbon trading initiatives, and the increasing use of lower carbon energy sources. China's coal consumption peaks in the 2030s, and earlier measures to reduce emissions begin to be implemented. This is greatly helped by the realization of carbon-capture storage on a large scale in China. However, it is still not enough to have a visible effect on the hazardous environmental conditions experienced in China's biggest cities. Europe continues to deepen its targets. Countries responsible for emitting 80 percent of global emissions are in various stages of policy action to implement increasingly stringent targets.

The Chinese Communist Party collapses under the weight of weak growth. The social contract between the party and the people—that the state would take care of them—is broken, and a series of mass public protests are brutally crushed. This only serves to strengthen the resolve of the people to form a solid resistance to the regime. The Communist's

Party's survival, predicated on the neglect of fundamental aspects of society's welfare in favor of short-term economic growth, proves unsustainable. Heavily subsidized industries, growing inequality, and poor use of labor reach a breaking point (Pei 2009). Lacking the personal charisma of past leaders, Xi Jinping proves disappointing.

When a new Chinese premier is selected in the mid-2020s, he resorts to the stolid conservative mold of previous leaders. Decades of greater education and access to education, combined with foreign travel, have resulted in a generation of middle-class Chinese who no longer believe that Community Party rule is the way for China to escape the doldrums of weak growth. What begins as a green movement against the hazardous environmental conditions in China ultimately challenges the viability of the leadership.

Attempts to institute a series of quick changes to allow greater political opening and economic reform are too late. Charitable, environmental, and human rights organizations gain autonomy from the party and the state, backed by influential Western organizations. In weakness, the Chinese leaders step down and allow for a transitional regime to establish a new constitution and hold contested elections at the local and federal level (Diamond 2013).

The 2040s

China is weakened in the late 2030s by slowing economic growth, demographic decline, political instability, and environmental fragility. A perfect storm of climate disasters, water scarcity, and crop failures hits in the early 2040s. Pollution in subsurface groundwater contaminates an increasing number of vital aquifers. Inefficient irrigation practices result in misuse of water and lower water productivity. Aridity increases, which reduces the flow of the vital Yangtze and Yellow Rivers (Moore 2013). The economy suffers a sharp decline, and the Chinese government has great difficulty keeping public order.

Faced with economic and political disaster, China overcomes local resistance to adopting legal and market reforms that rationalize water use. Water management is centralized, agricultural usage is marketed commercially and capped, and large investments are made to reduce waste, recycle, and desalinate (Moore 2013). A new low-growth economic equilibrium is eventually restored, but political tensions remain high because the expectations of the ever increasing wealth of the last two generations now seem to conflict with environmental reality.

China's geopolitical ambitions diminish as the nation's domestic, economic, and political problems rise. The government contents itself with the international respect it gets from its activism and leadership in the United Nations and other international forums and its newly acquired ability to deliver humanitarian assistance to troubled Pacific Asian and east African countries.

In the Middle East, water problems are more severe than in China, but the political tools to deal with them are better. IRENA helps to decouple water usage from GDP and population growth by shifting to marginal-cost pricing. Losses from leakage and wasteful irrigation practices prove relatively easy to reduce with some outside funding and technical assistance. An increasing amount of renewable energy production also helps to reduce water consumption. Improved desalination techniques are heavily exploited in the richer parts of the region.

By the mid-2040s, improvements in water management have helped to quell political tensions over the quality and quantity of water in Egypt and Yemen. Water disputes between Israel and Jordan and in the Nile River Valley are also calmed when it appears evident that enough water at a reasonable price will be available. Turkey's continued efforts to build environmentally sound dams along the Tigris and Euphrates enhances agricultural production in its southeastern region while reducing overall water usage. Rural-urban conflicts over water rights in all these areas are reduced by relying more on market-based pricing and giving voice to more stakeholders rather than making all decisions at the national level.

However, by 2050, it is understood that water supply is not keeping up with water usage in many parts of Eurasia, Africa, India, and Latin America. Falling water tables, saltwater intrusion, and evapotranspiration are among several urgent problems arising from the combination of climate variability and demographic pressures. The poor quality and quantity of the water supply hinders food and energy supplies and causes civil unrest. A global effort, led by the United Nations and several more specialized international organizations, is undertaken to apply several practical, policy, and market measures to ameliorate the situation.

Adaptive management techniques with citizen participation to utilize local knowledge and social learning are applied to enhance stewardship and collaboration in finding solutions among conflicting communities (Feldman 2012). Better models are adapted to evaluate the social cost of environmental externalities. It is found that total-cost pricing, including subsidies for the poor, are more efficient, sustainable, and peaceful ways of dealing with water shortages. Policy is adopted that addresses the complexity of water for energy usage. Best practices are found to conserve, clean, and replace water in energy production and generation. The notion of virtual water is quantified by an international agency that takes into account the use of water in product development and shipment. Finally, markets drive innovative ideas and changes for water use. Incentives are offered to companies to clean the water used in energy extraction and generation processes. Purified waste water is accepted globally, thanks to a massive global education campaign.

By 2050, countries still vary in their commitments and accomplishments in creating a more ecologically sound world. With a climate sensitively estimate of about 2.2 degrees Centigrade for a doubling of atmospheric CO_2, the global average temperature in 2050 is about 0.5 degrees Centigrade (0.9 degrees Fahrenheit) less than the projected value in scenario 1 (see table 7.4 for a comparison of all eight scenarios).

There is a great deal of popular satisfaction, at least in the OECD, in this achievement and an expectation that the positive trends will continue. The countries that are able to grow slowly while reducing emissions are claimed the victors. A postmortem of Energiewiende, the German government's plan devised in the 2010s to enhance future energy security while increasing the percentage of renewable energy, is conducted by a transatlantic group of energy experts, and a best practices plan is put forth to encourage the adoption of increased renewable energy and reduced carbon emissions, despite slower economic growth, for more OECD countries.

In the non-OECD countries, the effects of these policies are mixed. With the greatly reduced rate of economic growth, an estimated 1.3 billion more people are living in poverty ($1.25 a day or less) in 2050 than in scenario 1 (see appendix D online). The United States and the European Union—being rich in water, energy, and in the new energy technologies—come out ahead. Economic growth is not particularly high, but it is positive and more equitable as demographic changes increase labor demand for the young and the generation of workers starts to disappear from the retirement rolls. While the United States remains the leading great power, it sharply reduces the size of its military. A large armed forces is not as necessary in a world of environmental concerns, international cooperation, and reduced expectations.

Table 7.4
Environmental Calculations: Scenario 6 Compared to Other Scenarios*

	2010 values	Results for 2050							
		1	2	3	4	5	6	7	8
World GDP	$68	$269	$102	$214	$121	$187	**$109**	$176	$132
Fossil fuel use	78.0	146.4	99.2	103.3	59.7	71.6	**50.2**	102.0	102.8
Renewable energy	11.1	33.6	18.1	45.6	29.2	53.2	**36.8**	33.3	26.2
Carbon emissions	8.6	52.2	37.2	38.9	25.0	35.3	**22.2**	38.4	38.6
Atmospheric CO_2	390	525	497	497	474	503	**467**	502	500
World temperature	14.7	16.0	15.8	15.8	15.6	15.8	**15.5**	15.8	15.8

Note: *GDP measured in trillions of 2005 PPP dollars. Fuel use measured in billions of barrels of oil equivalents. Carbon emissions measured in billion tons. Atmospheric CO_2 in parts per million. Temperature in degrees Centigrade.
Source: Calculations with the IFs model.

Table 7.5
Eco World

	Energy	Economy	Harmony
High/Strong	Lower oil production, higher fuel taxes, and more expensive renewable sources raise prices.		More international cooperation deals with transnational problems. Considerable internal strife is spurred by low economic growth.
Low/Weak		High taxes, high energy costs, more regulations, and a true-cost accounting of globally traded goods curb growth.	

Source: Authors.

Conclusion

The challenge with this scenario was how high energy prices and weak growth could combine with global harmony. We assumed that there would be a fundamental shift in the way richer countries viewed development, more along the lines of sustainable solutions. A consensus, initially among the OECD countries, coalesced around the idea that the fossil fuel–driven global economy was environmentally unsustainable and that much higher fuel taxes were the solution, even if this resulted in slower economic growth.

The main drivers in this scenario were agreements among the bigger carbon emitters to exert financial penalties on emitters, international agreements on efficiency standards and technology adaptations, and increased spending on cleaner energy technology and its distribution. Although this scenario was desirable for some because it substantially lowered carbon emissions, sustained lower growth initially imposed a financial burden on the poor. At the same time, air and water conditions improved, positively affecting agricultural production in developing countries. Table 7.5 presents the combination of endogenous variables and how we assumed they would interact to create an eco world by 2050.

8 Ambition Fuels Rivalry

SCENARIO 7: LOW ENERGY PRICES, STRONG ECONOMIC GROWTH, GLOBAL DISHARMONY

In the seventh scenario, rapid technological change, particularly in energy and nanotechnology, is assumed to produce strong economic growth in the OECD countries, while improved economic governance propels growth in the non-OECD countries, particularly India. At first, this scenario has much in common with scenario 5, in which the world economy recovers from the derailment of 2008 and China asserts its newfound power against its neighbors and its great-power rival, the United States.

Different in this scenario, however, is growing energy abundance in the United States and increasing energy insecurity in China. Strong economic growth and cheap energy cause many countries to assert themselves internationally, especially to escape from U.S. hegemony but also to settle old scores with regional neighbors. Initially, this leads to military conflict and a nuclear arms buildup in south Asia. Internal conflict in Africa results from the successful production of vast new resources and the consequent wealth, which corrupts governments and weakens political and economic systems.

As China resorts to military force to challenge U.S. power in Asia, its primary policy tools to escape American hegemony are soft power, financial statecraft, and cyber attacks. In the end, nations in the East and the West join two major blocs: the League of Democracies or the Shanghai Pact. Russia, Brazil, Turkey, and Iran are left to influence their respective regions, and by the 2040s strong economic growth has turned India into a great power.

The 2010s

In the OECD countries, the business cycle eventually rights itself. The great surge in investment in energy resources (Maugheri 2012) and energy transportation routes in North America provides a major boost, and so does the huge decline in the U.S. energy trade deficit. By the middle of the decade, U.S. growth recovers to a rate of about 2 percent per year per capita (see table 8.1). As in scenario 5, a combination of entitlement and tax reform help governments in Europe and North America succeed in reducing deficit spending. In this recovery, fiscal consolidation, inflation targeting, and promarket reforms win the policy debate and are implemented by governments in North America and Europe (Phelps 2013).

After an agonizing debate over potential reforms to the international financial system as a result of the global financial crisis of the first decade of the 2000s, little change takes place. The U.S. dollar remains the primary reserve asset, international capital flow remains relatively free, no agreed-upon mechanism is put in place to force countries with large current account surpluses to reduce them, and no international central bank arises to backstop illiquid countries—a combination of factors that helped to create the 2008 financial crisis. As the main provider of the world's currency reserves, the United States continues to enjoy exorbitant privilege in good times but faces an equally exorbitant duty to provide a global insurance function during global financial crises (Gourinchas and Rey 2013). The United States is allowed to borrow in its own currency at lower than world-market interest rates and to sometimes pay back with depreciated dollars. These advantages continue to mean that while the United States has long had large and growing negative net foreign assets, it continues to record a large positive net foreign income in its balance-of-payment accounts. Fortunately, no significant global financial crisis occurs during the rest of this decade.

Chinese economic growth continues a strong upward trajectory. Higher wages and a higher real exchange rate lead to growing domestic demand, which helps Chinese industry restructure away from exports. This generates strong employment growth, greater consumer satisfaction, and more domestic tranquillity. Real GDP growth slows from more than 10 percent per year in the 2010s to a still exceptional 7 percent a year average. Rebalancing does not mean an end to mercantilist trade and investment policies, however, and China's power and

Table 8.1
Scenario 7: Ambition Fuels Rivalry
Low Energy Prices, Strong Economic Growth, Global Disharmony

Real GDP, billions of $, at 2010 exchange rates

	2010	2020	2040	2050
USA	14,447	18,332	27,117	32,815
		2.4%	2.0%	1.9%
China	5,931	12,060	31,465	38,623
		7.4%	4.9%	2.1%
India	1,684	3,239	17,406	34,439
		6.8%	8.8%	7.1%
OECD	38,646	45,149	57,113	64,397
		1.6%	1.2%	1.2%
Non-OECD	24,944	40,106	95,500	131,502
		4.9%	4.4%	3.3%
World	63,590	85,254	152,613	195,898
		3.0%	3.0%	2.5%

Real GDP per capita, 1000s of 2005 PPP $

	2010	2020	2040	2050
USA	42.1	49.1	64.4	74.6
		1.6%	1.4%	1.5%
China	6.8	10.6	19.9	23.3
		4.5%	3.2%	1.6%
India	3.0	4.3	12.6	20.3
		3.6%	5.5%	4.9%
OECD	34.9	39.7	49.8	56.6
		1.3%	1.1%	1.3%
Non-OECD	6.0	7.6	12.2	14.6
		2.4%	2.4%	1.8%
World	9.9	11.6	16.3	19.0
		1.6%	1.7%	1.5%

Source: See table 2.1.

sense of grievance against the transatlantic advantage in living standards and technological supremacy grow strongly.

Early Chinese oil and gas exploration in the contested areas of the East China and South China Seas is promising. China is eager to develop production, but Japan, South Korea, and Vietnam refuse to recognize the legitimacy of many of the Chinese stakes, and tension rises. By the end of the decade, there are numerous incidents of the

Chinese boarding foreign vessels, near misses in the air between Chinese and foreign military aircraft, and increasing nationalist-inspired looting of regional and international companies located in China. Military spending rises sharply in Japan, India, and most Southeast Asian countries, and military ties within the region and between the region and the United States are strengthened. A sense of the inevitability of a naval battle increases daily.

The Chinese feel annoyed that India's growth is surging. Unlike our assumptions about Indian humility in scenario 6, in this scenario the Indian government engages in a tremendous burst of progrowth activity: huge investments in infrastructure, a drastic reduction in regulations and red tape, reform of the legal system, and the development of a culture that encourages entrepreneurship in all sectors of the economy. India's large multinationals—Tata, HCL Technologies, Infosys, and many others—do very well in this environment, but so do millions of new small businesses, in the rural areas as well as the cities.

The increasing popularity of left-wing politics in Latin America that occurred in the first decade of the 2000s recedes in this scenario. The commodity boom of the first decade allows both the capitalist reformer countries (such as Chile, Colombia, Peru, and Mexico) and some of those that follow economic statism (such as Argentina, Ecuador, and Brazil) to record higher growth rates. But the latter group of countries use profligate spending and inefficient investment to cater to their populist clients, and the bills eventually become due. Decisions are made in most countries to backtrack on populist promises and to liberalize trade and investment policies to attract foreign capital and capitalist entrepreneurship in general.

A decade of fast economic growth is launched in the 2010s and extends well into the 2020s. The one exception to this is Venezuela, mired in post–Chávez power struggles between opposing groups. As Venezuelan leaders hold on to socialist state-driven notions of enterprise, oil sector revenues plummet and other sectors of the economy are crippled by stagnation and corruption.

Most of the other large non-OECD countries (especially Indonesia, Turkey, Nigeria, and South Africa) also resume high-growth trajectories. This is partly because of the overall improving health of the global economy and partly because of these countries' adoption of more investor-friendly policies. Turkey moderates its Islamic political path and gets back on the European Union membership track after the crisis in Syria is resolved. Nigeria and South Africa experience a commodities boom thanks to high demand from Asia and large new investments in production capacity. Indonesia and India expand their service sectors and invest large sums in their transportation and power infrastructures. Many of the poorer non-OECD countries are helped by the strong growth of demand in the rich countries.

New global oil and gas production spur economic growth. Angola and Nigeria have long been major oil producers, and now new technologies allow billions of barrels of exportable oil to come from a dozen new producers in east Africa's Great Rift Valley and west Africa's Gulf of Guinea. As a result, many African countries significantly increase their exports: Ethiopia, Kenya, Malawi, Mauritius, Tanzania, Uganda, Gambia, Ghana, Liberia, Sao Tome and Principe, Senegal, and Sierra Leone (Diamond and Mosbacher 2013). Sub-Saharan Africa produces an extra 2 million barrels of oil per day by 2020. New shale gas production also booms globally, especially in the United States but also in Australia, China, Mexico, Russia, and Saudi Arabia. Growth is spurred by declining production costs from efficiency gains as well as by declining fears about environmental damage.

In Iraq, the surge in investment leads to a potential production increase of 5 million barrels of oil per day by 2020 (Maugheri 2012). The political situation remains tense in Iraq, but the central government, thanks to significant external assistance, manages to keep Sunni terrorism to a low level, to work well enough with the Kurds to maximize oil revenue, and to keep foreigners motivated enough to keep investing in the area. The relative stability and increase in production support the construction of a Middle East to Europe gas pipeline originating in northern Iraq.

This worldwide surge in oil production capacity does not lead to cheap oil (see table 8.2). The world will probably never again see oil at $20 to $30 a barrel because much of the new global unconventional production is profitable only at $70 to $90 a barrel, depending on the geology and water availability and the rate of sustained production (Morse 2014). Nonetheless, the expectations about oil shortages that appeared to keep oil prices far above normal market clearing prices in the early part of this decade (Maugheri 2012) dissipate by 2020, and prices do drop for a few years to well below $100 a barrel. Moreover, the increased liquefied natural gas exports from the United States help to create an international spot market that spurs competition and pushes prices down globally, much to the discomfit of the major gas exporters.

Table 8.2
Energy Production

Billions of barrels of oil equivalents	2010	2020	2040	2050	Average annual percent change, 2011–2050
World	89.1	102.1	132.8	135.3	1.0%
Liquids	29.3	32.3	36.2	34.2	0.4%
Gas	22.2	24.7	35.5	36.7	1.3%
Coal	26.6	30.5	34.0	31.1	0.4%
Nuclear	4.6	5.0	5.9	5.8	0.6%
Renewable sources	6.5	9.4	21.3	27.5	3.7%
Hydro	5.4	6.4	6.9	7.1	0.7%
Other renewable sources	1.2	3.0	14.4	20.4	7.5%
World energy use/GDP ratio	100	87.6	70.1	58.4	–1.3%
World real price of energy (index: 2010 = 100)	100	104.8	107.8	119.8	0.5%
OPEC Middle East production of liquids	8.3	9.8	13.6	14.0	1.3%
Share of world liquids	28.3%	30.2%	37.5%	40.8%	
Share of world energy	9.3%	9.6%	10.2%	10.3%	
Other major liquid producers					
USA	2.4	2.5	2.6	2.4	–0.1%
Canada	1.2	2.6	3.8	3.2	2.5%
Russia	3.8	3.5	2.2	1.6	–2.1%
Major natural gas producers					
USA	4.0	6.2	11.5	12.3	2.8%
Canada	1.1	0.7	0.3	0.2	–4.0%
U.S. net energy imports as share of:					
Total energy use	23.5%	20.5%	–8.0%	–13.6%	
GDP (price adjusted)	1.9%	1.5%	–0.5%	–0.8%	
Chinese net energy imports as share of:					
Total energy use	13.6%	14.0%	18.5%	23.3%	
GDP (price adjusted)	3.0%	2.6%	2.5%	3.0%	
Indian net energy imports as share of:					
Total energy use	34.8%	39.6%	47.1%	39.7%	
GDP (price adjusted)	5.1%	4.7%	2.9%	2.1%	

Source: See table 2.2.

Russia suffers in this scenario, and not just because it has lost a good deal of its gas pricing power. By the later part of this decade, Russia finally starts to invest in production capacity in its gigantic Bazhenov shale oil field 2,000 miles east of Moscow. Unfortunately, after Russia has spent many billions of dollars on new production infrastructure, the fall in global energy prices makes much of the investment unprofitable, at least short-term. As the oil companies retrench, much of the idle and abandoned equipment is degraded, if not ruined, by the harsh Siberian environment. The vast expenditure of money in Bazhenov results in a diversion of funds from a possible renewal of existing Russian fields, which continue on a downward production spiral. As Russian economic growth falters, so does growth in Russia's periphery. As the nation becomes moribund economically, civil unrest grows across the former Soviet states. In addition to harshly clamping down on internal dissent, the Russian government lashes out at its many weak neighbors, taking sides with the governments against the protesters. Russia takes advantage of its neighbors' economic and political weakness to seize some valuable economic assets and to rearrange the borders in a few areas.

To deflect the failure of domestic economic and energy developments, Russia increases its rhetoric about sovereignty over the Arctic. Russian authorities use threats and militarization to claim seabed rights for a broad swath of territory that includes the North Pole. In response, the Canadian authorities ramp up their claims and heighten expeditions to the Arctic. Competition in the Arctic for resources, trade, and territory leads to a rise in militarization by rival Arctic states and raises concerns in Washington and Brussels of a potential naval conflict with Russia (Käpylä and Mikkola 2013). Russia also enhances its military presence in Latin America with the temporary stationing of naval assets in Nicaragua and Venezuela. Russia stakes a greater claim to patrolling navigation, including through the Panama Canal, which is met with an increased U.S. naval presence.

The 2020s and 2030s

With strong economic growth, technological superiority, and a surge toward energy independence, American prestige is on the rise. China, however, also rebounds sharply from its setback in the early part of the last decade and starts to assert itself more forcefully, not just on its Asian rim but also in Africa and wherever it can undermine U.S. power.

The weak African nations, which eagerly accepted Chinese aid and investment in the first decade of this century, come under increasing pressure as China begins requesting a military presence to protect its substantial investments and to discourage other outside interests. Arming and training African armies with Chinese oil funds, which has been done in Chad, has not proved adequate, particularly since the Chadian forces remain deployed in war-torn Mali and the Central African Republic. Recent investments in the new African oil-producing states of Kenya, Mozambique, and Madagascar, and the high potential for civil unrest in these places, heightens China's need for security forces in the area. In a change of policy, China requests an unofficial site in Sudan for military aircraft and security forces as well as ships to land onshore. Chinese forces conduct military exercises with neighboring states. The U.S. military sees this as a direct threat to its activities in the Horn of Africa and in North Africa and warns the Chinese to refrain from increasing their presence further.

But in this period, on the whole, high-intensity military conflict is avoided, and instead China's quest for comprehensive national power is led through its soft-power actions. Upon becoming president, Hu Jintao (2011) declares, "We should bring Chinese culture to the world, develop cultural soft power compatible with China's international standing, and increase the influence of Chinese culture in the world." The Confucius Institutes put down deeper roots in the West's universities, providing a positive image of China among the young, spreading the use of the Chinese language, and serving as a recruitment center for intelligence assets.

China uses some of its vast foreign earnings to buy media assets in the West to counter the criticism of the regime's human rights and environmental records and to downplay reports of civil unrest. Even when it does not directly control the media, the Chinese government heavily influences what journalists and academics write about China by granting or withholding favors. Tens of millions of dollars in travel and research grants are offered to Westerners who write and speak sympathetically about China. Critics of China are not just denied access but are also often criticized or even libeled in the Chinese press. The Chinese enhance their lobbying efforts in Western capitals and often directly bribe Americans and Europeans to bend decisions China's way.

Despite this growing rivalry between China and the United States, the global economy surges because of new technology. The boom in oil and gas production combined with continuing technological advances in both conservation and renewable energy leads to a trend of falling energy prices, which stimulates economic growth in most countries. New and cheaper robotic technology drastically increases labor productivity and leads to a huge new array of consumer and investment goods as well as weapons. The nanotechnology revolution allows the robotics industry to push its products into a multitude of new uses (Kaku 2012). The 3-D printing technology revolutionizes manufacturing, creates many new jobs in the OECD countries, and lessens the cost of goods worldwide.

Millions of semiskilled workers face short-term dislocation by the wave of creative destruction, but some, particularly younger, people eventually find new, higher-paying jobs in the vastly expanded leisure, entertainment, sports, and tourism industries; the booming robot-designing and robot-manufacturing industries; and start-up companies focused on creating more applications for personal and business use.

Many countries in Latin America and east Asia prosper through continuing domestic economic reforms in a promarket direction. Others, especially poorer countries in Africa and the former Soviet states, follow a more government-centered economic model, but that too works for them, at least in the early stages of development and with a booming global economy that spurs demand for their exports. A dozen new African oil exporters experience prolonged economic booms. Trade in other goods and services, however, has a diminished role in growth because many countries gradually increase protection, both directly and covertly, for old and new industries. Even the United States gradually begins to resort to countervailing duties to offset alleged unfair trade practices by China and others. The WTO loses relevance as its judgments are routinely ignored or evaded, and there is little serious effort to negotiate new treaties.

The dollar's role in world finance diminishes, partly because regional trade blocs increasingly use alternative currencies in cross-border trade and finance and partly because the Chinese and the Europeans, long critical of the dollar's exorbitant privilege, work assiduously to encourage the use of the euro and the renminbi in international trade and finance. In the 2020s, this movement makes global financial affairs less tumultuous because it forces governments to pursue more cautious policies in order to compete for financial assets. The United States, however, loses some of the gains (from the difference between the value of the money and the cost of producing and distributing it). This results in less growth and less power for the United States and more power and influence for Europe and China. The role of the United Kingdom as a global financial sector is severely tested until it opts to join the eurozone at the end of this period.

Toward the end of the 2020s, as oil prices rebound and some of Russia's earlier shale oil investment begins to pay off, the Russian government feels empowered enough to start acting on the global scene again, especially, if possible, to humiliate the United States. After trying for decades to switch the oil trade from the dollar to the euro, Russia creates a gold-backed currency aimed directly at undermining the dollar's exorbitant privilege. A new oil bank is created in London and begins trading in the new currency; anyone hoping to buy Russian oil or gas is required to use it. Russia ardently courts China and OPEC, encouraging them with significant price cuts to start using the new currency, not just for energy but for all of their trade.

Unfortunately for Russia, its potential allies demur. OPEC is having enough trouble selling the amount of oil it wants at a high enough price to keep its rickety economies afloat; it has no desire to risk upsetting the market, and Russia's inducements are not enough to make a difference. China would like to see the renminbi displace the dollar, but it has no interest whatsoever in raising the status of gold or of Russia. The Russian government finds its exports shriveling and its start-up costs a colossal waste. The effort is abandoned after only three years, leaving Russian leaders more frustrated than before.

As China's military activities continue to increase in the East China and South China Seas, the United States positions more military assets in the region. Chinese military vessels destroy a dock built by the Taiwanese on the largest of the Spratly Islands, Taiping, which Taiwan controls. China further threatens Taiwan with a series of strikes over the sovereignty of the Spratly islands. After a number of failed talks led by the United States, the Chinese signal their displeasure by launching a limited missile strike on Taiwan. Rather than capitulate, Taiwan declares war, and the United States mobilizes its forces and declares the formal recognition of Taiwan as a sovereign state at the United Nations. Japanese and South Korean forces join the fighting against China, and both take losses.

China takes several simultaneous actions to check Washington. First, China dumps a large part of its United States dollar reserves. Over decades, China accumulates excessive reserves of United States debt in the process of ensuring an undervalued exchange rate, the renminbi, and thus boosting its exports. The debt sell-off becomes possible in the 2030s when China is no longer so dependent on American markets for its manufactured exports. True, the value of China's holding is lessened, but that seems to be a price Beijing is willing to pay to see American interest rates skyrocket and the economy tumble into recession. In response, the United States blocks lucrative domestic investment deals by Chinese companies.

Second, China announces a ban on rare earth exports. The United States and allied nations, which require these rare earth minerals for the production of renewable energy and weapons systems, stockpile enough to maintain short-term manufacturing levels, but they could be in trouble long-term. In response, the United States imposes an import ban on all Chinese products using rare earth minerals, which includes most renewable energy designs.

Third, China launches a host of strikes on the most sensitive U.S. government systems, infiltrating the most highly secured intelligence systems. It executes a series of offensive attacks on the U.S. energy infrastructure, causing power outages in large metropolitan areas. It also infiltrates Wall Street trading systems and skews figures to simulate a crash. China next shuts down most official U.S. government websites.

Finally, Chinese hackers send out false news reports on major Western media websites about egregious American actions against innocent Chinese civilians and high U.S. military casualties by the Chinese military. Ultimately, the United States relents, and there is a truce over Taiwan, which reverts to an unrecognized entity—but not before the United States loses several planes and small ships to Chinese forces.

In the aftermath, China uses force to take over several territories. With Chinese support, communist rebels seize control of most of the Philippine Islands in the 2030s and declare their new government a devoted ally of China. The rump nationalist Philippine government, holding only a few of the western Visayan Islands, is promptly ejected from the United Nations under Chinese pressure. China seizes most of the contentious islands in the South China and East China Seas in the late 2030s. Many Western elected officials, exposed to decades of Chinese influence building and sometimes outright purchase of their influence or vote, urge their Asian allies to be calm as the natural regional power reestablishes its historical claims. All nations—but especially Russia, India, and Japan—must decide whether to increase their national capability to defend themselves or cede ground to China. The 2030s end with continuing minor political and military skirmishes in the western Pacific, along the Indian-Chinese border, and in Siberia.

Russia and the United States watch as China gradually builds up its nuclear arsenal with the goal of continuing to maintain a credible second-strike capability in relation to the United States. China is also concerned about vast improvements in U.S. espionage, surveillance, reconnaissance, missile defense, and long-range conventional precision munitions. India, which is also a nuclear power, feels threatened by the Chinese nuclear buildup. As China openly calls into question the policy of nuclear no-first use and links it to the future status of Taiwan, India increases its nuclear modernization efforts. India expands its arsenal of short- and medium-range weapons and deploys its first missile-equipped, nuclear-powered submarine. At the same time, Pakistan, supported by China, also builds up its nuclear arms to defend itself from India. China announces that it has submarine-based nuclear missiles covering targets in India. China assumes that the U.S. maintenance of missile defense shield systems deployed in California and Alaska is directed at China, rather than North Korea, and is intended to undermine China's second-strike capability.

Low oil prices and falling production levels in several Middle Eastern countries lead to chaos, and the dynamics within the Middle East change significantly. The region breaks into different camps, based on religion, politics, and economic ties. The Sunni-Shiite divide widens as a result of a prolonged proxy war fought in Syria and Iraq, headed by the extremist Sunni group ISIL, on one side, and a coalition of Iran- and Gulf-backed forces on the other. Iran weakens the role of its presidency and strengthens theocratic rule but also moderates its position toward Europe and the United States. Across North Africa, new Sunni-led Islamist-based governments suppress minority rights and foment a continuous cycle of street protests, civil conflict, and intervention by security forces.

In the 2030s, Africa's oil helps keep world energy prices down. It enriches the oil companies and the elites in a few countries but leaves most of Africa in a morass of underdevelopment and violent chaos. Despite a 20-year surge in revenues and a sustained rise in GDP, social conditions worsen in most places, and civil disorder intensifies. In many of the new oil-exporting nations, the new revenues have mostly served to enrich the political elite and poisoned the prospects for development. Diamond and Mosbacher (2013, 88–89) predicted, "The surge of easy money fuels inflation, waste and massive corruption, distorts exchange rates, and undermines the competitiveness of traditional export sectors such as agriculture."

The private sector and civil society shrivel as attention focuses on grabbing a share of the resource bounty rather than on finding new ways to profit from making and selling goods and services. Theft and kidnapping increase, and African governments try to secure the oil by paying thieves and insurgents rather than stopping them. However, that strategy soon breaks down; the theft of oil grows into a huge business, involving the local government, the police, and the military. At the national level, the practice of holding governments accountable diminishes, and it becomes more profitable to attach oneself to the vastly expanded pool of rents that make it to the capital, even if much of this is siphoned away near the production areas. Most of the 12 new energy exporters suffer recurrent coups, rigged elections, and active insurgencies as the benefits of seizing the state rise dramatically.

Russia feels marginalized by China's rise in the East and by continued U.S. technological dominance. The Russian government decides to divert attention from its domestic failures by making expanded claims to the Arctic: it builds military assets at Temp airfield on Koteny Island in the Novosibirsk region of the Arctic and expands the Tiksi airfield in Yakutsia. Russia claims to be safeguarding the Northern Sea Route shipping lane and the adjacent Arctic zone. However, its activities are viewed as counter to the agreements and dialogue among the Arctic Council members. Russia declares an exclusive air and sea defense zone in the area and threatens to block traffic that is undeclared to the Russian authorities. Relations with Canada become sour over numerous incidents of both sea and air violations by Russian military craft, which are clearly violating Canada's territorial sovereignty. The matter is reviewed by NATO, and plans are drawn up for a response, but no action is taken in this period.

The 2040s

By 2040, China's GDP is much larger than the U.S. GDP, and these continue to diverge sharply. China is no longer a poor country, but its per capita income is only about $20,000, so its people still badly lag behind the OECD citizens. The United States, fueled by technological innovation and protected by its own mercantilist policies, grows strongly, too (apart from the brief currency war and shooting war over

Taiwan), fueling China's resentment further. Despite this being a high-growth scenario overall, China's economic growth slows during the 2040s. The easy gains from convergence are long gone. High-tech productivity growth helps, but China has to divert increasing amounts of money to its military and to subsidies for its weak vassals. Instead of forging a harmonious high-consumption society, China opts to retain the kind of centralized and militarized state that ensures continued control by the Communist Party elite.

China has enjoyed decades of good growth and views its ascendance as being on a steady convergent path with the growth of the United States. Yet China is unable to use its soft power to seize the global moral and cultural high ground from the West, and faltering growth is even more discouraging. Economic dominance has allowed China to create an uneasy alliance in the western Pacific, but it has also alienated many countries with intelligence infiltration, unfair trade practices, and unappealing cultural values. While China's soft-power offensive is mostly a failure, its hard-power successes are more notable. It has seized disputed islands on its periphery; rolled the Philippines, North Korea, and Pakistan to its sphere; and profited by sending troops briefly into Kyrgyzstan and Tajikistan, all without too much bloodshed. But these efforts have left China with many enemies. Japan, South Korea, Vietnam, and India, relying on their growing military strength and ties to the United States, are able to escape domination by China. The status of Taiwan remains unresolved for now.

Two great global blocs of nations have formed; they are very different in construction from each other and from the blocs that were described in scenario 4. The United States forges strong bonds of economic and military cooperation with Western Europe, Canada, Mexico, the western countries of South America, Japan, South Korea, Australia, and New Zealand. This grouping is formalized as the League of Democracies in 2045 and comprises 1.5 billion people. The League of Democracies is a voluntary association, formed of nations from around the globe that share similar values and interests in pursuing commercial and security ties.

The second bloc, the Shanghai Pact, is composed of mostly east Asian states and of Tanzania. It is put together by statecraft pressure and the force of arms and is held together with great effort and expenditure by China. With 2.9 billion people, the Shanghai Pact is more populous than the League of Democracies, but it has a much smaller aggregate GDP: $51 trillion versus $79 trillion in 2050 (see table 8.3).

Table 8.3
Regional Blocs in 2050

	Number of countries	People, billion	Percentage of geopolitical power	GDP, trillion, 2010 $	GDP per capita, 1000s of 2005 PPP $	Average annual GDP per capita growth, 2041–2050
Shanghai Pact	26	2.9	24.7	51.3	15.3	1.4%
League of Democracies	55	1.5	38.2	79.5	45.9	1.4%

Source: See table 2.1. For composition of the blocs, see appendix C.

Asian output per capita is only about one-third of the income in the League of Democracies, and by the late 2040s convergence has stopped—the Shanghai Pact as a group is growing no faster than the league. Many countries, including all those in the League of Democracies, have migrated back to oil trade with the U.S. dollar; the gold-backed currency supported by Russia loses its attraction as a result of American manipulation of its value, and the renminbi is attractive only within the Shanghai Pact.

Elsewhere, other regional powers hold sway without much interference from the two major blocs. Brazil dominates eastern South America from Venezuela to Argentina. Based on the principles of Mercosur, Brazil forms an economic sphere of influence in which it leads industrial production, imports the resource wealth from its neighbors, and keeps the uneven arrangement palatable by playing on the simmering sense of grievance and populist fears that have long had appeal in Latin America. The fact that western South America, especially Colombia, Ecuador, Peru, and Chile has far higher living standards is judged insignificant compared to maintaining cultural independence from North America.

Turkey and Iran are rival regional hegemons in the Middle East. Turkey dominates Syria and Lebanon in order to pacify that area, and it maintains a peaceful accommodation with Israel, Armenia, and the Kurdish area of Iraq. This opens up new trade opportunities from the South Caucasus through the Middle East to Europe. Iran and allied Shiites gradually acquire influence, if not outright control, of most of the countries around the Persian Gulf. Iran renounces its development of a nuclear program and allows inspectors to verify its claims. Turkey hems Iran in on the west, and the United States and China refrain from engagement there beyond oil and gas exploration. Iran's regional dominance engenders more stability than the region has enjoyed for centuries, and support for terrorism withers.

Russia fades during this period. Russia's oil and gas rents decline, and the government elite focuses on how to use them to fund their fiefdoms rather than to build a postenergy economic future. The Eurasian Union withers, and all of the former non-Russian republics are gradually lost to competing spheres of influence in Europe, Asia, and the Middle East, except Belarus, which continues to be a drain on Russia. Russia becomes a third-world power, a police state with a disgruntled and dissatisfied citizenry. The young take every opportunity to emigrate.

India joins the great-power club in this scenario. It mostly avoids the conflicts of the 2030s and concentrates on a continuing series of reforms that propel its economy. It also significantly expands its military power and capabilities. By the late 2040s, India's geopolitical power surpasses China's and approaches that of the United States (see figure 8.1). India does not feel the need to join either the Western or the Eastern bloc, having grown powerful enough to achieve independent great-power status. India is hampered by being forced to spend huge amounts of money to maintain sufficient military strength to keep China's ambitions in check. It is also constrained by the need to keep trade relations open in all directions. With China encroaching on the northeast and

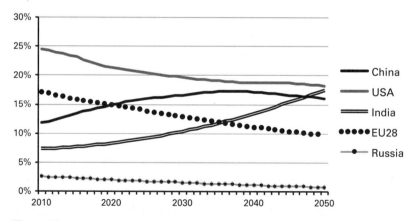

Figure 8.1
Share of Geopolitical Power in Scenario 7
Source: Calculations with the IFs model.

Pakistan now a Chinese vassal on its western frontier, India faces a challenging future securitywise.

Africa in the 2040s faces a perilous condition. Northwest Africa has aligned with Europe and thus the West. Egypt is dependent on aid provided both by the United States and Turkey. Southern Africa is dominated by prosperous and quasi-democratic South Africa, and southwestern Africa is dominated by Nigeria. But the vast middle of the continent, home to 1.5 billion extremely poor people, is increasingly violent. China brings some stability with troops and organization to a few select resource-rich microregions. However, neither the East nor the West has any taste for state building or even for humanitarian relief in countries that have proved to be ungovernable.

Conclusion

This scenario had the most potential for high-intensity conflict. Low energy prices with strong economic growth helped spur great-power convergence. That convergence in the face of a multitude of historical grievances and continued wide differences in political attitudes and governance styles led to many dangerous confrontations. The wars that did take place in this scenario were inventions that we think flow from the logic of the story line. Although we did not base these wars on IFs model projections, we referred to model simulations for guidance. In scenario 3, which had a peaceful power transition and global harmony, we reported (see table 4.4) that the probability of war for each of eight major nations declined over time.

In this scenario, besides altering the economic and energy assumptions, we increased military spending in many states, we assumed increased trade protection, and we assumed that the global impulse toward democratization and global comity diminished. The IFs model combined these assumptions to estimate that the probability of war rose for all eight countries, and the number of years of war for each country rose sharply (see table 8.4).

We assumed this was a multipolar world with several capable militaries and an overarching rivalry between China and the United States, creating two powerful blocs. The challenges we faced in this scenario were how far to take the conflict and how to ensure that the global economy kept growing despite conflicts of hard and soft power, including an attack on the U.S. financial center. It was interesting that neither rival power wanted to fight proxy wars, even in Africa, where both

Table 8.4
Probability of a Country Having at Least One War in a Given Year

	2015	2050	Number of War Years 2015–2040
China	6.4%	8.6%	17
United States	11.0%	10.8%	16
India	4.9%	7.3%	18
Russia	10.6%	9.0%	13
Japan	2.3%	2.4%	3
Israel	6.0%	6.3%	13
Iran	7.6%	7.2%	19
Turkey	5.8%	6.3%	8

Source: See table 4.4.

Table 8.5
Ambition Fuels Rivalry

	Energy	Economy	Harmony
High/Strong		Growth returns accrue to the OECD countries through rapid technological change. Improved economic growth raises regional powers.	
Low/Weak	Oil abundance and new energy technology keep prices low.		High growth and cheap oil fuel many conflicts. Major East and West blocs are formed, along with regional powers.

Source: Authors.

were heavily invested in oil production. The ambition that fueled rivalry was different for the United States than for China. The U.S. strategic goal was technological development and market dominance, whereas China's ambition was territorial and resource based. Global hegemony, in this scenario, was out of China's reach. Table 8.5 presents the combination of endogenous variables and how we assumed they would interact to foment the ambitions of the two great regional blocs.

9 Natural Disasters Promote Unity

SCENARIO 8: LOW ENERGY PRICES, WEAK ECONOMIC GROWTH, GLOBAL HARMONY

In the eighth scenario, a series of catastrophic natural disasters bring disparate countries together in humanitarian relief efforts, rescuing victims of floods, droughts, earthquakes, tsunamis, and fires. These transnational calamities forge a strong international will to address human security above all else. The majority of countries, particularly in the developing world, are unwilling as well as incapable of dealing with the wave of climate catastrophes, and domestic unrest increases.

Some of the more able countries take on an adaptive management approach to deal with the crises. The flood of refugees seeking haven in OECD countries increases, placing a burden on their economies, which are already severely stressed by decades of poor economic management. Energy prices stabilize because of the availability of hydrocarbons and the slow growth in energy demand in most of the world. An inability to overcome government inefficiency and growing domestic unrest prevent China and India from reaching the levels of development experienced by the OECD countries in the 20th century. With a few exceptions, low demand globally prevents large-scale investment in cleaner energy technology, and most countries choose to continue burning fossil fuels.

The 2010s

A series of revolutions sweep Asian countries, including Thailand, Vietnam, Cambodia, Indonesia, and Burma. Tired of decades of political patronage, corruption, interethnic strife, and poor government services, citizens rise up in a wave similar to that in Eastern Europe in the late 1980s and the Arab world in 2011. In some cases, the uprising leads to democratically elected leaders; in others, to new authoritarian leadership. The United States, Japan, Australia, and New Zealand make a unified effort to bring political and economic assistance to state-building efforts in postrevolutionary Asia. China expresses unease at the overthrow of governments but does not involve itself, other than to secure its previous commercial relationships, including those involving energy and trade.

After a crushing blow to ISIL in Iraq by a coalition of forces from within the region, the crisis in Syria is primarily contained within its borders but is further complicated by the influx of increasing numbers of jihadist-backed fighters. As a result, several factions are fighting one another in addition to fighting the government. The link between the North Caucasus Islamic fighters and Syria becomes disturbing for the Russian government, especially after a wave of calls from leaders of Muslim-majority republics within Russia for separation from Russia. Citizens in the North Caucasus support these calls, spurred by Russia's recognition of independent regions in neighboring Georgia and the annexation of Crimea from Ukraine.

President Vladimir Putin pushes for an end to the war through the UN Security Council and puts direct pressure on the Syrian government. The new leadership in Syria is beholden to both Russia and the West for reconstruction aid. Meanwhile, Russia increases its pressure on Ukraine and other states of the former Soviet Union in the name of its self-defined mission to protect Russian-speaking populations. It meets little resistance from the United States or the European Union.

This is a decade of slow growth for the United States and the European Union. In neither entity do strong governing coalitions come forth that can make coherent policy decisions, whether in a promarket, structural reform direction or in a spread-the-wealth interventionist approach. German Chancellor Angela Merkel tries, mid-decade, to force through a structural reform agenda in the European Union, but this proves much too favorable to German interests for the rest of the member states to adopt. Likewise, it is viewed as much too accommodating to the rest of the member states by most of the German population.

The new German government turns its focus inward while the rest of the European Union stagnates. Except for the Germans and the Nordic countries, the European Union remains profligate in budgetary matters, stifled by regulation, and unable to increase exports because of the overvaluation of the euro—overvalued, that is, from the viewpoint of all the non-German members of the eurozone.

In the United States, voters remain fairly evenly divided between those who favor more versus less government intervention in the economy. The result is a continuing seesaw in Washington, with no view managing to win the presidency, the House of Representatives, and the Senate all at the same time. Presidents tend to try to expand their executive and regulatory apparatus to empower their policy agendas, and a generational change at the Supreme Court leads to a new majority more in tune with an expansion of regulatory power.

Although this expansion of executive power leads to some new social safeguards and improvements in distribution, it also tends, on balance, to deter private investment and entrepreneurship and to lock in place enormous future claims on government resources. A lack of incentives and an uncertainty about the durability of policy decisions lead to an extended period of low growth.

China experiences economic difficulties in the latter part of the decade. China's growth model—moving unproductive rural workers to the city, where they can be employed in low-wage manufacturing geared for the world market—served the country and most of its people very well for several decades. When growth begins to falter because of falling world demand and diminished competitiveness in the middle of this decade, the Chinese government props up growth by an enormous amount of stimulus spending, which does little more than put off the crisis a few years. New Chinese leadership in the early part of the teens makes a show of launching new market-friendly reforms, but these prove mainly to increase the central government's power over the provinces. Overbuilding, an insolvent banking system, decentralized corruption, and growing labor unrest combine to reduce China's economic growth rate sharply.

Rather than work to find new ways to rekindle growth, many top Chinese leaders choose either to enrich themselves before their retirement or to emigrate. Below the top rank, however, a new generation of Chinese leaders emerges that consists of what Shambaugh (2013) calls the globalists. This new generation is less concerned with wealth and military power and is more interested in soft power and taking an active role in multilateral institutions and global governance. This group is not in a position to do much to influence policy in this decade, but the number of these leaders and their power grows to the point of gaining the top leaders' attention.

India also falls off the strong-growth track. The highly productive technology services sector is no longer able to propel the economy by itself, nor does it provide much in the way of forward or backward linkages that can lead to further industrial development. The Indian government fails to invest in enough new roads, railways, ports, and power generation to allow the country to continue to progress. Many Indians are not sure how much progress they want, anyway, lest modernity upset the old rural, caste-based, communal lifestyle that has prevailed for centuries. As the modern economic model fails to deliver, the political consensus weakens, politics are gridlocked, and Hindu nationalists gain more followers among the public.

Low growth in the United States, the European Union, and China result in hard economic times in most of the rest of the world, especially among the exporters of raw materials. At the start of the decade, Latin America is fairly evenly divided between the modernizing countries that favor market-based economic policies and those that favor centralized state control of national economic affairs. As world growth falters, the free market model seems much less appealing to both camps.

OECD growth is sputtering, and the whole world is still skeptical of the United States. After all, in 2008, "Wall Street produced and sold trillions of dollars of fraudulent securities and … it was aided and abetted in this racket by regulators on the make, politicians on the take, rating companies on the fake, and directors on a break" (Kotlikoff 2012, 10).

Africa has a few bright spots—mostly the countries that begin to exploit newfound oil wealth, especially Tanzania, Mozambique, and Kenya. Kenya is doubly blessed because it also starts to bring new lands into agricultural production, watered by the recently discovered Turkana aquifer. Kenya, like much of Africa, is still plagued by ethnic and religious conflict, poor governance, and extremely rapid population growth.

Even though the OECD has some positive effect on institution building in postrevolutionary Southeast Asia, respect for Western-style political and economic institutions recedes in Africa—especially respect for the United Kingdom. Gambia has already left the Commonwealth of Nations, citing neocolonialism and an oppressive insistence on human rights. Its departure is followed by many more: Cameroon, Ghana, Kenya, Lesotho, Mozambique, and Malawi are gone by 2020, and only Botswana and Mauritius remain.

Most Middle East regimes grimly hold on to power. Oil revenues remain sufficient to provide enough spending for public housing, food, fuel, and other subsidies, to keep popular dissatisfaction under control. Economic sanctions against Iran decay over time as that country and willing partners, such as China and Russia, find new ways to work around the sanctions. The United States and its allies began to lose interest. After Iran conclusively demonstrates that it possesses nuclear weapons in the late part of the decade, sanctions became pointless. The Iranian economy stages a strong recovery as the Western powers loosen the sanctions.

The United States also pulls back from its advanced positions in the Persian Gulf. It is obvious to all that Israel is unable to stop Iran's nuclear weapons program and is unwilling to launch an independent attack. This results in a weakening of Israel's influence, and the Jewish state becomes even more isolated politically. However, its wealth and deterrent power give it a measure of security in a sea of hostility.

The 2020s and 2030s

In the 2020s and 2030s, demographic and government debt challenges come to the fore and provoke profound social and economic dislocation. In the United States, Europe, China, and Japan, the aged population increases much more rapidly than expected, putting enormous strain on social welfare budgets. In Africa, Latin America, and Southeast Asia, fertility rates stop declining, and the size of the youth cohort grows much more quickly than expected. In countries with good governance and solid economic growth, this increase is not a problem, but most countries do not fall into that category; they are unable to employ the surging youth population and thus experience a sharp rise in civil unrest.

The United States and the European Union suffer a long period of slow growth because of massive debts and swelling expenditures on social welfare programs and climate mitigation. There is a growing disenchantment with the effect of globalization on richer societies, and this generates a wave of protest, particularly in the OECD countries, not unlike the Occupy Wall Street movement of the post-2008 global financial crisis. Recurring banking crises—and resentment over the opulent lifestyle of those who seem to create the crises—fuel the anger. Growing extremism among the youth leads to violence in European capitals and across North America, pitting groups against one another, the most violent of which target immigrants. Governments are increasingly unable to control cross-border movements of radical groups.

By 2025, the fiscal gap in the United States cannot be ignored. The baby boomers—the 78 million people born between 1946 and 1964—have mostly retired and are collecting Social Security, Medicare, and other benefits equal to about one-quarter of GDP (Kotlikoff 2012). As a result, by this period, 15 years of printing money and issuing government bonds leads to rising inflation, soaring interest rates, a plunging dollar, and a collapse in investor confidence.

In the midst of a deep recession (which becomes known as the Great Northern Recession of 2026–2029), the United States has no better choice than to start raising tax rates and cutting promised social benefits to levels that will facilitate an eventual return to solvency. The cutbacks are greeted with more massive civil disturbances: the elderly protest benefits cuts, and the young protest tax increases. There are many violent clashes and thousands of deaths, but civil war and fragmentation are avoided, and by 2030 the austerity measures are finally pushing the debt and deficit numbers in the right direction, and economic growth starts to rebound. The European Union faces similar problems but finds more peaceable ways of introducing austerity policies, and it too manages a modest revival in the 2030s.

Low world economic growth combines with ample supplies of conventional and unconventional oil and gas to keep world energy prices relatively low. Prices do not dip to $25 a barrel, which the big importing nations enjoyed in the early 2000s, but fluctuate between $70 and $90 a barrel (in 2010 prices), high enough to justify production from shale and tar deposits. Continuing advances in energy efficiency also help to moderate energy demand and prices. Subsidies for research on and production of alternative forms of energy are drastically cut because of budget difficulties in the United States and Europe, but efficiency continues to grow in wind, geothermal, and solar power, and the renewable share of total energy use grows.

The Kyoto Protocol's climate emissions reduction targets are not met by several major signatories, and no follow-up agreement is reached. Reduced estimates of climate sensitivity to carbon emissions and lower temperature predictions from the International Panel on Climate Change (IPCC) lessen the global commitment to reducing carbon emissions. In much of the Northern Hemisphere, this change of attitude lowers costs; some countries in Asia, the Middle East, and Africa, however, feel free to develop their industrial base without much concern about emissions and pollution. This has negative effects on global health, water supplies, and migration patterns.

The development of biofuels picks up in the 2030s. Brazil, Eastern Europe, and southern Africa become the major producers of biofuels, particularly sugarcane in Brazil and southern Africa. In the United States, land use for biofuels remains politically contentious, and production stagnates. However, in the 2030s, as extreme climate events hit North America, public demand for alternatives to oil increases, once again boosting the biofuel industry. The transition is made smoother this time by the increase in manufacturing of flex-fuel cars. Simultaneously, genetic modification makes biofuel production cheaper and less water- and land-intensive (Randers 2012).

The Great Northern Recession in the late 2020s has a profound effect on growth in the rest of world. Most countries are already struggling: unable to develop a competitive workforce because of domestic weaknesses in education, health, and technology; plagued by government corruption; and burdened by rapidly rising populations. Brazil and Russia, which were harmed by the leveling off of commodity prices in the 2010s, continue to suffer in this period.

China is hurt by falling demand from the OECD countries, and its demography brings problems, too. Its age structure becomes extremely top-heavy, with a sharply rising ratio of elderly (65 and older) to working-age people (15–64). China has a much less accommodating welfare state and has not promised nearly so much to its old people, but the burden of the growing dependency ratio puts a new hindrance on economic growth. As the younger generation pays increasing amounts of money to maintain the elderly, less money is available for investment and growth. Real economic growth for most of the world is much lower than in the 2020s, which in turn is lower than in the 2010s (see table 9.1).

In the BRIC countries, slowing economic growth causes increased inequality, tension, and social strife, which in turn help to accelerate the decline in labor productivity. The business climate deteriorates, and foreign investors become unwilling to operate in these increasingly nontransparent and corrupt systems. Fearful governments intensify their control of major industries, ensuring the personal prosperity of the governing elite but further depressing the economy. In the increasingly interconnected world, government greediness and incompetence are not as well hidden as in the past. Average citizens of the well-wired world are able to perceive—and resent—the differences between the

Table 9.1
Scenario 8: Natural Disasters Promote Unity
Low Energy Prices, Weak Economic Growth, Global Harmony

Real GDP, billions of $ at 2010 exchange rates

	2010	2020	2040	2050
USA	14,447	16,603	19,420	20,653
		1.4%	0.8%	0.6%
China	5,931	11,912	31,068	37,227
		7.2%	4.9%	1.8%
OECD	38,646	41,351	41,790	42,947
		0.7%	0.1%	0.3%
Non-OECD	24,944	38,696	77,732	99,025
		4.5%	3.5%	2.5%
World	63,590	80,048	119,522	141,972
		2.3%	2.0%	1.7%

Real GDP per capita, 1000s of 2005 PPP $

	2010	2020	2040	2050
USA	42.1	44.5	46.1	46.6
		0.6%	0.2%	0.1%
China	6.8	10.5	19.6	22.3
		4.4%	3.2%	1.3%
OECD	34.9	36.3	36.3	37.4
		0.4%	0.0%	0.3%
Non-OECD	6.0	7.4	9.9	10.9
		2.0%	1.5%	1.0%
World	9.9	10.9	12.7	13.6
		1.1%	0.8%	0.6%

Source: See table 2.1.

elite and everyone else in living standards, personal security, and human rights.

Western financial and commercial sanctions on Russia as a result of its aggression in Ukraine have a lasting effect. Russian oil and gas production declines because of a lack of investment and antiquated technology. The government continues to focus on extracting as much revenue as possible from the Russian energy industry and does not create an attractive climate that garners much domestic or foreign investment. Too much bureaucratic power, too few property rights, and a climate of extortion suppress Russian economic activity in general.

Russia also fails to reform its military, relying instead on undertrained conscripts commandeered by a top-heavy general officer corps reluctant to change.

This general state of inertia persists, and the existing conditions in the 2010s continue, including sluggish economic growth, a managed political scene, and an ongoing muddling through in foreign policy in which there is neither a breakthrough in relations with Russia's key Western partners nor a radical deterioration in relations (Sackwa 2011). Russia's brief flirtation with expansion into Ukraine meets an unhappy end and is not repeated.

Likewise, in China, new oil exploration and the exploitation of nontraditional sources of energy do not succeed. The Chinese shale energy revolution never takes off because most of the resources are far too deep to be easily exploited, and water resources are scarce. There is a brief period of exploration for coal-bed methane, but this effort results in little production because the extraction and transportation costs are too high. Most important, the state-controlled Chinese energy companies are too technologically backward, too immune to competitive forces, and too unattractive to potential foreign collaborators to take advantage of the opportunities that exist.

The Great Northern Recession speeds up the downward spiral. Russia ignores the WTO rules it agreed to in 2012 and raises tariffs on a variety of products. It hopes to repel foreign competition to aid Russian employment, but it is also eager to reduce imports of noncompeting goods, simply to keep the balance-of-payment deficit from exploding. Russia attempts to use the Eurasian Union to reorganize regional trade to its advantage, but few of the post-Soviet states opt to join, and those that do insist on terms much fairer than Russia can accept. Ukraine, Georgia, Moldova, and even Belarus and Armenia instead try to deepen ties with the European Union. It helps that they are less reliant on Russian energy supplies, by this time, and less dependent on the Russian market for their exports.

Russia also faces serious internal problems. The sense of civic nationalism is degraded by the prolonged economic downturn. Nationalist groups begin to rise that challenge the influx of immigrants from the South Caucasus and central Asia. Nationalist groups, as well as security services, commit violence against immigrants when politicians do not heed their concerns. The situation is further inflamed by an active Islamic insurgency operation in the North Caucasus that is successful in unseating Russian-supported regional leaders. The Russian Far East

experiences increased numbers of Chinese workers settling semiper-
manently in the region, and there is a similar backlash from locally
unemployed Russians.

After U.S. and allied troops scale down their presence in Afghanistan, there is little spillover of conflict into other central Asian
countries. Although the Afghani government remains weak and the
country's borders with Tajikistan, Uzbekistan, and Turkmenistan are
porous, fighting diminishes. The economies of these countries gradually reorient their trade from Russia to China. The economic integration
of central Asian nations also increases, including electricity provision
to Afghanistan, enhanced trade and travel across the borders, and
planned pipelines carrying natural gas to Pakistan and India.

Continued social inequality, corruption, and disregard for human
rights, coupled with slow growth and low prices for natural resources,
generates waves of protests in the 2020s. This opposition, however, is
dealt with swiftly by government security forces, often backed by the
Russian government. Changes in regime, where they happen, occur
within a closed circle of elites, with few if any changes in policy.

Many natural disasters hit Asia, Africa, and Latin America. The
IPCC (2013) downgrades the connection between global warming and
extreme weather events. By the late 2020s, this evaluation seems to be
repudiated by a horrifying parade of extreme events: droughts, earthquakes, heat waves, and coastal inundation that impoverishes and
displaces millions of people. In some places, water shortages reduce
agricultural production. Prices rise sharply, social discontent soars, and
cash-strapped governments are forced to use scarce foreign reserves to
import enough food to meet basic requirements.

Tensions increase between India and Pakistan over water rights in
the West and among China, India, and Bangladesh in the East. A large
part of Bangladesh becomes uninhabitable because of rising sea levels,
land subsidence, and amplification of tidal range (Pethick and Orford
2013), which forces the migration of many millions of people. Drought
also hits the Horn of Africa, which pushes the continent further into a
mire of civil wars, piracy, and communal violence. Palace coups became
a regular occurrence, and thoughts about economic development are
put aside as people fight for political and economic survival.

Latin America, already mired in slow growth, also experiences a
series of natural catastrophes, which cause regime turnover. Inept
disaster relief—particularly in Argentina, Bolivia, Ecuador, Peru, and
Venezuela—angers the masses. Educated youth seek to leave these

countries for better opportunities but find little welcome in North America or Europe. There is a great deal of violence among civil factions in the streets and between the civilians and the security forces.

In most countries, the military does not have the will or the inclination to suppress revolt. Governments in Colombia, Argentina, and Venezuela are replaced by a more youthful generation, which strives to create a more transparent, pluralistic, and responsive government. It works in some places but fails to end the cycle of instability in most countries. Whatever form of government is established, austerity measures are necessarily undertaken, hurting the working class and keeping the level of discontent high.

As extreme weather patterns increase, countries take on an adaptive management approach. In responding to natural disasters, slow-moving regional organizations and the United Nations are trumped by new ad hoc groups of governments and nongovernmental organizations ready and willing to assist. Countries with navies on the open seas (such as the United States, the United Kingdom, China, and Russia) increasingly cooperate globally to assist desperate communities. This cooperation in crisis builds strong relationships among the militaries and encourages a global consensus about improving human security regardless of borders.

Southeast Asia is spared the worst of the climate disasters. It benefits from improving economic governance and from a huge and prospering regional economy that self-consciously isolates itself as much as possible from the rest of the world. It is able to employ its young people in meaningful jobs, which ensures domestic tranquility. The highly capable navies of Australia and New Zealand are quick to provide disaster relief in their South Pacific neighborhood, but their governments refuse to provide homes for the new refugees.

The 2040s

The natural disasters become increasingly devastating globally. In some cases they ruin small nations' economies (Randers 2012). Several island nations are covered by the sea, and the survivors flee to nearby mainlands. Tidal waves hit Asian tourist towns; hurricanes hit U.S. tourist towns, and fires ravage forests in the United States and Europe. A drought hits south Asia and southern Africa, devastating agricultural production and resulting in people moving to the cities on the coasts. Cities are bursting with refugees, and rising temperatures result in an unprecedented number of deaths in the warmer months. Hohnen (2012, 31) described the situation as follows:

They [historians] will note ... that profound changes occurred in the earth's biophysical systems over the previous four to five decades. These will include changes in the chemistry of the planet's atmosphere and weather systems; in the diversity and regenerative capacity of terrestrial, freshwater, and marine systems; and in the quantity and quality of natural capital, both nonrenewable and renewable. The combined consequences of these developments, they will note, ... precipitated a new era of climate instability characterized by increased warming.

By 2050, there is a marked change in global cooperation in making decisions on policy issues such as setting a price for carbon, commissioning large-scale carbon-capture storage facilities, and funding the research and development of alternative energies. Governments gain more control over issues of pollution control and resource management. However, given the lack of capacity and legitimacy of the majority of the world's governments, along with the financial strain in a low-growth world, the majority of governments are unable to significantly contribute to global programs. Thus, rather than global solutions being found for global problems, smaller groups of nations with the capacity to execute such projects unite. Public-private partnerships are undertaken to meet the increasing regulation of the use of hydrocarbons.

In more advanced economies, new valuation models are adopted that take into consideration the full life cycle and environmental cost of energy sources, manufactured products, and food. Purely short-term market-based policy thinking is forced to give way to more long-term considerations. Many of the OECD and emerging economies adapt these measures to cooperatively create a green market, particularly in the energy, agriculture, and waste sectors. In non-OECD countries—the largest population-growth areas—governments lack the capacity and the will to adopt new valuation models. An underpinning rivalry remains with the West to achieve higher standards of living. The dramatic experiences of devastating climatic events, slow growth, and more polluted cities increase citizens' drive to adapt.

China's economic growth slows further in this decade, but it still outpaces the growth of the OECD countries. By 2050, China's total output (GDP, measured in 2010 prices and exchange rates) is almost as large as that of the entire OECD (as was shown in table 9.1). China's per capita income, however, is still far below that of the West, and income distribution continues to become more unequal. China's growth, and east Asia's growth in general, takes a heavy toll on the environment. Too many cars, factories, and coal plants generate too much unchecked pollution. Large-scale consumption, rather than spurring high growth, inflicts long-term costs that were not anticipated.

Across many of the non-OECD countries, conditions decline in most sectors. Most Asian governments refuse to relinquish control of agricultural and energy production, which leads to shortages in both sectors (Nair 2012). Food, water, and sanitation provisions and conditions decline. Public services also decline in many of the non-OECD countries, including the availability of low-cost housing, education, and health care. In regions with inadequate health-care systems, vector-borne and water-borne diseases increase. All this leads to more migration to cities and to OECD countries, placing further strain on their economies, infrastructures, and governments.

Freshwater resources are stretched with an increase in population. The agricultural, energy, and drinking-water suppliers all compete for a dwindling and nonreplenishing source of water. There is also an increase in the consumption of water by expanding industrial complexes in the developing countries. All this means a greater stress on the environment—perhaps bigger than the more often discussed climate change. Agricultural supply problems cause the relative price of food to rise sharply, which devastates the poor. Shortages, real and perceived, create severe tension among groups both within nations and across borders. The people most prone to conflict live along the Nile, Tigris-Euphrates, Mekong, Jordan, Indus, Brahmaputra, and Amu Darya Rivers. Water problems—combined with poverty, social tensions, disease, environmental degradation, ineffectual leadership, and weak political institutions—demand high-level attention.

Tools to address water shortages are still immature by the time the major crises occur. Treaties are a solution, but in general, regional organizations are underutilized and therefore lack the capacity to make treaties. The privatization of water utilities meets stiff protest from citizens. Efficiency gains never seem to be realized, and prices continue to rise. Sales and leases to foreigners for agricultural production place an additional strain on a country's yield; the benefits always seem to go the ruling class while the local population is displaced.

By 2050, China struggles with the effects of global warming (Bruntand and Reinvang 2012). Severe droughts in the north and floods and erosion in the south force China to be adaptive in food production

and water supply. China proves to be able to avoid large-scale instability, to mobilize resources constructively and effectively toward adaptation, and to relocate vulnerable populations. This propels Chinese
businesses to innovate by taking advantage of the massive scalable
economy to develop and market new technology. This includes not
only responsive technology to climate crises but also alternative energies to replace hydrocarbon-based fuels. By 2050, China is the most
important place globally for renewable energy production. Scalable
energy storage also allows for increasing amounts of renewable energy
to be used in OECD countries' energy mixes, including solar, wind, and
wave. However, this development is initially expensive and limited
globally.

Policy missteps lead to insolvency in many OECD countries. Their
poor policies and the poor governance in non-OECD countries keep
world economic growth very low. Climate change causes severe disruption in many areas, which leads to further economic decline. The
difference in prospects for the non-OECD countries between this scenario and the more optimistic scenario 1 are very great (see table 9.2).
Most significantly, the encouraging drop in poverty that was achieved
in sub-Saharan Africa in the early years of this century in many of the
scenarios is dramatically reversed in this scenario (see table 9.3).

By 2050, the world economic growth rate has been low for 40 years
because of a combination of poor governance and natural disasters
(see figure 9.1). World GDP per capita is slightly above the level reached
in scenario 6, Eco World, but in that scenario low growth is caused
by deliberate policy moves and is not entirely unwelcome. Carbon

Table 9.2
Real GDP Per Capita in the Non-OECD
Comparing scenario 1 to scenario 8 in 2050, 2005 PPP $

		Scenario 1	Scenario 8
	2010	2050	2050
Latin America and the Caribbean	10.1	25.7	16.7
Sub-Saharan Africa	2.0	11.1	2.6
Middle East and North Africa	8.9	18.6	7.9
Southeast Asia	5.0	34.3	14.0
China	6.8	57.5	22.3
India	3.0	16.6	8.7

Source: See table 2.1.

Table 9.3
Poverty Head Counts in 2050, Scenario 1 versus Scenario 8
Millions of People below the $1.25 a Day Standard

		Scenario 1	Scenario 8
	2010	2050	2050
Latin America and the Caribbean	32.3	16.5	38.7
Sub-Saharan Africa	413.7	152.0	1,248.9
Middle East and North Africa	8.0	2.5	68.1
Southeast Asia	76.8	2.1	9.2
China	155.5	0.6	24.8
India	400.2	13.9	103.0
Other	128.5	30.5	87.1
Total	1,215.0	218.2	1,579.8

Source: 2010 poverty numbers from the World Bank, at www.povcal.net; other figures estimated with the assistance of the IFs model.

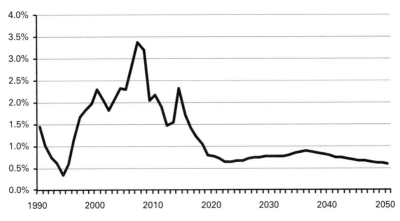

Figure 9.1
World Real GDP per Capita Growth Rate: Recent History and Scenario 8 Projections, 5-year Moving Average (2005 PPP $)
Source: Table 2.1.

emissions are almost 40 percent lower in scenario 6 and are on a sharp downward trend not evident in this scenario (as was shown in table 7.4).

By the 2040s, the governments of the bigger, more prosperous countries establish peaceful relations among themselves and are working together constructively to deal with humanitarian crises. There is more cooperation on climate policy, but they still do not come together with

Table 9.4
Natural Disasters Promote Unity

	Energy	Economy	Harmony
High/Strong			Nations unite to address natural disasters.
Low/Weak	Overproduction of hydrocarbons and biofuels lowers prices.	Recession in the West harms the rest of the globe. Natural disasters harm the poorer countries.	

Source: Authors.

a global solution sufficient to deal with the magnitude of the problem, and fossil fuels remain the primary source in the energy mix of every nation. The key to restarting global economic growth has not been found.

Conclusion

The key drivers in this scenario were policy failures that resulted in low economic growth compounded by climate disasters. A key challenge was why this undesirable combination might lead to global harmony rather than intensified conflict. Initially, intra-state conflicts occurred across the globe. However, over time, a factor leading to stability was low energy prices. Other factors were the debilitating effect that climate disasters had on populations, the inward turn that countries took to mitigate their circumstances, and the long-term effort to enhance international cooperation to deal with the humanitarian crises.

Finally, global harmony comes from the economic weakness of China and India, which are unable to overcome government inefficiency and growing domestic unrest. Table 9.4 presents the combination of endogenous variables and how we assumed they would interact to result in global unity as a result of natural disasters by 2050.

10 Summary and Conclusions

We have presented eight different scenarios covering a broad range of outcomes that we can represent in five graphs. Figure 10.1 shows the range of world GDP growth estimates presented in this book. Scenario 1, Catching Up to America, shows world economic output rising by more than 4 percent a year for 40 years. Scenario 2, Global Backtracking, shows world output rising by only 1.2 percent a year. All the other scenarios lie within these extremes, and the composition of growth—that is, which countries grow faster or slower—varies considerably.

World growth could, of course, be faster than shown in scenario 1, but this scenario already has very high growth by historical standards, and we think it is unlikely to be much higher. World economic growth could be much lower, but that would require more pessimism about geopolitical relations, resource constraints, governance failures, or environmental disasters.

The scenarios also contain a broad range of energy market scenarios. In scenario 6, Eco World, in which public opinion and government policies combine to shrink fossil fuel use, this use peaks in 2021 and falls 35 percent by 2050 (see figure 10.2). In scenario 1, fossil fuel use does not peak at all but continues to rise through 2050. This estimate is consistent with the reference case scenarios from the International Energy Agency (2013) and the Energy Information Agency (2013), which show fossil fuel use continuing to rise through 2035.

Renewable energy shows an even bigger range in our scenarios. In scenario 2, energy production from renewable sources and nuclear power grows only about 1.2 percent a year (less than in the last 20 years) and constitutes only 15 percent of total fuel use in 2050. In scenario 5, A New Bipolarity, optimistic assumptions about technological change leads to growth in production from non–fossil fuel sources of 4 percent per year.

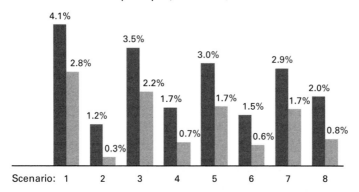

Figure 10.1
World Economic Growth in the Eight Scenarios: Average Annual Percent Change, 2011–2050
Source: See table 2.1.

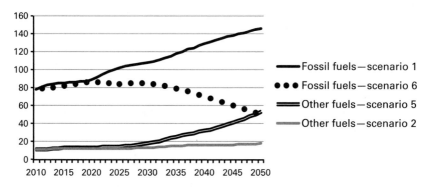

Figure 10.2
Highest and Lowest Use of Fossil Fuels versus Other Energy Sources: Billions of Barrels of Oil Equivalents. Note: Fossil fuels include oil, gas, coal, and liquid biofuels. Other fuel sources are nuclear, hydroelectric, wind, photovoltaic, and other noncarbon-based fuel sources.
Source: 2010 numbers from Energy Information Agency (2013); growth rates by assumption.

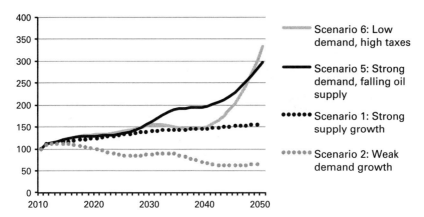

Figure 10.3
World Real Energy Prices in Four Scenarios.
Note: Average world energy prices relative to all other prices; 2010 ratio = 100.
Source: Calculations with the IFs model.

World average energy prices also range widely (see figure 10.3). In scenario 2, real energy prices fall an average of 1 percent a year because supply rises by more than enough to satisfy the energy required for low world economic growth. In scenario 6, energy prices rise 3 percent a year faster than the general price level because of constrained supply and high levels of taxation.

Our third key driver, geopolitical harmony, is harder to quantify. Findlay and O'Rourke (2007) suggest that trade openness is a possible measure of peaceful relations among nations. In our scenarios, we do not assume that hegemony is necessary; trade could still continue to flourish in an Ikenberry (2011) type of world, in which global institutions, not empire or hegemony, are viewed as salutary and hence are abided by. In either case—hegemony or strong global institutions—strong trade growth suggests that some political forces are working that allow peaceful pursuits to flourish.

Our comparative results are displayed in figure 10.4. World trade growth in relation to GDP is highest in scenarios 1, 3, and 8. All three scenarios experience global harmony by 2050. In scenario 1 and 3, a rising China outperforms the United States but decides not to risk disrupting the global trade regime, and allows the renminbi to appreciate to purchasing power parity to become a global reserve. In scenario 8, global cooperation in the face of natural disasters displaces rivalry among nations. In contrast, scenarios 4 and 7 involve the creation of

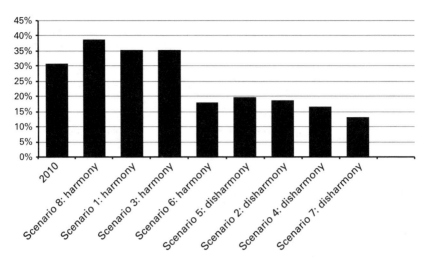

Figure 10.4
Trends in Trade Openness in 2050 as a Measure of Global Harmony
Note: Openness is defined as world exports as a share of world GDP.
Source: Calculations with the IFs model.

rival trade blocs, which lead to fractious behavior among nations and slower trade growth.

We have also used power transition theory and quantitative estimates of geopolitical power to frame the discussion of future geopolitical tensions. Kugler (2006) characterized that the most dangerous period is when a rising power approaches 80 percent of the power of the old hegemon. In all the scenarios, this dangerous period occurs between 2021 and 2025 (see figure 10.5).

In scenarios 1 and 8, China's progress in relation to the United States is rapid: China surges past the United States soon and keeps on growing. In those scenarios, harmonious relations ensue because China is confident it can become the new leading power without upsetting the existing order, and the United States seeks to make the best accommodation it can. Scenario 1 results in a Chinese superpower, and scenario 8 results in a multipolar system.

In all the other scenarios, however, the transition period either is longer or actually reverses, usually because of a serious slowdown in Chinese economic growth relative to the stronger growth in the United States in the 2040s. In scenarios 3 and 6, China achieves and maintains a preponderance of power, and harmonious relations ensue. In the four disharmonious scenarios, geopolitical relations are tenser, and the

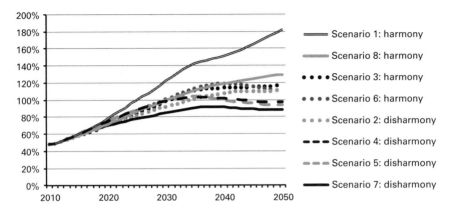

Figure 10.5
China's Geopolitical Power Relative to the United States
Source: Calculations with the IFs model.

probability of warfare increases. Internal strife occurs in nations with weak institutions in scenarios 2 and 4, and regional blocs create tensions in scenarios 5 and 7. Scenario 7 is complicated by the rise of India to great-power status. International organizations prove ineffective in finding solutions to disharmonious scenarios.

The Interconnectedness of the Three Key Drivers

We have presented two major opposing arguments about how to deal with current and potential problems of weak economic growth in the OECD countries. Proponents of the short-term, demand-side focus include some of the most prominent economists in the world, but other prominent economists focus on structural and long-term debt problems. We have tried to use both sets of arguments. The demand-side view wins the policy debate in scenario 3 and ushers in an era of strong growth. In scenario 4, however, the failure to deal with structural issues and growing government debt leads to more crises and weak growth. We show the implications of both policy strategies for economic developments in the rest of the world, for energy market developments, and for geopolitical alignments and the risk of war.

In addition to policy choices, debates about technological change are also key to our economic projections. In our four strong-growth scenarios (scenarios 1, 3, 5, and 7), the United States is assumed to continue to be the leading country (Gordon 2012), and the pace of technological change continues at a long-term trend of about 1.5 percent per year (Shackleton 2013). This trend-based forecast is similar to that used by Fouré et al. (2010), the Energy Information Agency (2013), and many others. The forecast is based on the expectation that previous techno-logical developments leave much room for further dispersion and improvement and that a large increase in the number of knowledge workers worldwide should produce a continued stream of productiv-ity-enhancing discoveries and innovations.

Our four weak-growth scenarios are not so optimistic. In these, the United States and the rest of the world face one or a combination of challenges such as growing dependency ratios, a decline in manufac-turing's share of the economy, a slowing of rural to urban migration, negative effects from globalization, resource or climate constraints, and geopolitical difficulties that prevent benign economic development (Gordon 2012).

Economic success of the United States is tied to the future of Africa (see table 10.1). In the scenarios in which the United States does relatively better economically, Africa tends to more closely follow the Western model of democratic capitalism. Governance improves,

Table 10.1
Sub-Saharan African Performance

		2050			
	2010 starting point	Scenario 1	Scenario 4	Scenario 6	Scenario 8
		Strong U.S. and Chinese growth, harmony	Weak U.S. and strong Chinese growth, disharmony	Weak, policy-induced, world economic growth	Weak world growth from climate and resource problems
GDP per capita, 1000s of 2005 PPP $	$2.0	$11.1	$3.8	$3.9	$2.6
Relative to OECD	5.7%	15.8%	13.0%	10.5%	6.9%
Poverty (millions below $2.50 a day)	667	323	1,096	908	1,780
As share of population	78.1%	17.5%	56.0%	57.5%	75.6%
Democracy and freedom*	7.3	10.1	8.5	8.6	7.4

Note: *Based on a scale from 2 to 14 in which 14 represents strong civil and political liberty.
Source: Calculations with the IFs model.

corruption declines, economic freedom is expanded, and poverty falls dramatically. In scenario 1, in which the United States and China both do well economically and China chooses to live with the existing rules of the liberal international order, sub-Saharan Africa registers its highest growth among the eight scenarios.

In the scenarios in which the United States does poorly and China follows a mercantilist state-capitalist model, especially scenario 4, Africa is still aided by China's demand for raw materials and its investment in infrastructure. But a Chinese-style growth model for Africa means a focus on resource exploitation and a turning away from trade and political liberalization. Becoming a supplier of raw materials to China and a market for China's manufactured goods, rather than trying to create niches of comparative advantage beyond resources, hurts Africa's long-term economic prospects. The African poverty rate decreases from its 2010 value in scenario 4, but the number of people living in absolute poverty increases. Sub-Saharan Africa also suffers from low growth and high poverty levels in scenarios 6 and 8, in which resource and climate fears as well as natural disasters affect Africa and the rest of the world.

Europe encounters even weaker economic growth factors than the United States, and projected per capita economic growth is lower than in the United States in six of the eight scenarios. Europe has a bigger demographic problem: the ratio of elderly to working-age people is higher to begin with and then increases. Furthermore, we assume that more rigid regulation and higher marginal tax rates hinder European entrepreneurship and innovation. The European Union members' average growth rate is boosted slightly by higher growth rates in the 13 newer members from eastern and southern Europe. Income convergence in these scenarios is very slow, however, and the 13 new members average less than two-thirds of the income level of the older 15 members by 2050.

Europe's global position as measured by our geopolitical power index weakens considerably in these scenarios, but it remains the leading voice on causes ranging from global climate change to human rights. Its security position does improve. The rising power, China, is far away and has no territorial ambitions anywhere that matter very much to Europe. A relatively weakened United States is of less concern to some European countries than it used to be, but, conveniently, the United States is still powerful enough to protect European security. Russia's population decline, economic weakness, and necessary preoccupation with the Chinese threat means that Russia is not much of a foreign policy problem for Europe after 2030. Trade and investment relations with Russia improve after sanctions are lifted in most scenarios. Europe's energy imports do not fall very much, but help comes from a rise in fossil fuel production outside OPEC and Russia, a rise in the production of renewable fuels, and sharp policy-induced reductions in energy demand.

We have explored in detail the rise of China. In scenario 1, China follows just such a path of liberal economic reforms and enjoys decades of strong economic growth, which leads to a dramatic rise in its international prestige and geopolitical power. Scenarios 6 and 7 could also be characterized as liberal, as could scenario 3, at least in the later years. In the other scenarios, however, we assume that state capitalism continues to predominate in China, with various degrees of success. In scenario 2, the state-directed allocation of resources and credit, a mercantilist trade policy, and a weak global economy result in very low long-term Chinese economic growth. But in scenario 5, we assume that state capitalism is refined, corruption is controlled, capital is allocated more rationally, and China manages strong growth for at least another 25 years.

China's economic growth, of course, has an effect on world energy demand and energy prices, but more interesting to us is the effect of China's growth on geopolitics and how it achieved that growth. China's level of growth has a significant effect on geopolitics. In scenario 1, we assume that a liberalizing China is a more globalized China, more able and willing to work harmoniously within the existing international system. In addition, China's economic rise is so powerful that the OECD countries have little option but to cede the government greater respect and a larger role in setting the rules of the international system. Strong Chinese growth also works out peacefully in scenario 3, in which China succeeds by refining its model of state capitalism and slowly adopts a more liberal domestic and foreign policy outlook.

A less successful China—which fails to liberalize and for whom the weaknesses of a state-centered business model are enhanced rather than reduced—sees lower growth, less domestic tranquillity, a more xenophobic foreign policy, and perhaps war. These issues are explored in scenario 4, in which Chinese state capitalism and a failure to live up to existing international norms and agreements leads to aggressive trade policy retaliation from the OECD. This backlash eventually leads

Table 10.2
China and the United States: Real GDP Per Capita in 2050 and Geopolitical Power in 2050

	1000s of 2005 PPP $		Average Annual Growth, 2011–2050*		China's Geopolitical Power as Percentage of U.S. Power
	China	USA	China	USA	
Scenario 1	57.5	78.9	5.5%	1.6%	182%
Scenario 2	16.8	37.0	2.3%	–0.3%	111%
Scenario 3	31.1	71.7	3.9%	1.3%	116%
Scenario 4	17.5	48.7	2.4%	0.4%	97%
Scenario 5	25.7	78.3	3.4%	1.6%	93%
Scenario 6	17.8	43.1	2.4%	0.1%	110%
Scenario 7	23.3	74.6	3.1%	1.4%	88%
Scenario 8	22.3	46.6	3.0%	0.3%	129%
Scenario average	26.5	59.9	3.2%	0.8%	116%

Note: *Chinese growth averaged 8.6 percent per year, 1979–2010; U.S. growth averaged 1.7 percent in the same period. China's geopolitical power is an estimated 48.3 percent of U.S. power in 2010.
Source: See table 2.1; calculations with the IFs model.

to the creation of powerful regional trade blocs and a stifling of world economic growth. In scenario 5, the combination of a successful state-capitalist model and growing turmoil in the world energy market leads to a much more aggressive Chinese foreign policy in east and south Asia and in Africa. China's growth falters in scenario 5, but its grievances and its military power are greater than ever. Its geopolitical power in 2050 is in the zone of near parity with the United States (see table 10.2).

China continues on a convergence path with the United States in all eight scenarios; the United States, after all, is not growing very fast in any of them. But China remains far poorer than the United States in all the scenarios, and only in scenario 1 does China's 2050 level exceed the average income of the OECD countries in 2010. China is perhaps satisfied with a $58,000 per capita income in scenario 1, and we assume that income does not quite matter as much in the sustainability model chosen in scenario 6. But in all the other scenarios, we doubt that China, after complaining so long and bitterly about not enjoying its rightful place in world affairs, would be satisfied with remaining so far behind the United States and its allies in living standards, if not in military power.

India does not significantly enhance its global position in any of these scenarios except one. In the strong world-growth scenarios, especially scenarios 1 and 3, Indian real per capita growth is about 5 percent a year for 40 years, and its people enjoy a far higher standard of living than they do today. However, China also grows strongly in those scenarios, and its increasing dominance in world affairs constrains Indian foreign policy. In scenario 6, philosophical and aesthetic considerations cause India to opt out of the race for economic growth and great-power status altogether.

Scenario 7 is much different. In the 2040s, our assumptions about China's bureaucratic rigidity and its military assertiveness result in a growth slowdown while India's economy keeps growing strongly. India improves its efficiency in water usage, increases domestic energy production, and raises agricultural productivity enough to provide its people with an improved diet. Its high-tech service industry and growing prowess in manufacturing make it a strong competitor in world markets. Its population is still growing, and its military is large and increasingly high-tech. By 2050, India surpasses China by our measure of comprehensive national power, making India more secure within its own borders and encouraging it to think about asserting itself more forcefully on the global stage.

Neither the United States nor any other country is an autonomous actor in these scenarios, able to choose its policies based on its own cultural and ideological considerations. If the U.S. economy thrives through a combination of good policies and felicitous technological change, its geopolitical future will be more sanguine. The United States can afford and will have the prestige to advance a globalized economic policy that encourages liberal political and economic reform in the non-OECD countries. It will also be able to afford a strong and technologically advanced military that will keep the ambitions of China and several important rising regional powers in check. If the U.S. economy does not thrive, respect for the Washington Consensus model will likely decline, along with American power and influence. Worse, if the United States, fearful of the economic challenge from China, retreats into mercantilism itself, its economic growth will likely decline even faster (scenario 4).

World energy demand varies in these scenarios, depending on world economic growth, reserves and exploitation of fossil fuels,

Table 10.3
World Energy Projections

Average Annual Percent Change, 2011–2050

Scenario	World GDP (PPP Terms)	World Energy Demand and Supply	Fossil Fuels	Nuclear and Renewable Sources	Real Energy Price	Middle East OPEC Oil Production as Share of World Energy Use
1	3.5%	1.8%	1.6%	2.8%	1.1%	10.8%
2	1.0%	0.7%	0.6%	1.2%	−1.0%	9.2%
3	2.9%	1.3%	0.7%	3.6%	2.6%	3.5%
4	1.5%	0.0%	−0.7%	2.4%	2.4%	4.8%
5	2.5%	1.3%	0.5%	4.0%	2.8%	3.6%
6	1.2%	−0.1%	−1.1%	3.0%	3.1%	4.9%
7	2.4%	1.0%	0.7%	2.8%	0.5%	10.3%
8	1.7%	0.9%	0.7%	2.2%	−0.5%	11.5%
					2010 value:	9.3%

Source: See tables 2.1 and 2.2.

technological change in the energy industry, and government policies, which affect all of the above (see table 10.3). In most of the scenarios, we assume there are sufficient global resources of fossil fuels to continue the increasing use of them through 2050, though at very slow rates and, in some cases, at very high prices. In scenario 4, production difficulties in the Middle East result in an overall decline in fossil fuel production and use by 2050. In scenario 6, low world economic growth, high energy taxes, and a popular will to reduce carbon emissions also result in a decline in fossil fuel use.

All scenarios except the eighth are marked by a certain technological optimism: energy supplied by renewable sources (e.g., hydroelectric, solar, wind, biomass) increase. We also anticipate some new nuclear power generation. If those anticipated increases turn out to have been overoptimistic, the energy prices necessary to clear the market would be quite a bit higher, and world economic growth would be weaker. However, in our modeling framework, the long-term effect of gradually rising energy prices is not severe.

Energy outcomes are shaped by the economic and geopolitical developments in the scenarios, but they also, in turn, help shape those economic and geopolitical outcomes. Low energy prices can be a sign of low energy demand that results from weak world economic growth, as in scenarios 2 and 8, or a sign of rapid expansion of the production of renewable sources. Low energy prices from either cause can be devastating to the Middle East oil exporters. But the Middle East plays a gradually diminishing role in world affairs in all our scenarios. With the exception of some of the smaller Persian Gulf nations, the region never manages to construct the institutions or enact the policies that lead to sustainable economic development. It experiences the weakest average per capita economic growth among the major regions. OPEC's Middle East oil exporters still produce and export a significant amount of oil, but oil plays a smaller role in the world economy in most of the scenarios, and imported energy plays a much smaller role in the U.S. economy and in foreign policy considerations in all the scenarios.

The energy variable is critical to the U.S.-China dynamic in the scenarios. The rapid rise of unconventional oil and gas production in the United States boosts economic growth in scenarios 3, 5, and 7. Strong economic growth and increased energy security (see table 10.4) lead to a high level of American geopolitical power in scenario 5. In scenario 7, however, China's economic growth is stronger, and its increasing energy insecurity might be a prelude to conflict.

China's energy insecurity has long been a factor in its foreign policy. Zhang (2006, 19–20) sums up the fears: "China cannot have control over development goals without corresponding control over the resources that fuel the economy. The simple fact is that China does not possess that control.... China is almost helpless to protect its overseas oil import routes. This is an Achilles heel to contemporary China, as it has

Table 10.4
Energy Security
Energy Imports as Share of Total Energy Consumption and as Share of GDP

		Scenario Results, 2050							
	2010	1	2	3	4	5	6	7	8
United States	23.5%	1.6%	19.8%	−7.1%	29.5%	−6.7%	17.4%	−13.6%	6.2%
	1.9%	0.1%	0.7%	−0.8%	3.3%	−1.0%	−2.8%	−0.8%	0.2%
China	13.6%	5.7%	−7.1%	0.5%	21.4%	6.5%	−2.8%	23.3%	13.5%
	3.0%	0.7%	−0.7%	0.2%	5.3%	2.1%	3.2%	3.0%	1.4%
India	34.9%	50.5%	43.9%	41.7%	44.5%	42.3%	3.2%	39.7%	56.2%
	5.1%	4.6%	2.5%	6.0%	7.0%	6.9%	8.3%	2.1%	4.3%

Source: 2010 energy numbers from EIA (2013); all other calculations from the IFs model.

forced China to entrust its fate to others." China could rely on the global economy and open markets—which we assume it does, in scenarios 1, 3, 6, and 8. Or it could take much more aggressive action such as trying to gain physical control of offshore energy resources and building up its fleet and bases to prevent the possibility of an adversary cutting off its imported energy.

China will almost certainly continue to expand its naval capabilities and perhaps establish a chain of bases to protect energy flow from the Persian Gulf. It will also probably vigorously pursue its claims to (presumed) undersea resources in the South China and East China Seas. It will seek new energy deals with corrupt and autocratic regimes in Africa. All these strategies involve an increased risk of confrontation and conflict with the United States and between China and its neighbors.

The danger from China's energy insecurity depends not just on Chinese energy demand and the global supply of fossil fuels, it also depends on how rapidly renewable sources of energy become important competitors. The technological optimism on renewable energy that is present in almost all our scenarios means that China produces between 16 and 48 percent of its energy needs in 2050 domestically through renewable energy—up from 7.7 percent in 2010. Before this huge rise in renewable energy comes to fruition, however, China's energy imports must increase, making China more vulnerable to supply interruption. If development of renewable energy proceeds at a slower pace than anticipated in our scenarios, or if oil peaks sooner, the Chinese security dilemma will worsen.

So far we have shown how our assumptions about technology, economic policy, and energy resources have acted as drivers, and we have made various assumptions about how those drivers affect geopolitical relations. But the interaction works both ways. Leaders who respond to their own fears and values and the interests of their constituents will act in ways that make a difference. Their actions could lead either to geopolitical harmony that encourages mutually beneficial trade and economic growth or to disharmony that at least restricts growth and at worst leads to war and the destruction of lives and property. We have assumed that many wars occur throughout the 40 years of our scenarios and that these wars flow plausibly from the assumptions we have made about the interactions of energy, economics, and geopolitics. Iran launches a nuclear attack on Israel in scenario 2, India and Pakistan fight in scenario 5, China violently expands its borders in scenario 7, and Russia retakes and holds some of its former Soviet territories in several scenarios. China and the United States fight only proxy and economic wars, but we could easily imagine a great-power war in the four disharmony scenarios.

The IFs model combines the openness estimates and the power calculations to determine the probability of war for each nation in each year (more than 34,000 probabilities for each scenario for each year). To condense this huge amount of information, we have calculated and reported the cumulative probability of nine significant countries having at least one war in 2015 and in 2050 (see table 10.5). The probabilities tend to go down over time in the harmonious scenarios and to go up over time in the disharmonious scenarios. The model was also run multiple times—using a random number generator operating on the probabilities, to predict individual wars, of various lengths and degrees of severity. We used these extra simulations to inform our judgments about warfare in these scenarios, but since they involve randomness— every model simulation produces different results—the individual wars described in the text flow from the logic of the story line rather than from our probabilistic estimates.

The rise of China both benefits and challenges its neighbors in Southeast Asia geopolitically. GDP growth per capita continues on a convergence path in all scenarios, with strong growth and faster convergence when the U.S. and Chinese economies do well and an open trading regimen is maintained (scenarios 1 and 3). Indonesia grows faster than the region as a whole. Since it is by far the most populous nation in the area, with a larger economy and a growing military presence Indonesia could choose to take on an independent leadership role in the region, but we assume that it does not. In scenarios 1 and 3, its passivity does not matter, because global growth surges and peaceful relations expand. But when it is threatened by China's increasing aggressiveness in the physical seizure of the islands and resources of the East China and South China Seas and the return of Taiwan (scenarios 1 and 7), in the annexation of North Korea or the Philippines (scenario 7), or in trade and currency wars (scenario 4), Indonesia jumps into the Chinese camp (the Asian League in scenario 4, the Shanghai Pact in scenario 7) or into a looser sphere of influence in the other scenarios. And it takes most of the rest of the region with it.

The majority of Latin American countries are fortunate not to have to choose sides in these scenarios. They can take shelter under the still strong leadership of the United States, choose to follow Brazil in

Probability of a Country Having at Least One War in a Given Year

	Harmony Scenarios				Disharmony Scenarios				Average of Scenarios	
	1	3	6	8	2	4	5	7	Harmony	Disharmony
China										
2015	5.9%	5.9%	6.4%	5.8%	5.9%	6.4%	5.9%	6.4%	6.0%	6.1%
2050	5.7%	5.8%	8.3%	4.9%	6.3%	8.4%	6.1%	8.6%	6.2%	7.3%
United States										
2015	10.5%	10.5%	11.0%	10.3%	10.5%	11.0%	10.5%	11.0%	10.6%	10.7%
2050	7.9%	8.0%	10.4%	7.1%	8.5%	10.6%	8.4%	10.8%	8.3%	9.6%
India										
2015	4.4%	4.4%	4.9%	4.3%	4.4%	4.9%	4.4%	4.9%	4.5%	4.6%
2050	4.3%	4.3%	6.8%	3.4%	4.8%	7.0%	4.7%	7.3%	4.7%	5.9%
Russia										
2015	10.4%	10.4%	10.7%	10.7%	10.4%	10.6%	10.4%	10.6%	10.6%	10.5%
2050	6.8%	6.8%	8.6%	6.7%	6.9%	8.7%	6.9%	9.0%	7.3%	7.9%
Japan										
2015	2.2%	2.2%	2.3%	2.1%	2.2%	2.4%	2.2%	2.3%	2.2%	2.3%
2050	1.4%	1.4%	2.5%	1.4%	1.5%	2.5%	1.5%	2.4%	1.7%	2.0%
Israel										
2015	5.4%	5.4%	6.0%	5.4%	5.4%	6.0%	5.4%	6.0%	5.6%	5.7%
2050	3.6%	3.6%	3.8%	3.5%	3.9%	6.0%	3.8%	6.3%	3.6%	5.0%
Iran										
2015	7.6%	7.0%	7.6%	6.9%	7.0%	7.6%	7.0%	7.6%	7.3%	7.3%
2050	4.6%	4.6%	4.6%	4.4%	4.8%	6.9%	4.6%	7.2%	4.6%	5.9%
Turkey										
2015	5.2%	5.2%	5.8%	5.2%	5.8%	5.8%	5.2%	5.8%	5.3%	5.6%
2050	3.6%	3.6%	5.9%	3.5%	4.4%	6.1%	3.9%	6.3%	4.2%	5.2%
Saudi Arabia										
2015	0.8%	0.8%	1.4%	0.8%	0.8%	1.4%	0.8%	1.4%	0.9%	1.1%
2050	0.7%	0.7%	3.0%	0.7%	0.9%	3.1%	0.8%	3.5%	1.3%	2.1%

Source: Calculations with the IFs model.

strengthened regional partnerships (scenarios 4 and 7), or follow no leadership in particular. Most Latin American countries continue to cycle between economic models, with the Pacific countries mostly following neoliberal policies and the Atlantic countries mostly following populist or state-centered policies, but with many reversals throughout the decades and among the scenarios.

Whichever policies are pursued, the growth differences are not very large. In scenarios 1 and 3, which are the most neoliberal, regional GDP per capita averages $26,900 in 2050, far above the $16,700 average in the two most populist scenarios (2 and 4). But much of that gap can probably be accounted for by the sharply higher world economic growth in scenarios 1 and 3. On average across the eight scenarios, Latin America continues on a slow convergence path with the OECD countries. Average GDP per capita rises from 29 percent of the OECD value in 2010 to an average of 43 percent in 2050.

Russia does not do very well in these scenarios in terms of economic growth, energy production, or geopolitical position. Russian performance is assumed to lag behind China and even the OECD countries (which it should be catching up with, given the normal convergence process), because it never manages to move much beyond the predatory state-centered model and it continues to focus on resource exploitation. In a nation with little rule of law or respect for property rights, and where innovative entrepreneurs run the risk of expropriation or prison, little dynamism can be expected. Russia's population falls, its economy barely grows, its energy leverage against its neighbors shrivels, and its ideological appeal to others is negligible. Russia has a hard time trying to hold on to its own territory in the face of an expansionist China (scenarios 1 and 7), although it does make some inroads in reacquiring some parts of its former Soviet territories.

Russian economic growth is buoyed by strong production of oil and gas in scenario 1 and by high energy prices in scenarios 3 through 6, but Russia never manages to turn its resource wealth into self-sustaining growth. Its population continues to decline by about 0.5 percent per year, and it has little more than 100 million people in 2050. In 40 years it slips from the 9th most populous country in the world to the 15th. In 2050 it holds only 1.5 percent of the world's comprehensive national power (slightly higher if nuclear weapons and energy security are taken into account). See appendix D online. While China, India, and the United States combine to increase their joint share of world power, Russia falls below Indonesia, Turkey, and Mexico in the world ranking.

This decline in power is reflected in the small success Russia has in rallying its neighbors to join the Eurasian Union (except in scenarios 4 and 7) and by its loss of influence over eastern Siberia to China in scenarios 1 and 7.

The Probabilities of the Scenarios

A summary of the scenarios in this book is depicted in table 10.6. We have made a subjective rating of the probability of each scenario relative to the others.

We give a low-probability rating to scenarios 1, 6 and 8. We believe scenario 1 to have a low probability because we do not think China can sustain such a high level of economic growth. No country has ever grown so fast for so long, and we discuss many factors in the other

Table 10.6
The Eight Scenarios

	Probability	Energy Prices	Economic Growth	Geopolitics
Scenario 1: Catching Up to America	Low	Low	Strong	Global harmony
				Chinese hegemony
Scenario 2: Global Backtracking	Medium	Low	Weak	Global disharmony
				Multipolarity
Scenario 3: Peaceful Power Transition	Medium	High	Strong	Global harmony
				Chinese hegemony
Scenario 4: Regional Mercantilism	Medium	High	Weak	Global disharmony
				Multipolarity
Scenario 5: A New Bipolarity	High	High	Strong	Global disharmony
				Bipolarity
Scenario 6: Eco World	Low	High	Weak	Global harmony
				U.S. hegemony
Scenario 7: Ambition Fuels Rivalry	High	Low	Strong	Global disharmony
				Multipolarity
Scenario 8: Natural Disasters Promote Unity	Low	Low	Weak	Global harmony
				Multipolarity

Source: Authors.

scenarios that we think are likely to limit Chinese growth. Scenarios 6 and 8 are wild cards. In scenario 6, fear of anthropogenic global warming in OECD countries and a call for more sustainable growth leads to a reduction in world economic growth. These assumptions lead to lower global political tensions and have the desired result of driving down energy use, CO_2 emissions, and world temperature, but at a significant cost in world incomes. We do not think it very likely that the more capitalist-minded countries of the United States, Australia, Japan, and South Korea, combined with the ambitious first and second echelon of emerging economies, would willingly make such sacrifices in growth. Nevertheless, a technological leap in innovation in the non-OECD countries could allow them to grow more slowly while still adapting to a more modern world. In scenario 8, natural disasters retard world economic growth but promote more harmonious relations among nations. There is a strain of thought in our theoretical and modeling work, especially that related to Inglehart and Baker (2000), that supports this outcome. However, the widespread and catastrophic nature of this scenario, combined with the almost passive responsive to economic challenges, makes it much less likely than the other scenarios.

We consider scenarios 2, 3, and 4 to have a medium probability. Scenario 2 has very weak economic growth for the United States. Although we think that the United States has significant long-term economic challenges, this scenario probably goes too far in its pessimism. Scenario 3 is somewhat more likely. A peaceful power transition is certainly plausible, given the theories and history we have examined and some of the actions and stated positions of leaders in both China and the United States. We judge that growing ambition in a rising China and growing fears in a fading United States could preclude harmony, however, and so we rate the probability of this scenario as medium. Scenario 4 is the most likely of our medium-probability scenarios. The failure to deal with structural issues because of political deadlock is highly plausible, particularly in the United States. We already see preliminary steps taken by many countries away from globalization and toward regionalization. We think those changes will intensify, but we are not sure they will get as severe as we lay out in scenario 4.

Scenarios 5 and 7 seem the most highly probable of our eight scenarios. They both have strong economic growth for the world, for China, and for the United States, midway between the higher estimates in scenarios 1 and 3 and the much lower estimates in the other four scenarios. We also think they are more probable because they assume that great-power rivalry will not go away and that China's anxieties are worsened by enhanced energy insecurity. In scenario 5, the combination of high energy prices and strong growth remind us of the 2010s, and before that the early 1970s. During both of these periods, the United States and its archrival, first the Soviet Union and then China, expanded its power and global reach. China will continue to pursue energy resources globally in order to feed its strong growth, and this will cause confrontation in Asia and Africa. But with U.S. confidence rising from strong energy production and rapid technological innovation, American leaders will probably not pull back from trying to lead the international system. Similarly, we can envision the formation of the two major archrival blocs as in scenario 7: democracies versus China's followers. We also like this scenario for the relative rise of India in the 2040s and the relative decline of a China that has overreached.

We began this book asking whether there will be more wars or peace. We asked what country or countries will dominate and which ones will fade in geopolitical significance. Will the unprecedented 60-year surge in world economic growth come to an end? Will shortages of energy or other resources constrain the global future?

We found that the declining trend in inter-state conflicts discernible from 1990 to 2010 (as shown in figure 1.2) may not be sustainable in the future. The model-estimated probabilities of war (as shown in table 10.5) are generally higher in the disharmonious scenarios than in the harmonious scenarios. For the rising great powers, China and India, the probabilities of war in 2050 are greater than they were in 2010 even in some of the harmonious scenarios. The probability of conflict for the United States remains relatively high, but it declines in all scenarios from its 2010 level, mainly because a rise in the probability of war with China is outweighed by the declining probability of war in the Middle East associated with assumed trends in energy vulnerability. It is important to note that these model-generated probabilities are not point forecasts of the future. They are conditional forecasts based on all the assumptions of the scenarios described above and the model's probability calculations based on the theoretical and empirical work described in the IFs model literature.

We also found that if strong world economic growth continues, but much less over time in the United States than in China, there will be a profound shift in geopolitical power, with the era of U.S. hegemony likely to come to an end. But an era of Chinese world hegemony seems unlikely. At the height of U.S. global power, shortly after World War II, the nation's economy accounted for roughly half of world output. In 2000 it still accounted for more than 30 percent. China is assumed to be the largest unitary power in 2050, but it reaches 30 percent only in scenario 1, and its share peaks in the late 2030s or early 2040s in most of the other scenarios. The Chinese economy also remains far more dependent on international trade than the U.S. economy ever was.

The United States will still be a large and relatively rich country with a powerful military in 2050, and it will probably be supported in resisting Chinese domination by large rich democracies: the European Union, India, Japan, Brazil, and Turkey. The Chinese people themselves will not wish to risk upsetting the global order that has allowed them to achieve a standard of living comparable to those in the West whom they have envied for so long. This picture of a generally peaceful power transition resembles scenario 3 or maybe scenario 1. Both scenarios are enabled by assumptions about continuing strong growth in global productivity generated by technological advances and by sufficient resources of fossil fuels to power the world economy at not too high a price until renewable energy sources increase.

The other scenarios explore how various factors can lead to less benign outcomes. Poor policy choices in China could lead to much weaker long-term growth, a more dissatisfied populace, and a heightened risk of great-power confrontation. In scenarios 2, 5, and 7, economic mismanagement leads to much slower economic growth in the 2030s and 2040s and leaves the Chinese people disgruntled and their leaders in search of a scapegoat. If we assume an increase in Chinese energy insecurity because of production decline in the Middle East or a failure to develop indigenous supplies, the risks of war are higher.

Lower technological growth will hurt the United States and the other OECD countries much more than it will slow China, which still has decades of catch-up growth to profit from. A poorer and weaker United States will feel more threatened by China and will be more tempted to retreat behind protectionist barriers that will undermine the global system and give China fewer reasons to restrain its great power ambitions (scenario 4).

Lessons Learned

From this scenario-planning exercise, we learned what combination of endogenous variables is more or less realistic. For example, combining strong economic growth and low energy prices is less realistic, since as demand rises, prices also rise. In this situation, the energy sector would have to experience commercial-scale technological advances to increase global production, or efficiency measures would advance and keep energy price inflation stable. We understood that advances in energy technology, particularly if cheaper hydrocarbons are displaced, could lead to expensive energy generation, keeping prices high. Or energy technology could spill into other sectors, spurring higher economic growth and more demand for energy.

Another unlikely pair is strong economic growth and global harmony, particularly if China reaches parity and challenges U.S. hegemony. It seemed farfetched to assume that China would not challenge something in the international system or that the United States would not challenge China's expansion of influence in Asia.

Yet another unlikely combination of variables is high energy prices and weak economic growth along with global harmony. We assumed that there was a fundamental shift in the way richer countries viewed development, more along the lines of sustainable solutions, such as higher taxes on hydrocarbons and penalties for carbon emissions. This necessitated cooperation among countries, adaptation by non-OECD countries, and gradual improvement in global environmental conditions.

We discovered that the combination of low energy prices and strong economic growth is the most likely combination for militaries to exert power and be confronted by other powers. This was because of an increase in military spending and trade protection, combined with a decline in global democratization and cooperation. At the same time, we were aware that too much war could curtail strong economic growth. We also found it less likely that low energy prices and weak economic growth could combine with global harmony. We attributed it to the possibility that low energy prices would generate less oil revenue. We also foresaw a slew of climate disasters forcing countries to turn to the OECD countries for help, and in this situation China and India would remain weak and turned inward.

We concluded from this exercise that the interaction of the three variables can result in a key driver shifting over time. For example, weak economic growth can keep energy prices down for a time, but it can also lead to desperate policies that breed mistrust, create disharmony, and place a further damper on growth (and with it, decreasing demand and lower energy prices). The effect of the interplay of the three variables over time can be even worse if a course correction does not occur.

Trade protectionism helped no one. When the three variables were all negative—high energy prices, weak economic growth, and global disharmony—we learned that a natural outcome could be a retrenchment from global affairs and into contentious economic and political regional blocs, leaving few winners. This could also happen with high energy prices and strong economic growth, particularly if China was unsatisfied with its gains from trade.

Finally, the high probability of scenarios 5 and 7 suggests that global disharmony is more plausible than harmony, particularly when combined with strong economic growth for China and the United States. At the same time, it does not appear to matter in the combination of strong economic growth and global disharmony whether energy prices are low or high. The energy market will be so dynamic between now and 2050 that supply will vary according to new technology, regulation, and new recovery of hydrocarbons. Economies are likely to grow despite energy prices as countries adapt to new supply realities. Greater energy efficiency and making renewable sources less expensive (possibly through storage) could be the deciding factor in sustaining growth alongside higher prices.

Limiting Factors

The scenarios cannot realistically cover all possible futures. There are, of course, some events that we cannot, or do not wish to, predict and that could change all the scenarios. These events are usually not foreseen and therefore do not affect government policy in a significant way to prepare for or prevent their occurrence. An example of this is the collapse of the Soviet Union in 1991, which forever changed the bipolar security paradigm. Another example is the attack on American financial and military sites on September 11, 2001, which resulted in the U.S. government launching a global war on terrorism for the next decade. The wave of protests across the Middle East that formed the Arab Spring and beyond saw the fall of several governments. A future geopolitical shock could be a debilitating sustained cyber attack on a major financial system or the detonation of a small nuclear device in a capital city, particularly in an OECD country that affects the global economy. The tsunami that impaired the nuclear power plant in Japan was a natural disaster that shocked the energy sector, similar to the hurricane that shut down the oil-refining capacity in the Gulf of Mexico in 2005.

On a more positive side, there can be technological breakthroughs that change the nature of global trade, such as the internet; that enhance transport, such as the airplane; or that create new energy technologies. Few foresaw the shale gas revolution that has taken hold in the United States and is now spreading to Europe and China. Many knew the gas was there, mostly beneath former oil fields, but not until a company used horizontal drilling to increase exposure to the resource-laden rock and hydraulic fracturing to increase permeability was it possible to extract trillions of cubic meters of gas.

Likewise, exploitation of deep water finds of unconventional oil is dependent on better and more reliable technology combined with substantial finance and supportive regulations. If solar and wind energy can be stored at sufficiently low cost, then renewable electricity generation could revolutionize not just electricity but also transportation. And should new sources of fusion be realized, this would almost certainly transform global energy supply. We attempted in several scenarios to suggest how technology could change the nature of the global economy, particularly manufacturing trends.

Although the IFs model does take into account social and human trends that could alter economic development in different countries, we did not feature them in our three endogenous variables or manipulate them as variables in our model. We are not quite sure how a global mass wave of urbanization would affect governance, energy use, or the environment. We are unsure of future military weapons developments, such as drones, and how they might alter power relations should other countries or groups gain access to or develop these systems. We also did not factor in the balance of the sexes, particularly how the empowerment of women could affect economic development in OECD countries in Asia and non-OECD countries in the Middle East. Nor do we account for the growing class divide, with children from poor and fragmented households disadvantaged in acquiring the human capital that is necessary to allow them to escape poverty.

We cannot fully account for how the lack of the rule of law and corruption could impair growth. We worry that "capital no longer flows to where it gets the best return but [flows instead] to where it can get the best tax subsidies, the deepest secrecy, and to where it can best evade the laws, rules and regulations it does not like" (Shaxson 2011, 70). Capital flight from emerging economies and poorer countries stunts economic growth. In poorer countries, there is a direct correlation between corruption levels, as measured by Transparency International, and poverty levels. In emerging economies, it is unclear how the diversion of assets affects economic growth; imagine how much richer and more stable Russia would be if, instead of the prevalence of capital flight, oil and gas dollars were reinvested into the system, properly taxed, and then spent by the government on infrastructure and technology development.

A limiting aspect of the quantitative assistance from the IFs model was the inability to estimate the probabilities of other variables besides war. The model is simply not sophisticated enough in this regard to help us. This precluded our ability to estimate the variability of individual scenarios and prevented us from producing conditional probabilities of the eight combinations. Instead, we had to rely on our qualitative and theory-informed exercise to suggest the most likely combinations. Another missing aspect in working with the IFs model was a detailed discussion of all the exogenous variables and parameters manipulated to produce each scenario. We have provided an overview of our general manipulations of exogenous variables in appendix B. A more extended discussion was beyond the scope of this book, but the interested reader is invited to examine the Sce files that are available along with the model itself at the IFs website.

Conclusion

The purpose of this book was to impose some discipline on the myriad efforts across several disciplines to describe the future based on the present scenario. The availability of energy resources, economic growth, and relations within and between nations are so codependent that it makes little sense to consider the long-term future for one key driver based on fixed assumptions about the others. This book portrays the interconnectedness of these three major drivers—energy prices, economic growth, and geopolitics—over the next 40 years in eight scenarios. Our work offers the first attempt to bring together the three driving factors as endogenous variables and generate primary and secondary implications. We found that maintaining an assumption of the exogeneity of certain variables was unrealistic and likely to lead to less than helpful forecasts.

Likewise, there is much to be gained from combining a quantitative model with the more subjective and qualitative approaches usually taken in scenario analysis. Economists, government organizations, energy industry analysts, and academics have all engaged with scenario analysis. It is thought that scenario analysis induces analysts to consider low-probability events that could have a large effect on project profitability. Scenario analysis also perhaps leads to the development of contingency plans that can be executed as events unfold. However, it is our opinion that these exercises could be better disciplined by quantitative constraints like those embedded in the IFs model. Practitioners could gain by combining the quantitative model with the more subjective and qualitative approach usually taken in scenario analysis.

The IFs model also allowed us to predict the probability of war in relation to high or low energy prices and strong or weak economic growth. Using the IFs model, we were able to manipulate the various ways energy prices would rise or lower and the types of energy available, which could then be measured against economic growth figures. It is clear that economic growth is not exogenous to energy markets, nor do energy markets exist beyond the confines of political factors. This adds to the usual forecasting exercises done by the International Energy Agency and the U.S. Energy Information Agency. Should practitioners maintain assumptions of the exogeneity of variables, we are concerned that this will lead to poor forecasts.

As for policy makers, the ideal combination of variables would at first seem intuitively to be low energy prices, strong economic growth, and global harmony. Yet in our scenario building, China catches up to the United States economically and also expands peacefully within the Asia-Pacific region. This might be acceptable to Chinese policy makers, but the ideal situation for American policy makers is more likely to be the one in which the United States remains the hegemon, which in our scenario building results from a combination of low energy prices, strong economic growth, and global disharmony. China actually challenges U.S. power militarily, and eventually two countering blocs are formed with the two major powers. Rather than a specific combination of variables, therefore, our prescription is for policy makers to consider in depth the endogeneity of a combination of variables. Policy, after all, is made in a dynamic environment of changing and interconnected factors that affect one another over time.

A multitude of futures is possible, of course, but we have concluded that this plausible and diverse set of assumptions about economic growth, energy production and demand, and geopolitical relations suggest a long period when global politics will be defined by relations between China and the United States. The peacefulness of those relations will be determined largely by the domestic economic conditions in each, by the economic connections between them, and by the political connections each maintains or fails to maintain with the smaller powers.

In follow-up work, we would like to explore further possible variants on China's rise using the IFs model. Although several are present in this book as the result of the interaction of combinations of three endogenous variables, factoring in more detail of how a change in microvariables could affect such a rise would help us to see whether our predictions are on track. We would also like to better incorporate corruption figures when forecasting economic growth of non-OECD countries. We believe that the absence of a true quantitative understanding of corruption impaired past predictions of the health of the Soviet Union in the 1980s and Russia in the first decade of this century and that it does so now with the Chinese Communist Party's state capitalism.

Likewise, we are not as confident as some banking institutions that the emerging economies will enjoy sustained robust growth, given poor governance and corruption. We would also like to revisit (with the assistance of Barry Hughes and others from the Pardee Center) the quantitative relationships that helped us to estimate the probabilities of inter-state war. We think those estimates were helpful in this book, but much work remains to be done.

Appendix A: Conference and Workshop Participants

Dr. Robert Aten, program economist emeritus, U.S. Agency for International Development.

Dr. Robert J. Brecha, professor, Department of Physics, and coordinator, Renewable and Clean Energy Program Sustainability & Environment Initiative, University of Dayton.

Ambassador Carey Cavanaugh, director, Patterson School of Diplomacy and International Commerce.

Dr. Stacy Closson, visiting lecturer, Patterson School of Diplomacy and International Commerce.

Dr. Yong Deng, professor, Department of Political Science, U.S. Naval Academy.

Dr. Richard L. Engel, major general (retired), U.S. Air Force, director, Environment and Natural Resources Program, Strategic Futures Group, National Intelligence Council.

Dr. Ralph Espach, analyst, Center for Naval Analysis.

Dr. Robert Farley, assistant professor, Patterson School of Diplomacy and International Commerce.

Dr. George von Furstenberg, professor of economics, Indiana University.

Dr. John Garen, professor of economics, University of Kentucky.

Dr. Audra Grant, political scientist, RAND Corporation, senior public opinion and policy analyst.

Dr. Paul Herman Jr., dean of academics, Florida State College at Jacksonville, formerly of the National Intelligence Council.

Dr. Evan Hillebrand, associate professor of geoeconomic studies, Patterson School of Diplomacy and International Commerce.

Dr. Sean Kay, professor of politics and government, Ohio Wesleyan University.

Steve LeVine, author, contributing editor to *Foreign Policy*, longtime foreign correspondent, and fellow at the New America Foundation.

Dr. Karen Mingst, professor, Patterson School of Diplomacy and International Relations.

Arch Puddington, director of research, Freedom House.

Appendix B: The International Futures Model

The International Futures (IFs) model is a large-scale, long-term, integrated global modeling system.[1] It represents demographic, economic, energy, agricultural, sociopolitical, and environmental subsystems for 186 interacting geographical units (mostly countries). The model is freely available from the IFs website at the University of Denver (http://pardee.du.edu/access-ifs). The model is written in BASIC and has a software interface that makes it easy to use by interested analysts. Although the model comes with a base case simulation of the world system to the year 2100, the IFs project does not routinely issue forecasts but has been developed primarily to help analysts think about evolving economic and social relationships within and between countries.

Like all social science models, the IFs model projects future values of endogenous variables—many hundreds for each country—based on assumptions about exogenous variables and estimated or assumed parametric relations among the variables. The key endogenous variables are economic variables such as GDP and its components; population; food demand, supply, and trade; energy demand, supply, and trade; human welfare indicators such as health, education, poverty, and inequality; the evolution of governance and social stability; and international war. The relationships among the variables are based on the relevant theoretical literature in each area, and the parameters are derived mostly from cross-sectional regression analysis. The model was constructed using data from 1960 to 2010, and it has performed well in extensive validation tests over the historical period (Hughes 2006).

The present volume is concerned with the interactions of three key drivers: economic growth, energy availability, and geopolitical relationships. Many forecasts of these three important factors are available in the literature, and a base case forecast is always presented with each new version of the IFs modeling system. We were not interested in making forecasts or evaluating the forecasts of others. Instead, we have tried to show how a plausible variation in any one of the factors (or variations in the factors across countries or energy sources) would affect the global system.

For example, a typical long-range economic forecast is based on assumptions about population growth, savings, and investment and the rate of technological change. For the OECD countries, the rate of technological change is the most important growth factor; for the non-OECD countries, the rate of catch-up to the technology level of the OECD countries is the most important factor. There is no universally accepted way of forecasting either of these two important rates, so the IFs base case, and most other long-range forecasts, are essentially an extrapolation of recent trends. In our scenarios, we make different assumptions about the rate of technological advance, the quality of economic and political governance, and the efficacy of policy choices to justify varying the rate of economic growth among countries and across time.

The different rates of economic growth affect energy demand, supply, and prices and also affect each country's perception of its power, vulnerability, and opportunities. When we force the model to follow a different growth trajectory (usually by assuming a different rate of technological change), the new model simulation calculates new estimates of energy security and geopolitical power, which we then use to make judgments about geopolitical outcomes. We want to emphasize that the economic growth trajectories are assumptions made by the authors and that the geopolitical outcomes are judgments also made by us, albeit with the assistance of some quantitative results from the IFs model.

Energy forecasts are handled in a similar fashion. The IFs base case forecast projects aggregate energy demand and energy supply (by five different fuel types) for every country through the year 2100. Energy demand is estimated in a straightforward fashion based on economic activity by country and the relative price of energy. The countries that are less efficient than the OECD countries in energy use relative to GDP are assumed to gradually converge toward (the increasing) OECD standard. In some scenarios, especially scenario 6, Eco World, we alter energy demand by raising domestic energy taxes sharply and by assuming that other policy measures are taken to both reduce aggregate demand and shift consumption more toward renewable fuels. Energy supply forecasts are based on known and estimated fossil fuel resources and assumed rates of drawdown and new discoveries, as well as many assumptions about the new production of energy from renewable sources.

The IFs base case forecast for energy supply shows world energy supply (and demand) growing at 2.1 percent per year through 2050 for a world GDP growth rate (in PPP terms) of 2.8 percent per year and a rise in the relative price of energy of 118 percent. The Energy Information Agency (EIA, 2013) forecast shows world energy supply growth somewhat less (1.5 percent per year), world economic growth somewhat higher (3.5 percent), and prices rising more (150 percent), thus suggesting a greater improvement in overall energy efficiency than the IFs base case.[2] The IFs model forecast assumes a much greater increase in the production of nonrenewable fuels at an affordable cost, thus pushing overall fuel use up and world prices down. Both forecasts assume no peak in the production of fossil fuels.

In scenario 1 we adjusted various assumptions in the IFs model so that the energy supply and demand forecasts approximate the EIA reference forecast, by major supplier as well as in the aggregate. In scenario 6 we adjusted the assumptions so the IFs numbers resembled the International Energy Agency's (2013) extreme conservation scenario. In the other scenarios, we adjusted supply estimates by fuel type for the United States, China, Russia, OPEC, and other countries to help us think about the effect on prices, economic growth, and geopolitical interactions based on the new energy numbers.

The IFs model also produces an estimate of comprehensive national power for each country in the world (the figure given is a share of world power). There is no generally accepted way to estimate national power. Most estimates (Hoehn 2011) combine factors such as GDP and population and military spending, but there is no consensus on exactly what factors to include or what weight to give each factor. The results reported in this paper use the default weighting scheme in the IFs model: 25 percent for population, 35 percent for GDP in PPP terms, 30 percent for military spending, and 10 percent for a measure of technology. The national power estimates are used in this book to help us think and write about the evolution of relationships among countries.

The IFs model uses the power calculations to make explicit probability estimates of the likelihood of inter-state war, based on power transition theory and a number of other factors, including past relations, geographic proximity, alliances, and the degree of economic and political connections (Hughes et al. 2004b). The probabilities are retrievable by the reader by accessing the model from the IFs website, running simulations with the files that were used for the eight scenarios, and observing the results. More than 5 million probabilities are estimated (the probability of war between each country and every other country in each year for the eight scenarios divided by 2).

Most of the probabilities are zero (the chances of Honduras going to war with Zambia, for example, are remote), but some are quite large, based on a history of hostility and on variations in relative power and other factors. To condense this huge amount of information, we have calculated and reported (see tables 4.4, 8.4, and 10.5) the cumulative probability of the significant countries having at least one war in 2015 and in 2050. These probabilities are not operational in the eight scenarios discussed in the book—they have no effect on other variables in the model. We have also run each of the scenarios at least one other time to allow a random number generator operating within the model to predict wars based on the probabilities.

The wars are of various duration and magnitude and differ somewhat in sequential simulations of the model (all other things being equal). In the simulation reported in scenario 3, the number of war years estimated is very low for all countries (see table 4.4). The number of war years estimated in scenario 7, Ambition Fuels Rivalry, is much higher even though the cumulative probabilities are not much different (because countries can fight more than one war in each year and because wars, once started, can last more than a year).

These wars affect economic growth, demography, and all the other endogenous variables within the model. Since these war results (and not the probabilities) are random, it means that every simulation is different. Slightly different bilateral wars of different duration and magnitude would change the economic and energy estimates for each iteration. We chose not to use the endogenous war-making possibilities of the IFs model in order to avoid this randomness, but we must note that all the economic results shown could be considered too high because they ignore the implicit costs of wars suggested by the nonzero probabilities.

The wars that we discuss in the scenarios are inventions that we think flow from the logic of the story lines. Although we did not base those wars on the IFs model results, we referred to multiple model simulations for help in constructing our scenarios. In our trials we also used an alternate definition of comprehensive national power that included the possession of nuclear weapons, and in several of the scenarios we assumed that some new nations acquired them (Moyer 2013). The new calculations of national power are not greatly different for the great powers, but they are quite different for some smaller countries, especially Israel, Iran, and Saudi Arabia. The online appendix (available at http://mitpress.mit.edu/geopolitical-futures) reports power calculations for these alternate simulations, as well as the eight preferred scenarios.

The IFs model also contains a wealth of material related to population growth, health, education, poverty, and income distribution. The assumptions and relationships embedded in the model in relation to these variables were unchanged in our scenarios (except in scenario 6, where certain assumptions about fertility and mortality were changed). Thus, the model itself is relied on to give us an estimate of the effect our assumptions about growth, energy, and geopolitics have on these factors. The most dramatic results are the effect of different economic growth rates on poverty.

The online appendix shows the poverty head count numbers in 2050 at $1.25 a day by country for the eight scenarios according to 2005 PPP dollars. There is an enormous range of results, from global poverty being almost wiped out in scenario 1 to a large increase in the number of people living in poverty in scenario 8. The poverty numbers for all the countries for all years and all scenarios (at $1.25 a day, at $2.50 a day, as well as Gini coefficients for each country) are available if the reader chooses to employ the IFs model as described above.

Appendix C: The Composition of Regional Aggregations

World (186 units) Afghanistan, Albania, Algeria, Angola, Argentina, Armenia, Australia, Austria, Azerbaijan, Bahamas, Bahrain, Bangladesh, Barbados, Belarus, Belgium, Belize, Benin, Bhutan, Bolivia, Bosnia and Herzegovina, Botswana, Brazil, Brunei, Bulgaria, Burkina Faso, Burma, Burundi, Cambodia, Cameroon, Canada, Cape Verde, Central African Republic, Chad, Chile, China, Colombia, Comoros, Congo (Democratic Republic), Congo (Republic), Costa Rica, Cote d'Ivoire, Croatia, Cuba, Cyprus, Czech Republic, Denmark, Djibouti, Dominican Republic, Ecuador, Egypt, El Salvador, Equatorial Guinea, Eritrea, Estonia, Ethiopia, Fiji, Finland, France, Gabon, Gambia, Georgia, Germany, Ghana, Greece, Grenada, Guatemala, Guinea, Guinea-Bissau, Guyana, Haiti, Honduras, Hong Kong, Hungary, Iceland, India, Indonesia, Iran, Iraq, Ireland, Israel, Italy, Jamaica, Japan, Jordan, Kazakhstan, Kenya, Korea (North), Korea (South), Kosovo, Kuwait, Kyrgyz Republic, Laos, Latvia, Lebanon, Lesotho, Liberia, Libya, Lithuania, Luxembourg, Macedonia, Madagascar, Malawi, Malaysia, Maldives, Mali, Malta, Mauritania, Mauritius, Mexico, Micronesia, Moldova, Mongolia, Montenegro, Morocco, Mozambique, Namibia, Nepal, Netherlands, New Zealand, Nicaragua, Niger, Nigeria, Norway, Oman, Pakistan, Panama, Papua New Guinea, Paraguay, Peru, Philippines, Poland, Portugal, Puerto Rico, Qatar, Romania, Russian Federation, Rwanda, Samoa, Sao Tome and Principe, Saudi Arabia, Senegal, Serbia, Seychelles, Sierra Leone, Singapore, Slovak Republic, Slovenia, Solomon Islands, Somalia, South Africa, Spain, Sri Lanka, St. Lucia, St. Vincent and the Grenadines, Sudan, South Sudan, Suriname, Swaziland, Sweden, Switzerland, Syria, Taiwan, Tajikistan, Tanzania, Thailand, Timor-Leste, Togo, Tonga, Trinidad and Tobago, Tunisia, Turkey, Turkmenistan, Uganda, Ukraine, United Arab Emirates, United Kingdom, United States, Uruguay, Uzbekistan, Vanuatu, Venezuela, Vietnam, West Bank and Gaza, Yemen, Zambia, Zimbabwe

Organisation for Economic Co-operation and Development (OECD) (23 nations) Australia, Austria, Belgium, Canada, Denmark, Finland, France, Germany, Greece, Iceland, Ireland, Israel, Italy, Japan, Netherlands, New Zealand, Norway, Portugal, Spain, Sweden, Switzerland, United Kingdom, United States

Non-OECD (163 units) The remaining entities under "World" that are not listed as OECD nations.

European Union (28 nations) Austria, Belgium, Bulgaria, Croatia, Cyprus, Czech Republic, Denmark, Estonia, Finland, France, Germany, Greece, Hungary, Ireland, Italy, Latvia, Lithuania, Luxembourg, Malta, Netherlands, Poland, Portugal, Romania, Slovak Republic, Slovenia, Spain, Sweden, United Kingdom

Latin America and the Caribbean (30 nations) Argentina, Bahamas, Barbados, Belize, Bolivia, Brazil, Chile, Colombia, Costa Rica, Cuba, Dominican Republic, Ecuador, El

Salvador, Grenada, Guatemala, Guyana, Haiti, Honduras, Jamaica, Mexico, Nicaragua, Panama, Paraguay, Peru, St. Lucia, St. Vincent and the Grenadines, Suriname, Trinidad and Tobago, Uruguay, Venezuela

Middle East and North Africa (19 units)   Algeria, Bahrain, Egypt, Iran, Iraq, Jordan, Kuwait, Lebanon, Libya, Morocco, Oman, Qatar, Saudi Arabia, Sudan, Syria, Tunisia, United Arab Emirates, West Bank and Gaza, Yemen

Southeast Asia (15 nations)   Bangladesh, Brunei, Cambodia, Indonesia, Laos, Malaysia, Myanmar, Papua New Guinea, Philippines, Singapore, Sri Lanka, Taiwan, Thailand, Timor-Leste, Vietnam

Sub-Saharan Africa (48 nations)   Angola, Benin, Botswana, Burkina Faso, Burundi, Cameroon, Cape Verde, Central African Republic, Chad, Comoros, Congo (Democratic Republic), Congo (Republic), Cote d'Ivoire, Djibouti, Equatorial Guinea, Eritrea, Ethiopia, Gabon, Gambia, Ghana, Guinea, Guinea-Bissau, Kenya, Lesotho, Liberia, Madagascar, Malawi, Mali, Mauritania, Mauritius, Mozambique, Namibia, Niger, Nigeria, Rwanda, Sao Tome and Principe, Senegal, Sierra Leone, Somalia, South Africa, Sudan, South Sudan, Swaziland, Tanzania, Togo, Uganda, Zambia, Zimbabwe

BRICs (4 nations)   Brazil, Russia, India, China

STICKs (5 nations, scenario 3)   South Africa, Turkey, India, Colombia, Kazakhstan

SANZ (7 nations, scenarios 2 and 8)   Singapore, Australia, New Zealand; later also includes Korea (South), Japan, Malaysia, Taiwan

Asian League (22 units, scenario 4)   Bangladesh, Bhutan, Brunei, Cambodia, China, Hong Kong, Indonesia, Korea (North), Korea (South), Laos, Malaysia, Maldives, Mongolia, Myanmar, Nepal, Pakistan, Papua New Guinea, Philippines, Taiwan, Thailand, Timor-Leste, Vietnam

Trans-Pacific Partnership (25 nations, scenario 4)   Australia, Bahamas, Barbados, Belize, Canada, Chile, Colombia, Costa Rica, Cuba, Dominican Republic, Ecuador, El Salvador, Fiji, Guatemala, Honduras, Jamaica, Japan, Mexico, New Zealand, Nicaragua, Panama, Peru, Puerto Rico, Singapore, United States

EU2050 (41 nations by 2050, scenario 4)   Albania, Austria, Belgium, Bosnia and Herzegovina, Bulgaria, Croatia, Cyprus, Czech Republic, Denmark, Estonia, Finland, France, Germany, Greece, Hungary, Iceland, Ireland, Israel, Italy, Kosovo, Latvia, Lithuania, Luxembourg, Macedonia, Malta, Moldova, Montenegro, Morocco, Netherlands, Norway, Poland, Portugal, Romania, Serbia, Slovak Republic, Slovenia, Spain, Sweden, Switzerland, Turkey, United Kingdom

Eurasian Union (11 nations, scenarios 1 and 4)   Armenia, Azerbaijan, Belarus, Georgia, Kazakhstan, Kyrgyz Republic, Russian Federation, Tajikistan, Turkmenistan, Ukraine, Uzbekistan

Mercosur (8 nations, scenario 4)   Argentina, Bolivia, Brazil, Guyana, Suriname, Trinidad and Tobago, Uruguay, Venezuela

African Union (31 nations)   Angola, Benin, Botswana, Burkina Faso, Burundi, Cameroon, Cape Verde, Comoros, Cote d'Ivoire, Equatorial Guinea, Ethiopia, Gabon, Gambia, Ghana, Guinea, Guinea-Bissau, Kenya, Lesotho, Liberia, Madagascar, Namibia, Rwanda, Sao Tome and Principe, Senegal, South Africa, Swaziland, Tanzania, Togo, Uganda, Zambia, Zimbabwe

Islamic Brotherhood (17 units, scenario 4)   Afghanistan, Algeria, Bahrain, Egypt, Iran, Iraq, Jordan, Kuwait, Lebanon, Libya, Oman, Qatar, Saudi Arabia, Syria, Tunisia, United Arab Emirates, West Bank and Gaza

Greater India (4 nations, scenario 4)   India, Mauritius, Seychelles, Sri Lanka

Shanghai Pact (26 units by 2050, scenario 7)   Bangladesh, Bhutan, Brunei, Cambodia, China, Hong Kong, Indonesia, Kazakhstan, Korea (North), Korea (South), Kyrgyz Republic, Laos, Maldives, Mongolia, Myanmar, Nepal, Pakistan, Papua New Guinea, Philippines, Tajikistan, Tanzania, Thailand, Timor-Leste, Turkmenistan, Uzbekistan, Vietnam

League of Democracies (54 nations by 2050, scenario 7)   Albania, Australia, Austria, Bahamas, Barbados, Belgium, Bosnia and Herzegovina, Bulgaria, Canada, Chile, Colombia, Croatia, Cyprus, Czech Republic, Denmark, Estonia, Finland, France, Germany, Greece, Hungary, Iceland, Ireland, Israel, Italy, Japan, Kosovo, Latvia, Lithuania, Luxembourg, Macedonia, Malaysia, Malta, Mexico, Moldova, Montenegro, Morocco, Netherlands, New Zealand, Peru, Poland, Portugal, Puerto Rico, Romania, Serbia, Singapore, Slovak Republic, Slovenia, Spain, Sweden, Switzerland, Ukraine, United Kingdom, United States

Notes

Chapter 1

1. In this work, "OECD countries" refers to the 24 nations that were members of the Organisation for Economic Co-operation and Development as of 1991, except for Turkey, which we put in a different aggregation for thematic reasons (see appendix C).

2. For our work, we use IFs model version 6.75, August 2013. The model is freely available at http://pardee.du.edu/access-ifs. The IFs model is constantly being revised and updated through the institutional support and structure of the Pardee Center at the University of Denver.

3. The starting point, based on Hughes, Hossain, and Irfan (2004b) manipulating the Political Instability Task Force's "State Failure Problem Set" (Marshall, Gurr, and Harff 2009), are probabilities in 2010, ranging from 0.1 percent for very stable regimes (mostly the rich democracies of the OECD) to 100 percent for regimes actually in the midst of an internal war (e.g., Afghanistan). The mean probability for instability for the 163 non-OECD countries in 2010 was 16.4 percent.

4. South Africa attends BRIC meetings and is considered a partner as of 2010. For our study, however, we consider them instead as a second-echelon emerging market.

Chapter 2

1. The International Comparison Project (2014) rebased its benchmark PPP numbers to 2011 and substantially raised its estimate of the size of the Chinese economy. The major implication that the new numbers have for the present volume is that Chinese GDP, in PPP terms, surpasses U.S. GDP sooner than 2024. The 2050 numbers, however, would not be substantially different, since a richer China in the early years suggests less opportunity for catch-up growth and hence slower growth in the later years.

Appendix B

1. This section has been written with the assistance of the founder of the IFs model project, Professor Barry B. Hughes. Further details of the model are given in Hughes, Hossain, and Irfan (2004a, 2004b), Hughes (2006), and Hughes et al. (2008–2012).

2. The EIA forecast only goes through 2040. The numbers cited above extrapolate through 2050 based on the reported growth rates from 2030 to 2040.

References

Abdollohian, Mark, Carole Alsharabati, Brian Efird, Jacek Kugler, Douglas Lemke, Allan C. Stam III, Ronald L. Tammen, and A.F.K. Organski. 2000. *Power Transitions: Strategies for the 21st Century*. London: Chatham House.

Acemoglu, Daron, and James Robinson. 2012. *Why Nations Fail: The Origins of Power, Prosperity, and Poverty*. New York: Random House.

Alexadratos, Nikos. 2011. "World Food and Agriculture to 2030/2050 Revisited." In *Looking Ahead in World Food and Agriculture: Perspectives to 2050*, edited by Piero Conforti, 11–46. Rome: UN Food and Agricultural Organization.

Archibald, David. 2012. "A Look at Oil Production." *Watts Up with That Blog*, May 31. http://wattsupwiththat.com/2012/05/31/a-look-at-oil-production.

Baroliche Foundation. 1976. *Baroliche Foundation World Model*. San Carlos de Baroliche, Argentina: San Carlos de Bariloche.

Barro, Robert, and Xavier Sala-i-Martín. 1995. *Economic Growth*. New York: McGraw-Hill.

Berkowitz, Bruce. 2008. *Strategic Advantage: Challenges, Competitors, and Threats to America's Future*. Washington, DC: Georgetown University Press.

Bhagwati, Jagdish. 2009. "Does the U.S. Need a New Trade Policy?" *Journal of Policy Modeling* 31:549–51.

Binningsbø, Helga Malmin, Cyanne Loyle; Scott Gates; and Jon Elster. 2012. "Armed Conflict and Post-Conflict Justice, 1946–2006: A Dataset." *Journal of Peace Research* 49: 731–740.

Bisley, Nick. 2011. "Biding and Hiding No Longer: A More Assertive China Rattles the Region." *Global Asia* 6:62–73.

Bobbitt, Philip. 2002. *The Shield of Achilles: War, Peace, and the Course of History*. New York: Random House.

BP. 2013. *BP Energy Outlook 2030*. http://www.bp.com/energyoutlook2030.

Brainard, Lael, and Leonardo Martinez-Diaz, eds. 2009. *Brazil as an Economic Superpower? Understanding Brazil's Changing Role in the Global Economy*. Washington, DC: Brookings Institution Press.

Brecha, Richard. 2011. "Ten Reasons to Take Peak Oil Seriously." Paper presented at the annual conference of the Patterson School of Diplomacy and International Commerce, Lexington, KY, October 12.

Bremer, Stuart A. 1977. *Simulated Worlds: A Computer Model of National Decision-Making.* Princeton, NJ: Princeton University Press.

Bremmer, Ian. 2006. *J Curve: A New Way to Understand Why Nations Rise and Fall.* New York: Simon and Schuster.

Bremmer, Ian. 2010. *The End of the Free Market: Who Wins the War between States and Corporations?* New York: Penguin.

Bremmer, Ian, and Nouriel Roubini. 2011. "A G-Zero World." *Foreign Affairs* 90:2–7.

Bruinsma, Jelle. 2011. "The Resources Outlook: By How Much Do Land, Water, and Crop Yields Need to Increase by 2050?" In *Looking Ahead in World Food and Agriculture: Perspectives to 2050*, edited by Piero Conforti, 233–78. Rome: UN Food and Agricultural Organization.

Bruntand, Bjorn, and Rasmus Reinvang. 2012. "China—the New Hegemon." In *2052: A Global Forecast for the Next 50 Years*, edited by Jørgen Randers, 279–83. White River Junction, VT: Chelsea Green.

Bush, George H.W. 2006. "The National Security Strategy." Washington, DC: The White House.

Campbell, Colin. 2005. *The Coming Global Oil Crisis.* New York: Multi-Science.

Cline, Ray. 1975. *World Power Assessment: A Calculus of Strategic Drift.* Boulder, CO: Westview Press.

Closson, Stacy. 2011. "A Comparative Analysis on Energy Subsidies in Soviet and Russian Policy." *Communist and Post-Communist Studies* 44:343–56.

Closson, Stacy. 2013. "The Military and Energy Security: Moving the U.S. beyond Oil." *Energy Policy* 61:306–16.

Closson, Stacy, Evan Hillebrand, and Jeremy Bervoets. 2013. "Russia's Sanctions Expectations in Eurasia Diminished." Paper presented at the International Studies Association conference, Buenos Aires, Argentina, July 24, 2014.

Collier, Paul. 2007. *The Bottom Billion: Why the Poorest Countries Are Failing and What Can Be Done about It.* Oxford, UK: Oxford University Press.

Conforti, Piero, ed. 2011. *Looking Ahead in World Food and Agriculture: Perspectives to 2050.* Rome: UN Food and Agricultural Organization.

Cooper, Richard. 2002. *What the Future Holds: Insights from Social Science.* Cambridge, MA: MIT Press.

Cornish, Edward. 2004. *Futuring: The Exploration of the Future.* Bethesda, MD: World Future Society.

Curry, Judith, and Peter Webster. 2011. "Climate Science and the Uncertainty Monster." *Bulletin of the American Meteorological Society* 92:1667–82.

Daly, Herman E. 1996. *Beyond Growth: The Economics of Sustainable Development.* Boston: Beacon Press.

Diamond, Larry. 2013. "Chinese Communism and the 70-Year Itch." *Atlantic*, October 29.

Diamond, Larry, and Jack Mosbacher. 2013. "Petroleum to the People: Africa's Coming Resource Curse—and How to Avoid It." *Foreign Affairs* 92:86–98.

Drezner, Daniel. 2009. "Bad Debts: Assessing China's Financial Influence in Great Power Politics." *International Security* 34:7–45.

Drezner, Daniel. 2010. "Three Ways of Looking at Chinese Economic Statecraft." *Foreign Policy Blog*, October 20. http://drezner.foreignpolicy.com/posts/2010/10/20.

Duval, Romain, and Christine de la Maisonneuve. 2010. "Long-Run GDP Growth Scenarios for the World Economy." *Journal of Policy Modeling* 32:314–29.

Economist. 2013. "How to Stop the Fighting, Sometimes." *Economist*, November 9.

Edwards, Sebastian. 2010. *Left Behind: Latin America and the False Promise of Populism.* Chicago: University of Chicago Press.

Eichengreen, Barry. 2011. *Exorbitant Privilege: The Rise and Fall of the Dollar and the Future of the International Monetary System.* Oxford, UK: Oxford University Press.

El-Gamal, Mahmoud A., and Amy Myers Jaffe. 2011. *Oil, Dollars, Debt, and Crises: The Global Curse of Black Gold.* Cambridge, MA: Cambridge University Press.

Energy Information Agency (EIA). 2011. *International Energy Outlook.* Washington, DC: U.S. Department of Energy.

Energy Information Agency (EIA). 2013. *International Energy Outlook.* Washington, DC: U.S. Department of Energy.

European Commission. 2012. *Energy Roadmap 2050.* Brussels: European Union.

European Union Institute of Strategic Studies. 2011. *Futures Study to 2025: Citizens in an Interconnected and Polycentric World.* Paris: European Union Institute of Strategic Studies.

Evans, Gareth. 2008. *The Responsibility to Protect: Ending Mass Atrocity Crimes Once and for All.* Washington, DC: Brookings Institution Press.

Fallows, James. 2008. "Be Nice to the Countries That Lend You Money." *Atlantic*, December.

Feldman, David. 2012. *Water.* Malden, MA: Polity.

Fettweis, Christopher. 2010. *Dangerous Times? The International Politics of Great Power Peace.* Washington, DC: Georgetown University Press.

Findlay, Ronald, and Kevin O'Rourke. 2007. *Power and Plenty: Trade, War, and the World Economy in the Second Millennium.* Princeton, NJ: Princeton University Press.

Fortune. 2011. "The Global 500." August 25. http://money.cnn.com/magazines/fortune/global500/2011/full_list.

Fouré, Jean, Agnés Bénassy-Quéré, and Lionel Fontagné. 2010. "The World Economy in 2050: A Tentative Picture." Center for Economic Perspectives and International Information Working Paper 27, Paris.

Fouré, Jean, Agnés Bénassy-Quéré, and Lionel Fontagné. 2012. "The Great Shift: Macroeconomic Projections for the World Economy at the 2050 Horizon." Center for Economic Perspectives and International Information Working Paper 3, Paris.

Friedman, George. 2009. *The Next 100 Years: A Forecast for the 21st Century.* New York: Doubleday.

Gilpin, Robert. 1988. "The Theory of Hegemonic War." *Journal of Interdisciplinary History* 18:591–613.

Giustozzi, Antonio. 2013. "The Next Congo: Regional Competition for Influence in Afghanistan in the Wake of NATO Withdrawal." Paper presented at the Afghanistan Regional Forum 10, Elliott School of International Affairs, Washington, DC, September 13.

Glenn, Jerome C., Theodore J. Gordon, and Elizabeth Florescu. 2011. *State of the Future.* Washington, DC: Millennium Project.

Goldstein, Joshua. 2011. *Winning the War on War: The Decline of Armed Conflict Worldwide.* New York: E. P. Dutton.

Goldstone, Jack, Robert Bates, Ted Robert Gurr, Michael Lustik, Monty G. Marshall, Jay Ulfedler, and Mark Woodward. 2005. "Political Instability Task Force Report: Phase V Findings." Paper presented at the annual meeting of the American Political Science Association, Washington, DC, September 1–4.

Goldstone, Jack, Robert Bates, Ted Robert Gurr, Michael Lustik, Monty G. Marshall, Jay Ulfedler, and Mark Woodward. 2010. "A Global Model for Forecasting Political Instability." *American Journal of Political Science* 54:190–208.

Gomory, Ralph E., and William J. Baumol. 2001. *Global Trade and Conflicting National Interest.* Cambridge, MA: MIT Press.

Gordon, Robert J. 2012. "Is U.S. Economic Growth Over? Faltering Innovation Confronts the Six Headwinds." National Bureau of Economic Research Working Paper 18315, Cambridge, MA.

Gourinchas, Pierre-Olivier, and Hélène Rey. 2013. "External Adjustment, Global Imbalances, and Valuation Effects." NBER Working Paper 19240, Cambridge, MA.

Haber, Stephen, and Victor Menaldo. 2011. "Do Natural Resources Fuel Authoritarianism? A Reappraisal of the Resource Curse." *American Political Science Review* 105:1–26.

Halper, Stefan. 2010. *The Beijing Consensus: How China's Authoritarian Model Will Dominate the Twenty-First Century.* New York: Basic Books.

Hartley, Peter. 2011. "Energy Sector Innovation and Growth: On Optimal Energy Crisis." Paper presented at the Convention of the International Association of Energy Economists, Stockholm, Sweden, June.

Hartley, Peter, Kenneth B. Medlock III, Ted Temzelides, and Xinya Zhang. 2013. "Energy Sector Innovation and Growth." Paper presented at the Convention of the International Association of Energy Economists, Stockholm, Sweden, June.

Heinberg, Richard. 2010. *Peak Everything: Waking Up to the Century of Declines.* Gabriola Island, BC: New Society Publishers.

Heinberg, Richard. 2011. *The End of Growth? Adapting to Our New Economic Reality.* Gabriola Island, BC: New Society Publishers.

Helpman, Elhanan. 2004. *The Mystery of Economic Growth.* Cambridge, MA: Harvard University Press.

Herb, Michael. 2005. "No Taxation without Representation? Rents, Development, and Democracy." *Comparative Politics* 37:297–317.

Hillebrand, Evan. 2008. "The Global Distribution of Income in 2050." *World Development* 36:727–40.

Hillebrand, Evan. 2010. "Deglobalization Scenarios: Who Wins? Who Loses?" *Global Economy Journal* 10:1–19.

Hillebrand, Evan. 2011. "Poverty, Growth, and Inequality over the Next 50 Years." In *Looking Ahead in World Food and Agriculture: Perspectives to 2050*, edited by Piero Conforti, 159–90. Rome: UN Food and Agricultural Organization.

Hoehn, Karl. 2011. "Geopolitics and the Measurement of National Power." PhD dissertation, University of Hamburg, Hamburg, Germany.

Hohnen, Paul. 2012. "The Future of Sustainability Reporting." London: Chatham House. http://www.hohnen.net/highlights2012.html.

Howard, Philip, and Muzammil Hussain. 2013. *Democracy's Fourth Wave? Digital Media and the Arab Spring*. Oxford, UK: Oxford University Press.

Huang, Yasheng. 2008. *Capitalism with Chinese Characteristics: Entrepreneurship and the State*. Cambridge, MA: Cambridge University Press.

Hufbauer, Gary Clyde, and Jeffrey J. Schott. 2009. "Buy American: Bad for Jobs, Worse for Reputation." Peterson Institute for International Economics Policy Brief PB09-02, Washington, DC.

Hughes, Barry. 2006. "Assessing the Credibility of Forecasts Using International Futures (IFs): Verification and Validation." International Futures Working Paper. June, Denver, CO.

Hughes, Barry, and Evan Hillebrand. 2006. *Exploring and Shaping International Futures*. Boulder, CO: Paradigm Press.

Hughes, Barry, Anwar Hossain, and Mohammod Irfan. 2004a. "Long-Term Socio-Economic Modeling." International Futures Working Paper. Denver, CO.

Hughes, Barry, Anwar Hossain, and Mohammod Irfan. 2004b. "The Structure of International Futures (IFs)." International Futures Working Paper. May. Denver, CO.

Hughes, Barry, et al. 2008–2012. *Patterns of Potential Human Progress*. 5 vols. Oxford, UK: Oxford University Press.

Huntington, Hillard G. 2005. "The Economic Consequences of Higher Crude Oil Prices." Paper presented at the Energy Modeling Forum, Stanford, CA, October 3.

Huntington, Hilliard G. 2007. "Oil Shocks and the Real Economy." *Energy Journal* 29:31–46.

Huntington, Samuel P. 1991. *The Third Wave: Democratization in the Late 20th Century*. Norman: University of Oklahoma Press.

Ikenberry, John. 2011. "The Future of the Liberal World Order." *Foreign Affairs* 90:58–68.

Inglehart, Ronald, and Wayne Baker. 2000. "Modernization, Cultural Change, and the Persistence of Traditional Values." *American Sociological Review* 65:19–51.

International Comparison Project. 2014. "Purchasing Power Parities and Real Expenditures of World Economies: Summary of Results and Findings of the 2011 International Comparison Program." Washington, DC: The World Bank.

International Energy Agency. 2013. *World Energy Outlook*. Paris: International Energy Agency.

International Panel on Climate Change (IPCC). 2007. *Special Report on Emissions Scenarios*. Geneva: United Nations.

International Panel on Climate Change (IPPC). 2013. *Fifth Assessment Report on Climate Change*. Geneva: IPCC Secretariat.

Jintao, Hu. 2011. Speech at meeting commemorating the 90th anniversary of the founding of the Communist Party, July 1. http://in.china-embassy.org/eng/zt/cpc90/t835812.htm.

Kagan, Robert. 2012. *The World America Made*. New York: Alfred A. Knopf.

Kahn, Herman, William Brown, and Leon Markel. 1976. *The Next 200 Years: A Scenario for America and the World*. New York: William Morrow.

Kaku, Michio. 2012. *Physics of the Future: How Science Will Shape Destiny and Our Daily Lives by the Year 2100*. New York: Anchor Books.

Käpylä, Juha, and Harri Mikkola. 2013. "Arctic Conflict Potential: Towards an Extra-Arctic Perspective." Finnish Institute of International Affairs. September 24. http://www.fiia.fi/en/publication/361/#.Uq83H-KzK8s.

Kaufman, Daniel, Art Kraay, and Massimo Mastruzzi. 2003. "Governance Matters III: Governance Indicators for 1996–2002." World Bank Policy Research Paper 3013, Washington, DC.

Kegley, Charles, and Eugene Wittkopf. 2005. *World Politics: Trends and Transformation*. 10th ed. Boston: Wadsworth.

Kennedy, Scott. 2010. "The Myth of the Beijing Consensus." *Journal of Contemporary China* 19:461–77.

Kindleberger, Charles P. 1973. *The World in Depression: 1929–1939*. Berkeley: University of California Press.

Klare, Michael T. 2001. *Resource Wars: The New Landscape of Global Conflict*. New York: Henry Holt.

Kotlikoff, Lawrence. 2004. *The Coming Generational Storm: What You Need to Know about America's Economic Future*. Cambridge, MA: MIT Press.

Kotlikoff, Lawrence. 2012. *The Clash of Generations: Saving Ourselves, Our Kids, and Our Economy*. Cambridge, MA: MIT Press.

Krepinevich, Andrew. 2009. *7 Deadly Scenarios: A Military Futurist Explores War in the 21st Century*. New York: Bantam Books.

Krugman, Paul R. 2008. "Trade and Wages Reconsidered." *Brookings Papers on Economic Activity* (Spring): 103–137.

Krugman, Paul R. 2012. *End This Depression Now!* New York: W. W. Norton.

Kugler, Jacek. 2006. "The Asian Ascent: Opportunity for Peace or Precondition for War?" *International Studies Perspectives* 7:36–42.

Kunstler, James H. 2005. *The Long Emergency: Surviving the End of Oil, Climate Change, and Other Converging Catastrophes of the Twenty-First Century.* New York: Atlantic Monthly Press.

Kupchan, Charles. 2012. *No One's World: The West, the Rising Rest, and the Coming Global Turn.* New York: Oxford University Press.

Landes, David. 1999. *The Wealth and Poverty of Nations: Why Some Are So Rich and Some Are So Poor.* New York: W. W. Norton.

Leeb, Stephen. 2006. *The Coming Economic Collapse: How You Can Thrive When Oil Costs $200 a Barrel.* New York: Warner Business Books.

Leontief, Wassily, Ann P. Carter, and Peter Petri. 1977. *The Future of the World Economy.* New York: Oxford University Press.

Levy, Jack. 2003. "Economic Interdependence, Opportunity Costs, and Peace." In *Economic Interdependence and International Conflict: New Perspectives on an Enduring Debate,* edited by Edward D. Mansfield and Brian M. Pollins, 127–147. Ann Arbor: University of Michigan Press.

Lipman, Maria, and Nikolay Petrov. 2011. *Russia in 2020: Scenarios for the Future.* Washington, DC: Carnegie Endowment for International Peace.

Looney, Robert. 2011. "Recent Developments on the Rare Earth Front." *World Economy* 12:47–78.

Luong, Pauline Jones, and Erika Weinthal. 2010. *Oil Is Not a Curse: Ownership Structure and Institutions in Soviet Successor States.* New York: Cambridge University Press.

Maddison, Angus. 2001. *The World Economy: A Millennial Perspective.* Paris: Organisation for Economic Co-operation and Development.

Maddison, Angus. 2007. *Contours of the World Economy, 1–2030 AD.* Oxford, UK: Oxford University Press.

Malleret, Thierry. 2012. *Disequilibrium: A World Out of Kilter.* BookBaby. Kindle edition.

Manning, Robert. 2013. *Global Trends 2030: Challenges and Opportunities for Europe.* Washington, DC: Atlantic Council.

Mansfield, Edward. 1994. *Power, Trade, and War.* Princeton, NJ: Princeton University Press.

Mansfield, Edward. 2003. "Preferential Peace: Why Preferential Trading Arrangements Inhibit Interstate Conflict." In *Economic Interdependence and International Conflict: New Perspectives on an Enduring Debate,* edited by Edward D. Mansfield and Brian M. Pollin, 222–238. Ann Arbor: University of Michigan Press.

Marshall, Monty G., and Benjamin R. Cole. 2013. "Global Conflict Trends." Center for Systemic Peace. http://www.systemicpeace.org.

Marshall, Monty G., Ted Robert Gurr, and Barbara Harff. 2009. "State Failure Problem Set: Internal Wars and Failures of Governance, 1955–2008." Political Instability Task Force, April 29. http://www.systemicpeace.org.

Maugheri, Leonardo. 2012. "Oil: The Next Revolution." Harvard University Belfer Center, June. http://belfercenter.ksg.harvard.edu/publication/22144/oil.html.

McCloskey, Deirdre. 2010. *Bourgeois Dignity: Why Economists Can't Explain the Modern World*. Chicago: University of Chicago Press.

Meadows, Donella, Jørgen Randers, and Dennis Meadows. 1992. *Beyond the Limits: Confronting Global Collapse, Envisioning a Sustainable Future*. White River Junction, VT: Chelsea Green.

Meadows, Donella, Jørgen Randers, and Dennis Meadows. 2004. *Limits to Growth: The 30-Year Update*. White River Junction, VT: Chelsea Green.

Meadows, Donella, Jørgen Randers, Dennis Meadows, and William Behrens. 1972. *Limits to Growth: A Report for the Club of Rome's Project on the Predicament of Mankind*. New York: Universe Books.

Mearsheimer, John J. 2001. *The Tragedy of Great Power Politics*. New York: W. W. Norton.

Mesarovic, Mihajlo, and Eduard Pestel. 1974. *Mankind at the Turning Point*. New York: E. P. Dutton.

Millennium Project. 2011. "State of the Future Index." World Federation of United Nations Associations. http://www.millennium-project.org/millennium/SOFI.html.

Mills, Robin M. 2008. *The Myth of the Oil Crisis: Overcoming the Challenges of Depletion, Geopolitics, and Global Warming*. Westport, CT: Praeger.

Moore, Scott. 2013. "Water Scarcity and Politics in China." Paper presented at the annual conference of the Patterson School of Diplomacy and International Commerce, Lexington, KY, October 18.

Morris, Ian. 2010. *Why the West Rules—for Now: The Patterns of History, and What They Reveal about the Future*. New York: Farrar, Straus and Giroux.

Morse, Edward L. 2014. "Welcome to the Revolution: Why Shale Is the Next Shale." *Foreign Affairs* 93:3–7.

Mowery, David C., and Nathan Rosenberg. 1989. *Technology and the Pursuit of Economic Growth*. New York: Cambridge University Press.

Moyer, Jonathan. 2013. "The China-U.S. Power Transition: Challenges for Measurement and Forecasting." PhD dissertation, University of Denver.

Msangi, Siwa, and Mark Rosegrant. 2011. "World Agriculture in a Dynamically Changing Environment: IFPRIs' Long-Term Outlook for Food and Agriculture. In *Looking Ahead in World Food and Agriculture: Perspectives to 2050*, edited by Piero Conforti, 57–94. Rome: UN Food and Agricultural Organization.

Nair, Chandran. 2012. "Constraining Asian Consumption." In *2052: A Global Forecast for the Next 50 Years*, edited by Jørgen Randers, 23–27. White River Junction, VT: Chelsea Green.

Nasr, Vali. 2013. *The Dispensable Nation: American Foreign Policy in Retreat*. New York: Doubleday.

National Intelligence Council (NIC). 2004. *Global Trends 2020: Mapping the Global Future*. Washington, DC: NIC.

National Intelligence Council (NIC). 2008. *Global Trends 2025: A World Transformed*. Washington, DC: NIC.

National Intelligence Council (NIC). 2012a. *Global Trends 2030: Alternative Worlds*. Washington, DC: NIC.

National Intelligence Council (NIC). 2012b. "Global Water Security: The Intelligence Community Assessment." February. Washington, DC.

Naughton, Barry. 2010. "China's Distinctive System: Can It Be a Model for Others? *Journal of Contemporary China* 19:437–60.

Nordhaus, William. 2008. *A Question of Balance: Weighing the Options on Global Warming Policies*. New Haven, CT: Yale University Press.

North, Douglass C. 1990. *Institutions, Institutional Change, and Economic Performance*. Cambridge, UK: Cambridge University Press.

Notestein, Frank. 1945. Population: The Long View. In *Food for the World*, edited by Theodore Schultz, 36–57. Chicago: Chicago University Press.

Organski, Abramo, and Kenneth Fimo. 1968. *World Politics: The Stages of Political Development*. New York: Alfred A. Knopf.

O'Rourke, Kevin H., and Alan M. Taylor. 2013. "Cross of Euros." *Journal of Economic Perspectives* 27:167–192.

Pachauri, Rajendra K. 2004. "The Future of India's Economic Growth: The Natural Resource and Energy Dimension." *Futures* 36:703–713.

Pardee Center for International Futures. 2009. *Reducing Global Poverty*. Boulder, CO: Paradigm.

Pei, Minxin. 2006. *China's Trapped Transition: The Limits of Developmental Autocracy*. Cambridge, MA: Harvard University Press.

Pei, Minxin. 2009. "Looming Stagnation." *National Interest*, March.

Pethick, John, and Julian Orford. 2013. "Rapid Rise in Effective Sea Level in Southwest Bangladesh: Its Causes and Contemporary Rates." *Global and Planetary Change* 111: 237–245.

Phelps, Edmund. 2013. *Mass Flourishing: How Grassroots Innovation Created Jobs, Challenge, and Change*. Princeton, NJ: Princeton University Press.

Pinker, Steven. 2011. *The Better Angels of Our Nature: Why Violence Has Declined*. New York: Viking Press.

Ramo, Joshua Cooper. 2004. *The Beijing Consensus*. London: Foreign Policy Centre.

Randers, Jørgen, ed. 2012. *2052: A Global Forecast for the Next 50 Years*. White River Junction, VT: Chelsea Green.

Roberts, Paul. 2005. *The End of Oil: On the Edge of a Perilous New World*. Boston: Houghton Mifflin.

Romer, Paul M. 1986. "Increasing Returns and Long-Run Growth." *Journal of Political Economy* 94:1002–1037.

Rosenberg, Nathan, and L. E. Birdzell. 1987. *How the West Grew Rich: The Economic Transformation of the Industrial World*. New York: Basic Books.

Ross, Michael. 2012. *The Oil Curse: How Petroleum Wealth Shapes the Development of Nations*. Princeton, NJ: Princeton University Press.

Sachs, Jeffrey, and Andrew Warner. 1997. *Natural Resource Abundance and Economic Growth*. Harvard University Center for International Development and Harvard Institute for International Development. www.cid.harvard.edu/ciddata/warner_files/natresf5 .pdf.

Sackwa, Richard. 2011. "Transition as a Political Institution: Towards 2020." In *Russia in 2020: Scenarios for the Future*, edited by Maria Lipman and Nikolay Petrov, 233–254. Washington, DC: Carnegie Endowment for International Peace.

Samuelson, Paul. 2004. "Where Ricardo and Mill Rebut and Confirm Arguments of Mainstream Economists Supporting Globalization." *Journal of Economic Perspectives* 18:135–146.

Schwartz, Peter. 1991. *The Art of the Long View: Planning for the Future in an Uncertain World*. New York: Crown.

Schwartz, Peter. 2003. *Inevitable Surprises: Thinking Ahead in a Time of Turbulence*. New York: Gotham Books.

Shackleton, Robert. 2013. "Total Factor Productivity Growth in Historical Perspective." Congressional Budget Office Working Paper 1, Washington, DC.

Shambaugh, David. 2013. *China Goes Global: The Partial Power*. New York: Oxford University Press.

Shaxson, Nicholas. 2011. *Treasure Islands: Uncovering the Damage of Offshore Baking and Tax Havens*. New York: Palgrave Macmillan.

Shell. 2013. *New Lens Scenarios*. The Hague, Netherlands: Shell.

Shirk, Susan. 2007. *China: Fragile Superpower*. Oxford, UK: Oxford University Press.

Simmons, Mathew R. 2005. *Twilight in the Desert: The Coming Saudi Oil Shock and the World Economy*. Hoboken, NJ: John Wiley & Sons.

Slaughter, Richard. 2010. *The Biggest Wake-Up Call in History*. Melbourne, Australia: Foresight Institute.

Song, Guoyou, and Jin Yuan Wen. 2012. "China's Free Trade Agreement Strategies." *Washington Quarterly* 35:107–19.

Spence, Michael. 2011. *The Next Convergence: The Future of Economic Growth in a Multispeed World*. New York: Farrar, Strauss, and Giroux.

Speth, James, and David Zinn. 2008. *The Bridge at the Edge of the World: Capitalism, the Environment, and Crossing from Crisis to Sustainability*. New Haven, CT: Yale University Press.

Summers, Lawrence, and Bradford DeLong. 2012. "Fiscal Policy in a Depressed Economy." *Brookings Papers on Economic Activity* (Spring): 233–297.

Systems Analysis Research Unit (SARU). 1977. *SARUM 76 Global Modeling Project*. London: Departments of the Environment and Transport.

Taleb, Nassim N. 2007. *The Black Swan: The Impact of the Highly Improbable.* New York: Random House.

Taleb, Nassim N., and Mark Blyth. 2011. "The Black Swan of Cairo: How Suppressing Volatility Makes the World Less Predictable and More Dangerous." *Foreign Affairs* 90:33–39.

Taylor, John. 2011. "An Empirical Analysis of the Revival of Fiscal Activism in the 2000s." *Journal of Economic Literature* 49:686–702.

Taylor, John. 2012. *First Principles: Five Keys to Restoring America's Prosperity.* New York: W. W. Norton.

Terrill, Ross. 2005. "What Does China Want?" *Wilson Quarterly* 29:50–61.

Treisman, Daniel. 2011. "Russia's Political Economy: The Next Decade." In *Russia in 2020: Scenarios for the Future,* edited by Maria Lipman and Nikolay Petrov, 149–164. Washington, DC: Carnegie Endowment for International Peace.

Trenin, Dmitri. 2012. "Russia's Foreign Policy Outlook." In *Russia in 2020: Scenarios for the Future,* edited by Maria Lipman and Nikolay Petrov, 45–66. Washington, DC: Carnegie Endowment for International Peace

United Nations. 2004. *Global Environment Outlook (GEO-4).* http://www.unep.org/geo4/media.

U.S.-China Economic and Security Review Commission. 2011. *Annual Report to Congress.* Washington DC: U.S. Government Printing Office.

Van der Mensbrugghe, Dominique, Israel Osorio-Rodarte, Andrew Burns, and John Baffes. 2011. "Macroeconomic Environment and Commodity Markets: A Longer-Term Outlook. In *Looking Ahead in World Food and Agriculture: Perspectives to 2050,* edited by Piero Conforti, 191–232. Rome: UN Food and Agricultural Organization.

Van der Ploeg, Frederick. 2011. "Natural Resources: Curse or Blessing?" *Journal of Economic Literature* 49:366–420.

Victor, David. 2008. "What Resource Wars?" *National Interest,* January/February.

Victor, David, Amy M. Jaffe, and Mark Hayes, eds. 2006. *Natural Gas and Geopolitics: From 1970 to 2040.* New York: Cambridge University Press.

Ward, Karen. 2011. *The World in 2050: Quantifying the Shift in the Global Economy.* HSBC Global Research, January. http://www.hsbc.com/1/content/assets/about_hsbc/2011_in_the_future/120508_the_world_in_2050.pdfx.

Waslekar, Sundeep, and Semu Bhatt. 2004. "India's Strategic Future: 2025." *Futures* 36:811–821.

Webb, Michael D., and Stephen D. Krasner. 1989. "Hegemonic Stability Theory: An Empirical Assessment." *Review of International Studies* 15:183–198.

Williamson, John. 2004. "A Short History of the Washington Consensus." International Institute of Economics, September. http://www.iie.com/publications/papers/williamson0904-2.pdf.

Wilson, D., and R. Purushotham. 2003. *Dreaming with BRICs: The Path to 2050.* Goldman Sachs Global Economics Paper 99, New York..

Wolf, Martin. 2013. "Germany's Strange Parallel Universe." *Financial Times*, September 25.

World Bank. 2010. "Development Indicators." http://data.worldbank.org/indicator.

World Bank. 2011. "Development Indicators." http://data.worldbank.org/indicator.

Yergin, Daniel. 1990. *The Prize: The Epic Quest for Oil, Money, and Power*. New York: Free Press.

Yergin, Daniel. 2011. *The Quest: Energy, Security, and the Remaking of the Modern World*. New York: Penguin.

Zakaria, Fareed. 2008. *The Post-American World*. New York: W. W. Norton.

Zakaria, Fareed. 2011. *The Post-American World: Release 2.0*. New York: W. W. Norton.

Zhang, Wenmu. 2006. "China's National Interests in the Course of Globalization." *Chinese Contemporary Thought* 37: 7–40.

Index